TEXTBOOK OF
CULINARY AND BAKERY WORLD

TEXTBOOK OF
CULINARY AND BAKERY WORLD

Chef Ishita Kirar
Lecturer
Food Production Incharge
IHM Faridabad

TECHSAR™
NEW DELHI

Published and Printed by
TechSar Pvt. Ltd.
4435-36/7, Ansari Road, Daryaganj
New Delhi-110002 (India)
E-mail: tech_info@techsarworld.com
Website: www.techsarworld.com

ISBN 978-93-86768-88-9

Reprint 2025

DEDICATION

Every challenging work needs self efforts as well as guidance specially those who were very close to our heart.

My humble effort I dedicated to my distracting little daughter, Akira 4 years old, and my son Saatvik 3 years old, my father, my mother.

My husband Chef Satish Kumar, whose affection, love, encouragement and prays of day and make me able to get such success and honour.

Preface

The material of study has been driven by a trend away from substantial meal at traditional and modern times. Within this context *culinary and bakery world* strives to cater for the aspirations of trainees and apprentices preparing food for presentation in a wide range of settings. This requires the student and practitioner not only to have a solid grasp of the theory but also a thorough knowledge of food quality with their details. Ingredients information and there availability in market as well.

In this edition we have included recipes that reflect current style and different flavourings. This has enabled us to retain the old recipes and add new ones. The book includes comprehensive study notes and questions that match the latest competency based training guide.

Culinary and Bakery World is designed both as an introduction to the subject of 'B.Sc. in Hospitality and Hotel Administration" course offered by National Council for Hotel Management and Catering Technology, New Delhi.

The students who join catering courses have little or no background in bakery and culinary area. They need a textbook that relates to what they practice in sessions. They find technical and practical difficulties to comprehend. From my experience of teaching the subject to students of catering, I have developed this text that concentrates on those aspects of bakery and culinary of particular relevance to the catering industry.

The text is divided in five units. In section of Basic commodities is cover details knowledge about milk, cream, cheese, butter, and flour. Next unit covers shortening (fats and oils), raising agent, and thickening agent, sugar. Unit 3 covers all pastry cream preparation. Unit 4 deals with basic pastries. Unit 5 covers all icing and topping used in bakery, frozen desserts, chocolate and bread. The book concludes with some more delicious recipes and the important culinary terms.

The main strengths of the book are concise notes on the principles and practice of culinary and bakery, the references to food identification and selection and supporting.

Using the recipes I have selected to expose to a wide range of menu items and bakery items.

Chef Ishita Kirar

Acknowledgements

I would like to give sincere thanks to all those individuals who have given me assistance and support in the preparation of this book. I like to thank the following sources from where I get the all online materials. The completion of this book has drawn upon a variety of experience & literature. I also want to owe to my sincere gratitude to the following who have given their precious time for my book and assist in its completion through their knowledge, experience and guidance.

I pay my deep sense of gratitude to Dr. Satvir Singh, Director of Studies NCHMCT, Noida. Mr. Satvir Singh is a very dynamic personality who believes in working attitude and always encourages and supports to his subordinates. He has given me a lot of guidance and moral support in the successful completion of this book.

I extend special thanks to Mr. Atul Shukla Principal of IHM Faridabad & IHM Panipat, for your guidance and moral support.

There are lots of people behind the successful completion of this work, some of them includes – Satish Kumar (Lecturer, Latit Suri Hospitality School), Anil Rustagi (HOD- IHM Faridabad), Alok Kumar Mishra (Lecturer IHM Faridabad), Shweta Kumar (Lecturer, IHM Faridabad), Mr. Sumeet Malhotra Administrative Officer, IHM Faridabad).

Finally, I acknowledge with gratitude, the support and love of my family – my parents, my husband and my loving kids.

Chef Ishita Kirar

Contents

Preface *vii*
Acknowledgement *ix*

Part 1: Basic Commodities

1. Milk **3**
Kinds of Milk 4
Processing of Milk 5
Storage of Milk 11
Types of Milk 12
Milk Products 15
Uses of Milk 16
Composition of Milk 16

2. Cream **18**
Processing of Cream 19
Types of Cream 20
Classification of Cream 22
Storage 23
Handling / Using Cream 23

3. Cheese **25**
Processing of Cheese 25
Classification of Cheese 26
Cooking Quality 30
Different Varieties of Cheese and Their Uses 30
Storage of Cheese 34

4. Butter **35**
Processing and Manufacturing of Butter 36
Storage of Butter 37

Uses of Butter	37
Packing & Storage	37
Butter Making Process	40
Types of Butter	43
Shortenings	45
Margarine	45
5. Flour	**47**
Composition of Flour	47
Milling	47
Types of Flour and Their Use	48
The Wheat Plant	53
Processing of Wheat Flour	59
Baking Process	62
6. Shortenings (Fats & Oils)	**65**
The Culinary Fruit Oils and Their Characteristics	71
The Culinary Seed Oils and Their Characteristics	73
Types of Fats and Oils	76
Processing and Refining of Fats	76
Refined Oils	77
Specific Fats	77
Flavour Reversion	79
Rancidity	79
Smoking Point	80
Changes in Fat on Heating	81
7. Raising Agents	**83**
Classification of Leavening Agents	84
Methods of Leavening	84
Use of Filler in Baking Powder	88
Types and Uses of Raising Agents	89
Action and Reactions	91
8. Thickening Agents	**94**
Classification of Thickening Agents	96
Role of Thickening Agents	97
Types of Leavening Agents	100

9. Sugar **106**
Various Stages of Cooking Sugar 108
Importance of Sugar 108
Types of Sugar 109
Sugar Substitutes 112
Other Natural Sweeteners 118

Part 2: Bakery and Confectionery

10. Pastry Creams **123**
Basic Pastry Creams 124
Preparation and Care 126

11. Pastry **130**
Short Dough 130
Puff Pastry 131
Principles of Pastry Making 131
Types of Pastry 132
Some Important Instructions 132
Types of Pastries 132

12. Icings & Toppings **142**
Six Types of Icings 143
Decorating Equipment 145
Points to be Considered while Using Fillings and Toppings 146
Types of Icings 147
Balancing Cake Recipes 156
Mixing Methods 157
Various Types of Cakes and Their Recipes 159

13. Frozen Desserts **164**
Types of Frozen Desserts 164
Italian Ice 166
Ice Cream Manufacture 168
Gelatine-based Desserts 181
Egg-based Desserts 182

Cream-based Desserts 183
Rice Desserts 183
Fruit-based Desserts 183
Ice Cream-based Desserts 184

14. Chocolate **185**
Manufacturing and Processing of Chocolate 186
Types of Cocoa and Chocolate Products 187
Candy 194
Assorted Preparation of Chocolate 197

15. Breads **199**
History 199
Ingredients Used in Bread Making 200
Bread Making Process 215
Bread Improvers 222
Ovens 224
Other Equipment Used in Bread Making 231
International Bread Varieties 238
Bread Varieties with Recipes 244
Bread Faults 251

16. Meringues **256**
French Meringue 256
Swiss Meringue 256
Italian Meringue 256

Part 3: Recipes

Pastry Recipes 261
Bread Recipes 314
Cookies Recipes 335
List of Culinary (Common and Basic Terms) 343

References **361**
Index **363**

PART 1

BASIC COMMODITIES

Unit 1

Milk

Milk is composed of water, calcium albumen, milk protein (casein), milk sugar (lactose), milk fat and vitamins. The final product depends on how the milk is processed and how one or more of its main constituents are treated.

In many countries, the milk sold has, by law, to be pasteurised, that is, free of any bacteria which could cause milk-borne diseases. Usually, the milk is heated below the boiling point, held at this temperature for a few seconds, and then cooled immediately that results in pasteurised milk.

Whole milk usually contains about 3.25 % milk fat and a cream line is clearly visible. **Homogenised milk**, on the other hand, has no cream line because the fat has been broken up and dispersed evenly throughout. **Skim milk** has less than 1 % milk fat but all the proteins, and minerals of whole milk, apart from the fat-soluble vitamins, are added. Whereas fortified skim milk has some of these vitamins added. **Condensed milk** has its water content reduced by about half and a sweetener is added; **evaporated milk** undergoes a similar process but without adding water and sugar. **Powder milk** is made by reducing the water content to less than 3 %, milk that has been subjected to ultra- high temperature, rapidly cooled and vacuum packed.

Milk represents a major ingredient in our diet— poured over cereals, drunk in glasses, in tea and coffee— but it is also a part of many dishes, especially desserts, such as ice cream, custard, pancakes, rice puddings, etc. It is particularly high in calcium, and is also fairly rich in fat.

Milk is a nutritive liquid, produced by the female mammals for feeding their young ones. Milk is one of the most complete foods containing a wide range of essential nutrients for proper functioning of the human body. Milk is a good source of proteins, calcium and B group vitamins. Milk is an oil-in-water emulsion.

KINDS OF MILK

(a) **Whole milk:** This contains at least 3.5 % of butterfat, which gives it the wholesome taste.

(b) **Homogenised milk:** Homogenisation is the process of breaking down the fat molecules in milk, so that they stay integrated rather than separate as cream. It is a physical process; nothing is added to the milk. Homogenised milk reduces the size of fat and then mixes them together. This is the best milk to use for tea and coffee. Grass milk, grass milk yogurt and heavy whipping cream, all other organic valley fluid milk products are homogenised.

Advantages of homogenisation:

- Less cream line formation.
- Whiter and more appetizing.
- More flavoured and fully boiled.
- Stability of the cultured product.
- Soft curd and a better digestive product.

Disadvantages of homogenisation:

- Increased cost of products.
- These types of milk products might not be suitable for certain products.
- Difficult to handle, sometimes.

(c) **Skimmed milk:** This milk is without any fat. Basically, it is a fat buster, low calorie produce.

(d) **Buttermilk:** It was originally a by-product while making butter. Today, buttermilk is made from pasteurised milk with addition of lactic acid bacteria.

(e) **Milk powder:** This is whole milk from which the water is removed by either spray drying or by roll drying processes.

PROCESSING OF MILK

It helps to produce milk that has initial low-bacterial count, good flavour and satisfactory keeping quality. There are three operations of milk processing:

Milk is a valuable nutritious food that has a short shelf-life and requires careful handling. Milk is highly perishable because it is an excellent medium for the growth of microorganisms – particularly bacterial pathogens – that can cause spoilage and disease to the consumers. Milk processing preserves milk for days, weeks or months and helps to reduce food-borne and many more other diseases.

Butterfat content accounts for several types of products. Whole milk(2%), non-fat (1 %), and half & half cream are some examples. A machine called a separator separates the cream and skims portions of the milk. A separator is a large centrifuge that spins about 2,000 rotations per minute. The different types of milk products are then "standardized" by blending the components (skim milk, raw milk and cream) in the correct proportion to give the desired end-products. Water is never added to lower the butterfat content of fluid milk. Excess cream is used to make ice cream, butter and a few other products. Milk is homogenised to prevent the cream portion from rising to the top of the package. The expression "cream rises to the top," is accurate because cream is lighter in weight than milk. The cream portion of unhomogenised milk would form a cream layer at the top of the carton. A "homogeniser" forces the milk under high pressure through a valve that breaks the butterfat globules to an extent that they actually not "coalesce" (stick together). Homogenisation does not affect the nutrition or quality of the product; it is done entirely for aesthetic purposes.

Vitamin quantities may be reduced by the heating process and removing the butterfat. Therefore, to replace the natural nutrition of nature's perfect food, liquid vitamins are added to fortify most fluid milk products. Many states have their own milk standards that require addition of milk solids. These solids represent the natural **minerals (calcium, iron), protein (casein) and sugar (lactose)** portions of non-fat dry milk. Quality control personnel conduct tests on the raw and pasteurised products to ensure their optimum quality and nutrition. A sample is analyzed for the presence of microbiological organisms with a **standard plate count** (SPC) and ropy milk test. The equipment used to analyze butterfat and solids (non-fat) is calibrated on a regular basis to insure a consistent, quality product that meets or exceeds government requirements.

All milk products have a sell-by date printed on the package. This is the last date the item should be offered for sale. However, most companies guarantee the quality and freshness of the product for at least 7 days past the date printed on the package. Samples of each product packaged each day are saved to confirm that freshness is maintained 7 days after the sell-by date.

- Once the milk has been separated, standardized, homogenised and pasteurised, it is held below 40 °F in storage tanks, then packaged for sale.
- The packaging machines are maintained under strict sanitation specifications to prevent bacteria from being introduced into the pasteurised product.
- All equipment that come in contact with the product (raw or pasteurised) are being washed daily. Sophisticated automatic clean-in-place (CIP) systems guarantee consistent sanitation with minimum manual handling which helps in handling the task easily, reducing the risk of contamination. Once packaged, the products are quickly conveyed to a cold storage warehouse. They are stored there for a short time and shipped to

the refrigerated trailers. Once at the store, the milk is immediately placed into a cold storage or refrigerated display case.

Clarification

Milk is passed through a centrifugal clarifier. The speed is adjusted in such a way that cream is not separated but dirt, filth and cells from the udders and some bacteria are removed. The clarified milk is ready for pasteurisation.

Pasteurisation

Pasteurisation derives its name from the French scientist Louis Pasteur, who found that heating of certain liquids to a high temperature improves their heating quality. In general terms, it is the heating of milk to a temperature which destroys organisms responsible for tuberculosis and fever and nearly all the other microorganisms present in the product without seriously affecting the composition or properties of the product. Pasteurisation should be followed by immediate cooling of the product to the temperature sufficiently low to check the growth of microorganisms which are resistant to the temperature used. At present, pasteurisation is considered an essential feature in the manufacture of butter, ice cream and also in cheese industry. Pasteurisation can also activate some of the natural enzymes like lipase.

Three general methods are in use nowadays:

1. **Holding or batch system:** The holding system is defined as bringing the milk or cream to a specific temperature, usually to 65 °C for at least 30 minutes, followed by rapid cooling. A higher temperature is sometimes used, in which case the time of holding may be short. For example, holding at 68.3 °C for 20 minutes. Careful control of both temperature and heating is important. In more recent years, it is found that the organism causing Q fever, Coxiellaburnetii, is slightly more resistant than the tuberculosis organism and requires a treatment of 63 °C for 30 minutes to ensure its destruction.

2. **High Temperature Short Time Method (HTST) or the Continuous System:** The machine used makes possible a continuous operation and for this reason, the system is called "continuous flow or flash pasteuriser". The system depends upon the raising of temperature of the milk to at least 72 °C for 15 seconds as it passes through the machine. This is followed by quick cooling. This method does not impart cooked flavour and cream line is not affected.
3. **Ultra-High Temperature System:** The UHTS system results in complete pasteurisation of milk. In this system, milk is held for 3 seconds at 93.4 °C or for 1 second at 149.5 °C. This system is also used extensively for the treatment of the milk or cream in dairy industry. This product has a longer shelf life than milk pasteurised by other methods. After pasteurisation, the milk is cooled rapidly to 7 °C or lower. There is more pronounced cooked flavour to UHT milk. Pasteurised milk is not sterile. It must be cooled quickly following pasteurisation, to prevent the multiplication of the surviving bacteria.

Role of Phosphatase in Pasteurisation

Raw milk contains alkaline phosphatase.This enzyme serves as a built-in indicator by which the adequacy of pasteurisation may be gauged. This enzyme has heat destruction characteristic that closely approximates the time, temperature and exposure of proper pasteurisation.

Heating of milk destroys disease causing bacteria and increases milk's shelf life.

$$\text{Disodium phenyl phosphate (substrate)} \xrightarrow[\text{(enzyme)}]{\text{Phosphatase}} \text{Phenol + Phosphate (endproudct)}$$

This test is so sensitive that it gives positive in the presence of 0.1 % raw milk added or if the pasteurisation temperature is less than 1 °F.

Effects of Pasteurisation

1. **Nutritive value :** Due to pasteurisation, there is no major change in nutritive value, except for the slight decrease in the heat labile vitamins, like thiamine and ascorbic acid. Proteins are denatured along with the loss of heat labile water soluble vitamins, there is slight denaturation of whey protein. Mineral precipitation is not appreciable. On the other side, there is protection from microorganisms and production of a fine curdon digestion.
2. **Flavour:** The flavouring compounds present in milk are not destroyed by pasteurisation.
3. **Microorganisms:** Pasteurised products are not sterile. They contain vegetative organisms and spores still capable of growth. Approximately 99 % of bacteria, yeast and moulds are destroyed by pasteurisation. Pasteurisation is required to destroy unwanted microorganisms. Milk does not contain heat-resistant moulds and yeast.
4. **Enzymes:** Apart from phosphatase, lipase also gets inactivated, which adversely affects the quality.

After pasteurisation, tests for temperature, fat, specific gravity, solids-not-fat, acidity and bacterial analysis are conducted. For pasteurised milk, we say, it should be stored for a week or more in good condition. At room temperature, it may be spoilt in a day. If it is too hot, it is stored in refrigerator only.

Homogenisation

The process of making a stable emulsion of milk fat and milk serum by mechanical treatment and rendering the mixture homogeneous is homogenisation. This is achieved by passing warm milk or cream through a small aperture under high pressure and velocity. Milk is a oil-in-water emulsion, where the fat globules are dispersed in a continuous skimming process.

Mixed milk (cows + buffalos)

↓

Cooled at 5 °C for 6-8 hours

↓

Assessment of the quality of milk

↓

Pumped into plate, chilled to 0 °C

↓

Passed to raw milk storage tank

↓

Pasteurised at 80 °C at the rate of 10,000 /hr

↓

Passed into silo

↓

I stage – homogenised under 500 psi

↓

II stage – homogenised under 2000 psi

↓

Processing of Milk at Dairy Farm

The fat globules have a tendency to gather into clumps and rise, due to their lower density than skimmed milk. This results in decrease in the size of the fat globules and increase in their number and surface area. A film of absorbed protein or lipoprotein immediately surrounds each of new globule, acting as an emulsifier and prevents it from reuniting. The newly formed fat droplets are no longer coated with the original membrane material.

There are three factors which enhance the stability of homogenised milk:

1. Decrease in the mean diameter of the fat globules (a factor in Stokes' law).
2. Decrease in size distribution in the mean diameter of the fat globules (result is: they don't tend to cluster during creaming).
3. Increase in density of the globules.

Homogenised milk is a result of creamier structure, bland flavour and whiter appearance. It has a greater whitening powder when added to coffee and tea. Soft curd is formed when coagulated and is easily digested. In the manufacture of evaporated milk (condensed milk) and ice cream homogenisation deaccelerates the action of lipase and rancidity of fat takes place. Homogenisation is done before pasteurisation.

Freezing

When milk or cream is frozen at a relatively slow rate,the film of protein that acts as an emulsifying agent around the fat globules is weakened and ruptured. As a result, the fat globules tend to coalesce. The dispersion of protein and calcium phosphate is also disturbed by freezing. Both constituents tend to settle on thawing and standing, thus, reducing the whiteness of milk.

STORAGE OF MILK

Milk should be stored in the refrigerator (for up to 5 days), and consumed within 2 days.

- Fresh milk should be kept in the container in which it is to be developed.

- It should always be stored covered, as it absorbs strong smells of onion, fish, spices, etc.
- Tinned milk should be stored in cool, dry and ventilated rooms.
- Pasteurised milk can be stored for 5 days when kept in refrigerator.
- Dried milk should be stored in airtight containers.
- Sterilised milk, if not opened, can be stored for 2-3 months.
- UHT (ultra-heat treated) milk if not opened, can be kept unrefrigerated for several months (nearly 6 months) but once opened, it can be stored only for 4-5 days under refrigeration.

TYPES OF MILK

The most common type sold milk is whole milk, 2 % (reduced fat), 1 % (low fat), and skim (fat-free).

Whole milk contains 3.5% milkfat.

Fat-free milk contains no more than 0.2 % milkfat.

1. **Whole milk:** Milk that has none of its fat removed. It usually contains about 3.25 % and has not been homogenised, so that it has a cream line. It can be kept for 4-5 days in a refrigerator and is used in drinks, pudding and for baking.
2. **Homogenised milk:** It contains the same percentage of ingredients as whole milk but it is processed so that the cream does not separate. It is used in beverages, puddings, soups and a variety of baked goods.
3. **Skimmed milk:** Milk with less than 1 % milkfat but contains all the proteins and minerals of the whole milk, except the fat-soluble vitamins.

   Fat content is reduced to 0.5-2 % by centrifugation. By removing fat from the milk, not only the taste or flavour is reduced but fat-soluble vitamins, like vitamins A and D, are also reduced. Usually, this milk is fortified with vitamins A and D. Condensed skim milk finds extensive use in the baking industry and manufacture of confectionery. Skimmed milk is used for low-calorie diets and for children, who need high protein.

4. **Buttermilk**

   It is the residue of butter-making but now, it is usually made from pasteurised skimmed milk. Popular in biscuit making and it can also be used as a substitute for sour milk.

5. **Condensed milk**

   Milk from which half of the water content is removed and sugar is added. It can be poured over fruit salads, and is useful for reconstituting and confectionery.

6. **Dried milk (solid form)**

   Milk from which most of the moisture is removed, is stored in powdered form and it can be included with the dry ingredients used in baking, reconstituted for drinking or added to coffee and tea. Dry milk can be made with whole milk or skimmed milk. Milk powder can be dehydrated to about 97 %

by spray drying and vacuum drying. Good shelf life, without refrigeration of dry milk, makes it a valuable product. Milk powder can be reconstituted into fluid milk. It is highly hygroscopic. Whole milk powder can be stored for only 6 months, because of the propensity of fat to oxidise.

No-fat dry milk powder is usually made from fresh pasteurised skimmed milk by removing about two-thirds of the water under vacuum and then spraying this concentrated milk into a chamber of hot filtered air. This process produces a fine powder of very-low moisture content, about 3 %. Instant non-fat dry milk disperses readily in cold water. To make an instant product, regular non-fat dry milk is remoistened with steam to induce small particles into large, porous particles that are creamy white and free flowing.

7. **Baked milk**

   It is boiled milk, made by simmering milk for around one hour.

8. **Evaporated milk:** It is the milk from which about 50-60 % of water has been evaporated. Raw milk is clarified and concentrated in a vacuum pan at a temperature of 74-77 °C for 15 minutes and cooled. This heat treatment gives evaporated milk a light brown colour owing to sugar-protein interaction and its characteristic flavour. As per PFA rules, the condensed milk should contain 26 % milk solid, of which 8 % is fat.
9. **Fortified skimmed milk:** It is skimmed milk with vitamins added. It has less than 1 % milkfat, yet contains the fat-soluble vitamins because these have been added after the milk is skimmed.

10. **Pasteurised milk**: It is the milk that has been subjected to heat treatment to destroy bacteria. It should be kept for 4-5 days in the refrigerator. It spoils but does not sour.

MILK PRODUCTS

Butter

Churning fresh or fermented cream or milk. Its used as spread or in the production of flavouring ingredients.

Cheese

It is available in wide range of flavours, textures and forms by coagulation of milk protein 'casein'. It comprises proteins, fat and milk. Milk is usually of cows, buffalos, goats or sheep.

Khoa

Khoa is semi-solid, obtained from milk by evaporating it in open pans. Milk is cautiously stirred in a circular motion to prevent scorching. When milk becomes viscous, the rate of stirring is increased to maintain a uniform

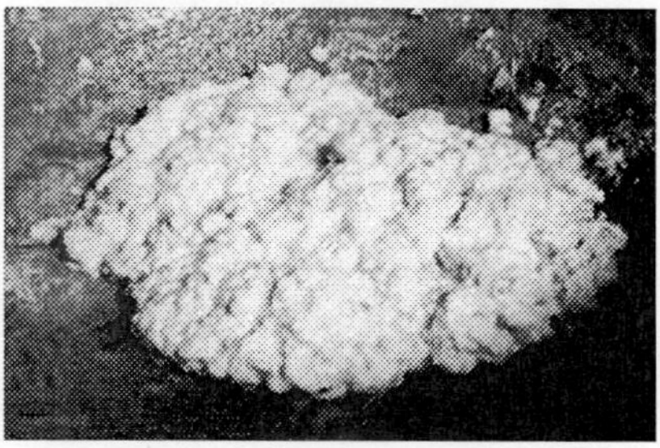

consistency. After cooling, it becomes solid. The yield is about 20 % of the weight of the milk used with cottage cheese.

During the preparation of khoa, all the milk protein is coagulated because of appreciable homogenisation that occurs during vigorous boiling. When coagulation of proteins sets in, all the fat decreases in vitamin A and some water-soluble vitamins. Buffalo's milk khoa contains 46 % fat and cow's milk contains 35 % fat.

It is used in the preparation of gulab jamun, carrot halwa, etc.

Ghee (Clarified butter)

Ghee is a type of clarified butter that originated in ancient India. It is basically prepared by simmering the butter, which is churned from the cream thus skimming any impurities from the surface and then pouring and retaining the clear liquid fat while discarding the solid residue that has settled to the bottom.

USES OF MILK

1. In soups and sauces;
2. In vegetable preparations;
3. For making puddings, cakes and sweet dishes;
4. For the preparation of non-alcoholic drinks, such as milk shakes; and
5. In preparation of hot drinks, such as tea, coffee, hot chocolates, etc.

COMPOSITION OF MILK

Protein	11 %
Fats	3 %
Minerals	1 %
Vitamins	1 %

Carbohydrates	2 %
Water	82 %

The composition of milk is affected by:

1. Breed of animals.
2. Phase of lactation period.
3. Type of food given to the animals.

Nutritive Value of Milk

The main protein in milk is casein. It is easily coagulated by the action of acids, e.g., renin (enzyme present in calf's intestine). Other proteins present in milk are: lacto-albumin and lacto-globulin.Lactose is the primary carbohydrate present in milk sugar. The minerals present in the milk are Ca, Na, S, K, Mg, etc., and vitamins of A and B groups.

CHECK YOUR PROGRESS

1. What is pasteurisation? Explain the different methods of pasteurisation.
2. Describe different kinds of milk.
3. Write a short note on homogenised milk.
4. Write a short note on nutritive value of milk.
5. Write the full form of HTST and UHT.
6. Explain the manufacturing of milk powder?
7. Write the advantages and disadvantages of homogenised milk.
8. Explain the steps involved in the storage of milk.

Unit 2

Cream

Cream is a dairy product,constituting that part of milk which is rich in fat and has been separated by skimming or otherwise. Originally, the cream was separated from the milk by gravity. When milk is left to stand in a vessel, fat globules cluster or aggregate and being lighter than rest of the milk, rise to the surface to form a layer of cream, which may be skimmed off by hand or can be skimmed with the help of a ladle as well.

Nowadays, commercial cream manufacturers use centrifugal force to separate the cream. Commercially, the viscosity of cream can now be controlled by manufacturing processes, giving a variation in the thickness of creams of the same fat content.

The principal difference between the various types of cream – single cream, double cream, whipped cream, clotted cream and soured cream – is the balance between the water and butterfat. This makes them liquid of a thick consistency. Other differences are in the way they have been made and their time of maturing, which results in different tastes.

Types of Cream

S. No	Cream varieties	Fat percentage
1	Single cream	18 % fat
2	Double cream	45 % fat
3	Whipping cream	38-40 % fat
4	Clotted cream	55 % fat
5	Sour cream	20 % fat
6	Double thick cream	50% fat
7	Sterilized cream	55% fat

PROCESSING OF CREAM

The most critical phase of production is the separation of cream from the raw milk. This process takes time and attention. After separation, there are several possible directions to go.

- You can put some fat back into the milk to make it creamier (e.g., semi-skimmed milk with 1.5 % fat);
- You can also pasteurise or UHT-treat the remaining hot (60 °C) cream to sell as whipping cream;
- It can be cooled, stored and later turned into crème fraîche, coffee cream, cooking cream, sour cream, etc.

The production of cream varies slightly in the different types of cream; however, the production of most involves the separation of fat from milk which is done through centrifugation. Centrifugation involves the rotation of milk at high speed by an electric motor; the force of this process causes the milk-fat globules to separate from the denser liquid. This process is continued until cream of the desired fat content is produced.

The cream is then pasteurised (heat-treated) to kill any bacteria that may be present. Pasteurisation also destroys lipases (enzymes) which can affect the flavour of the cream and reduce its shelf life. Whipped and whipping creams are made by mixing cream with air to roughly double the volume. The air bubbles are captured in the network of fat droplets.

Clotted cream involves a slightly different method of production. Traditionally, cow's milk is strained into a shallow pan and then left for 6-14 hours. We keep this to allow the cream to rise to the surface of the milk. This milk with a cream layer is then heated in the pan over a water bath to 80-90 °C and is kept there for 40-50 minutes. It is then allowed to cool for 24 hours, during which time the cream layer forms a solid crust which can be lifted clear of the skimmed milk, creating a product with more than 55 % fat. The commercial production of clotted cream involves a float cream method. This involves scalding a layer of double cream poured over skimmed milk or whole milk held in shallow trays. Sterilised cream undergoes a more severe form of heat treatment than pasteurised cream. Sterilisation destroys nearly all the bacteria present, meaning it can be kept unopened for several months without refrigeration. The cream is put into cans and heat treated. The high temperatures involved give the cream a caramelised flavour.

Sour cream contains 18 % or more milkfat and is subjected to a bacterial culture resulting in the production of lactic acid, which sours and thickens the product.

TYPES OF CREAM

Following are the most common types of cream available with the legal minimum milk fat content by weight.

(a) **Clotted cream:** It has about 55 % of milk fat and is traditionally produced by pouring milk into shallow pans, which is then left undisturbed for 12-24 hours for the cream to rise. The pans are then heated or scalloped to about 82 °C (180 °F) and held at this temperature for about an hour. The surface cream develops a rich yellow wrinkled crust. The pans are cooled slowly and the cream crust skimmed off. The heating of the cream improves its keeping qualities by destroying bacteria, which may cause souring. Clotted cream is traditionally served with scones, fruit and fruit pies.

(b) **Double cream:** It has about 48 % of milk fat and is produced commercially by centrifugal separation and sometimes slightly homogenised and may also be pasteurised. It can be used for pouring, for making baucorises, ice creams, etc.

(c) **Whipped or whipping cream:** It has about 35 % of milkfat and is produced commercially by centrifugal separation. It is pasteurised and may or may not be homogenised. Whipping cream will double its volume and is less likely to curdle through over-whipping. It is ideal for piped decoration on desserts and gateaux. It is also sold in the market after whipping and is known as whipped cream.

(d) **Single cream:** It has about 18 % of milkfat and is normally homogenised to prevent separations during storage. It may be pasteurised. Single cream is used as a pouring cream in coffee, on fruit and cream and to enrich soups and sweet and savoury dishes.

(e) **Half cream**: It is homogenised to prevent separation and it may also be pasteurised. It is also known as coffee cream.

(f) **Soured (dairy sour) cream**: 18 % is pasteurised-homogenised single cream, sourced by the addition of a culture of harmless bacteria which grows in cream and converts the natural sugar, lactose into lactic acid. It has a piquant refreshing flavour used for enhancing sweet and savoury dishes.

(g) **UHT cream:** It is subjected to ultra-heat treatment, which destroys microorganisms present in the cream without significantly affecting its nutritional value. However, there is a slight change in the flavour. The heat treatment is carried out by heating cream up to 140 °C (284 °F) for about 2 seconds. The treated cream is homogenised, poured into sterile containers and sealed under antiseptic conditions. Double, whipping and single cream can all be presented by UHT.

(h) **Frozen cream:** Any or all the creams can be pasteurised and cooked and, commercially frozen by blast freezing up to 18 °C.

(i) **Aerosol cream:** Cream is ultra heated and filled into aerosol containers. Nitrous oxide is used as a propellant to release the whipped cream and acid aeration. Volume increases by 400 %. It is good for instant use as it collapses soon.

CLASSIFICATION OF CREAM

Type	Fat %	Processing & packaging	Storage	Characteristics & uses
Half cream	12 %	Homogenised (usually UHT).	2 months (unopened), 2-3 days (refrigerated).	Cannot be whipped. Used for coffee & sauces.
Single cream	18 %	Homogenised (usually UHT).	2-3 days (refrigerated).	Cannot be whipped. Used for coffee & sauces.
Sour cream	18 %	Pasteurised/ homogenised + Bacterial culture	2-3 days (refrigerated)	Cannot be whipped. Suitable for sweet & savoury preparations, salad dressing, etc.
Whipped cream	35 %	Pasteurised/ homogenised (usually UHT).	2-3 days (refrigerated).	It whips up to double it. Ideal for piping into cake and deserts.
Double cream	48 %	Pasteurised/ homogenised (usually UHT).	2-3 days (refrigerated).	It whips up to 1 ½ times of its volume. Ideal for piping into cakes and deserts.
Clotted cream	55 %	Pasteurised/ homogenised (usually UHT).	4-6 days (refrigerated). If frozen, can be kept for 1 month.	Suitable for pies. Not recommended for cooking.
Sterilised cream	55 %	Homogenised/ sterilised .	2 years (unopened), 2-3 days (refrigerated).	Cannot be whipped.

(Contd...)

Type	Fat %	Processing & packaging	Storage	Characteristics & uses
Crème Fraiche	30-40 %	Pasteurised/ homogenised + Bacterial culture.	3 weeks (refrigerated).	Cannot be whipped. Suitable for sweet & savoury preparations, salad dressing, etc.
Frozen cream	18 % (S.C) 35 % (W.C.) 48 % (D.C) 55 % (C.C.)	Pasteurised, cooled & frozen (blast freezing).	1 year in deep freezer.	As per variety.
Non-dairy cream	Varies	Cream substitute based on fat and oil, which are emulsified in water.	It varies from product to product. Normally, stored in refrigerator.	Pouring and whipping.

STORAGE

1. Fresh cream should be kept in containers in which it is to be delivered.
2. Stored in refrigerator.
3. Keep covered.
4. Use frozen cream after thawing.
5. Canned cream should be stored in cool, dry and ventilated area.

HANDLING / USING CREAM

1. Whip in clean and chilled bowl.
2. If over-whipped, fold 30 mL of cream to 150 mL of whipped cream.
3. When adding the cream to hot liquids, dilute the cream with some of the liquid, then add.

CHECK YOUR PROGRESS

1. Explain the processing done for cream.
2. Discuss the points to be remembered while using cream.
3. Describe the role of cream.
4. Write a short note on frozen cream.
5. Write a short note on whipped cream.
6. Describe the characteristics and uses of clotted cream.
7. Describe the characteristics and uses of sour cream.
8. Explain the steps involved in the storage of cream.

Unit 3

Cheese

Making cheese is both an art and a science. Cheese is made of milk. It comprises protein 'casein'. It is a preserved form of milk made by the coagulating, draining or pressing, and salting for milk and fats. It is popular for versatility, longevity, portability, and nutritional values. Cheese is a stable food with a longer shelf life than other products of milk. Cheese is available in numerous styles, shapes, tastes and textures, all developed in different regions, climates, and cultures of the world.

Cheese comprises

Water	38 %
Fat	35 %
Protein	25 %
Others	2 %

Nutritional value of cheese

Protein	–	for growth
Calcium	–	for strong bones & teeth
Vitamin A	–	important for immune system, bone growth & vision
Vitamin B12	–	for red blood cells
Vitamin D	–	to help absorb calcium

PROCESSING OF CHEESE

Processed cheeses are made from one or several cooked or uncooked pressed cheeses that are re-melted, and to which, milk, cream or butter is added; they keep for a long time. Depending on the product, stabilizers, emulsifiers, salt, colours, sweeteners and seasonings, may be added.

There are six important steps in cheese making: acidification, coagulation, separating curds and whey, salting, shaping, and ripening.

CLASSIFICATION OF CHEESE

1. **Fresh:** Fresh cheeses are coagulated under the action of lactic acid fermentation in the milk instead of adding rennet. While they are drained after formation of the curd, they are neither ripened nor fermented. This category includes cottage cheese, ricotta, mascarpone, cream cheese and quark.
2. **Soft:** Soft cheeses are ripened for a relatively short period before being drained and turned into moulds without being pressed or cooked. They have a moisture content of 50-60 % and their fat content is 20-26 % of the cheese's weight. They develop a soft rind that can be more or less satiny and are usually eaten with bread. They tend to lose flavour when heated.
3. **Semihard:** Semi-firm cheeses are uncooked pressed cheeses that are dense and usually pale yellow. They include- Cheddar, Cantal, Reblochon, Edam, Gouda and Monterey Jack. Firm cheeses are cheeses that have been cooked and pressed. The curd is heated for an hour in order to make it more concentrated, which, upon pressing, produces a more compact cheese. Their texture is usually firm, although some hard cheeses, like Parmesan and Romano, may have a rather granular texture.
4. **Blue vein:** Blue veined (or blue) cheeses are neither cooked nor pressed; the curd is inoculated with a species of blue-green mould, which is injected into the cheese

Classification of Cheese

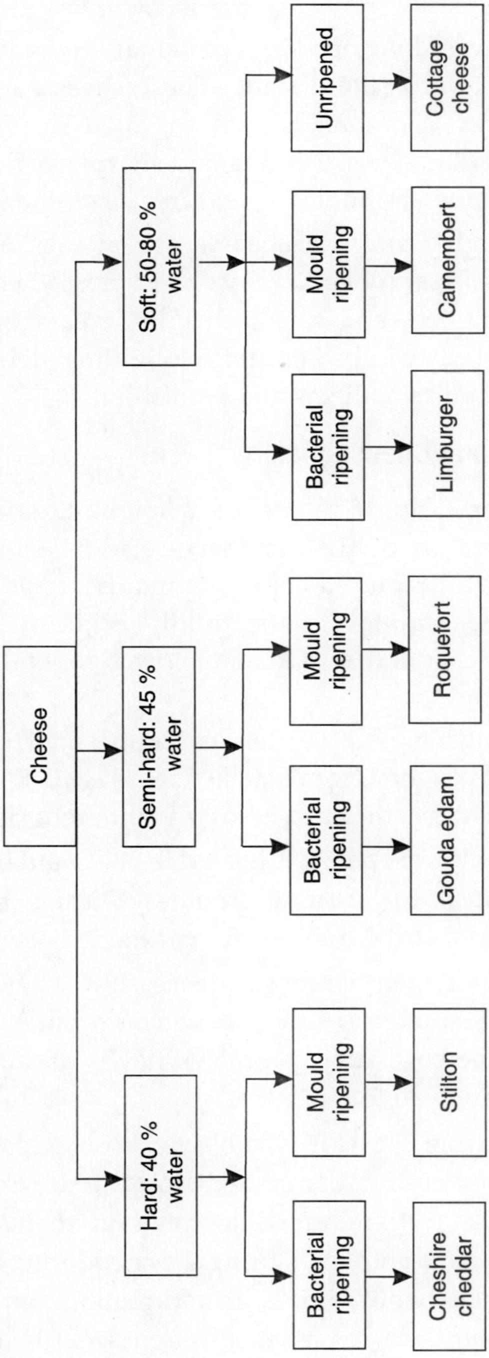

by means of long needles. Fermentation occurs from the inside towards the outside. These cheeses – including Roquefort, Gorgonzola, Stilton, Bleu de Bresse and Danish Blue – have a strong and sharp, peppery flavour and are often crumbled in texture.

5. **Processed:** Processed cheeses are cheeses made from one or several cooked or uncooked pressed cheeses that are re-melted, and to which milk, cream or butter is added. They can be kept for a long time, depending on the product, stabilizers and emulsifier.

Steps Involved in Cheese Making

1. **Curd formation:** Pasteurised whole milk is brought to a temperature of 31 °C and lactic acid producing starter culture and required colouring matter are added. After about 30 minutes to the mildly acidic milk, rennin solution is added, stirred and allowed to set the curd for 30 minutes.
2. **Curd cutting:** The curd is cut into small cubes. The removal of whey from small cubes is easy. For different type of cheese, the curd is cut into different sized cubes.
3. **Curd cooking:** Then, it is heated to 38 °C and held at that temperature for about 45 minutes. During this period, the curd is stirred to prevent matting.
4. **Curd drainage:** Heating squeezes out whey from the cubes. Heat increases the rate of acid production, which makes the curd cubes shrink. Whey is drained off and curd is allowed to mat.
5. **Cheddaring:** Next, it is subjected to cheddaring. This consists of cutting the matted curd into blocks, turning the block at 15-minute intervals and then piling the blocks on one another. During the cheddaring operation, which takes about 2 hours, acid formation continues. The cheddared curd is passed through a curd mill, which cuts the slabs into strips.

6. **Salting the curd:** Whey is eliminated during this process. Salt is added to draw whey out of curd by osmosis and also acts as a preservative. Salt also holds down spoilage of organisms and adds flavour.
7. **Pressing:** The cheese cubes are pressed under pressure overnight. This pressing determines the final moisture content of the finished products and then the cheese is ripened from 60 days to 12 months, depending on the strong or mild flavour of cheese required.
8. **Ripening:** Ripening takes place under controlled conditions of temperature and humidity for varying periods of time and makes cheese easily digestible. During this process, cheese changes from a bland tough rubbery mass to a full-flavoured soft product. During ripening, rennin splits the protein of cheese into peptones and peptides. Enzymes formed by the microorganisms act on these and other substances, to form products like amino acids, amines, fatty acids, esters, aldehydes, alcohols and ketones, that give its characteristic flavour. There is also an increase in B-vitamins during ripening. Ripening also improves the cooking quality. The increased dispensability of the protein of ripened cheese is a factor in the blending of cheese with other food ingredients.

The types of starters used also contribute to flavour and consistency of cheese.

Cheese has limited shelf-life and requires refrigeration, should be kept cold and dry, i.e., it should be wrapped in wax paper or metal foil.

Nisin is naturally produced in cheese by a number of strains of cheese starter organisms. It inhibits some clostridia. Nisin is a bio-preservative and is generally recognised as safe (GRAS).

COOKING QUALITY

Hydrolysis of the proteins of the cheese occurs during ripening. Cooking quality of cheddar cheese of normal fat content improves as the product of protein hydrolysis is increased.

Moisture content is also related to cooking quality, since cheese of high-moisture content is superior compared to low-moisture cheese.

When fat content is low, the tendency for mat formation is exaggerated. The fat of normal samples melted during cooking contributes to the consistency and tenderness of the heated product, preventing the formation of a continuous protein mass. The cooking quality of processing cheese is better than the natural cheese (cottage cheese). The presence of emulsifying agent does not help in keeping the fat emulsified but in increasing the alkalinity of cheese, which, in turn increases the solubility of casein. As casein is rendered more soluble, it is less likely to be tough or form firm string on cooking. It is possible that both ageing and the addition of emulsifying salts improve the cooking quality of cheese because they make the protein more soluble. We can also add smoky flavour, herbs and spices at the time of processing of cheese.

DIFFERENT VARIETIES OF CHEESE AND THEIR USES

Sulguni

A pickled Georgian cheese from the Samergrelo region. It has a sour, moderate salty flavour, a dimpled texture, and an elastic consistency. These attributes are the result of the process used, as is the source of its moniker "pickle cheese". Its colour ranges from white to pale yellow. Sulguni is often deep fried, which masks its odour. It is often served in wedges.

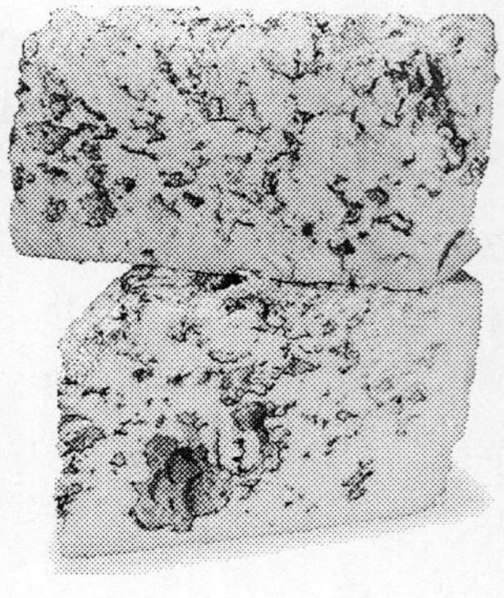

Sakura Cheese

A soft cheese created in Hokkaido, Japan. It is creamy white and flavoured with mountain cherry leaves. Sakura means "cherry blossom" in Japanese.

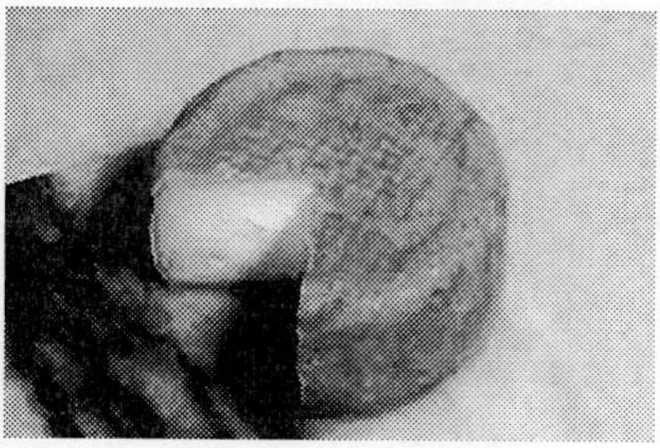

Byaslag

This cheese from Mangoliais prepared with cow or yak milk, has a lumpish curd and is somewhat sour in flavour.

Herve Cheese

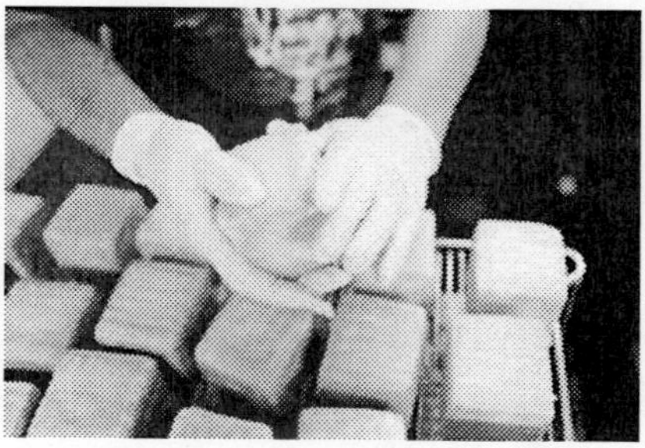

An aged cheese made from unpasteurised cow's milk. It is traditionally aged in humid caves. It is from Belgium.

Limburger Cheese

It originated during the 19th century in the historical Dutchy of Limburg, which is now divided among modern-day Belgium, Germany and Netherlands. The cheese is especially known for its pungent odour. Order of the most traditional forms of eating Limburger is the Limburger Sandwich.

Danish Blue

Danish blue cheese (Danablu) is from Denmark. Danablu is a strong, blue-veined cheese. This semi-soft cheese is typically drum or block-shaped and has white to yellowish, slightly moist, edible rind. Made from full fat cow's milk and homogenised cream, it has a fat content of about 25-30 % and is aged for 8-12 weeks.

Camembert

Camembert is handmade and a soft cheese. It originated in a village called Camembert, in Normandy, France. There are very good Camemberts made in Normandy from pasteurised milk, of which "Le Châtelain" is one. Because of their short aging period (just over three weeks), you will not find any raw milk Camembert. It is rich, buttery, and spreadable. Camembert has a mild, mushroomy aroma.

Best uses: Eaten as it is on sandwiches, baked in a crust, breaded and deep-fried.

Cheddar

Cheddar is a cow's milk cheese that originated in Somerset, England. In this cheese making process, the curds of the cow's milk are cooked and then milled into rice-size pieces. The pieces are then pressed into large blocks, and the blocks are stacked one on top of another to remove the remaining moisture. Cheddar cheeses, made in this traditional fashion, are dry and crumbly in texture, with a deep, tangy, nutty flavour. Cheddar-style cheeses vary in quality, so it is a good idea to talk to your cheesemonger about them. The colour ranges from ivory to straw to deep yellow in colour, depending on the season and the feed of the cattle.

Best uses: In sandwiches, grilled cheese, casseroles, etc.

Emmental

Emmental is what many people think of when they hear "Swiss cheese" (yes, holes and all). It is considered an "Alpine-style" or "mountain" cheese, as it originates from the milk of cows that are led up the Alps to graze over multiple seasons, and the curds are cooked and pressed together firmly. The holes you find are bubbles of carbon dioxide created as the bacterium *Propionibacterium freudenreichii* consumes lactic acid. This cheese has certain sweetness with a piquancy that hits the back of the tongue on the finish. Like all Alpine cheeses, it is a great melter.

Best uses: Fondue, grilled cheese, casseroles, etc.

Mozzarella

Mozzarella is a fresh, pulled-curd cheese, made from the milk of water buffalo (for *mozzarella di bufala*) or cows (for *mozzarella fior di latte*). The curds are heated in warm water and stretched by hand before being rolled into moist balls. The balls of cheese can then either be sold fresh, or packed in a salty brine to add flavour. Fresh and dairy-rich, Mozzarella is prized for its texture and mild creamy flavour.

Best uses: Fresh with a drizzle of olive oil, coarse salt and pepper,in sandwich, pizza, etc.

STORAGE OF CHEESE

A resalable plastic bag will do the job, but it is not the ideal storage solution for your cheese. The best way to wrap leftovers depends on the particular type.

Whatever the type of cheese, stash it in the vegetable crisper of the refrigerator, where the temperature is cold and stable.

Use a fresh piece of plastic wrap or wax paper to wrap cheese after each use.

The length of time you can keep cheese also differs according to the variety; in general, the harder the cheese, the longer it will last.

The varieties of cheese are differentiated according to their flavour, body and the texture, which, in turn, depends upon the type of milk used, manufacturing and processing method adopted, salts and seasoning added and the type of bacterial and mould species used in the ripening. Cheese is classified as hard-semi-hard or soft, depending on its moisture content and whether it is ripened by bacterial or mould ripening or whether it is unripened.

CHECK YOUR PROGRESS

1. What is cheese? How is it manufactured?
2. Write the nutritional importance of cheese.
3. Write a short note on cottage cheese.
4. What is Mozzarella cheese? Where is it used?
5. Identify three categories of cheese and give one example for each.
6. What is pasteurisation?
7. Identify five key factors considered while storing cheese.

Unit 4

Butter

Butter is made by churning cream until the fats separate from the liquid (buttermilk). It is believed that the nomads first discovered butter making. They are said to have collected milk from cattle and goats, separated the cream from the milk, and continuously mixed the cream until it turned into butter. Farm made butter uses the cream directly from whole milk whereas commercially made butter is made by extracting small amounts of cream from whey, a by-product of cheese making, using large centrifuges. Butter is essentially the fat of the milk. It is usually made from sweet cream and is salted. However, it can also be made from acidulated or bacteriological soured cream and saltless (sweet) butters are also available.

In the 19th century, butter was still made from cream that was allowed to stand and sour naturally. The cream was then skimmed from the top of the milk and poured into a wooden tub. Butter making was done by hand, in butter churns. The natural souring process is, however, a very sensitive one and infection by foreign microorganisms often spoils the result.

Commercial butter making is a product of the knowledge and experience gained over the years in such matters as hygiene, bacterial acidifying and heat treatment, as well as the rapid technical developments that have led to the advanced machinery. The commercial cream separator was introduced at the end of the 19th century; the continuous churn was commercialized by the middle of the 20th century.

In detail, butter should come from the churning process of butter- milk, which should have a fat content of 80 %. The cream made in butter making can either be fresh or soured, although most of the butter produced is from the former. The residue that is left after butter making is buttermilk, although nowadays buttermilk is often made from pasteurised skimmed milk. Margarine was originally invented as a low-cost alternative to butter by a French chemist. He made an emulsion of beef fat extract, water and skimmed milk.

Margarine consists of refined and purified edible oils, such as sunflowers, palm, soy and coconut. These are then hydrogenated (a process which adds hydrogen and solidifies the oils). A similar but more expensive technological process blends together the oil and high proportion of water (up to 60 %), enabling some commercial producers to market a low-calorie polyunsaturated spread. The hard or block margarine contains saturated or animal fats. All animal fats need some processing before use. Suet, raw, hard fat of beef or mutton found around the loins and kidneys must be skinned and cleaned. Dripping (the fat separated from meat during cooking) has to be strained or clarified, while lard (pork fat) is purified. It is heated, liquefied and then strained.

PROCESSING AND MANUFACTURING OF BUTTER

Holding: Cream is pasteurised for 2-4 seconds at 95 °C & then temperature is lowered to 4-5 °C. Then, it is kept for several hours to ensure uniformity of fat particles.

Ripening: When the end-product is going to be lactic butter only, then this step is carried out in which bacteria culture is added. In this case, the holding temperature is 15-18 °C for 3-4 hours before being cooled to 4-5 ° C. This gives butter a good flavour.

Churning: It is carried out in which stainless steel contains about 100 gallons of cream and the internal churning is passed through the cream. This breaks the layers of fat, which are released and combined to form a large group of butter,which gets separated from buttermilk and floors to the surface.

Washing and salting: The butter grains are now washed, with ice cold water to remove any buttermilk left on the surface of each grain, in order to maximize the keeping quality. Salting is carried out in two ways: by adding fine grains dairy source and by dipping butter grains into brine solution (solution formed from salt and vinegar) for 10-15 minutes and allow the butter grains to absorb it.

STORAGE OF BUTTER

1. In a refrigerator from 2 to 5 °C.
2. It should be properly wrapped and covered, so that it does not absorb any flavour from outside.
3. If purchased in bulk, it should be stored at 25-30 °C (can be kept for several months).
4. It should not be exposed to the sunlight, as it can lose vitamin A and become sour.
5. Salted and sweet cream butter can be kept for a longer duration as compared to basic butter.

USES OF BUTTER

1. As a spread on bread,
2. as a basic ingredient in cakes & pastries,
3. as a cooking medium but should be treated at high temperature,
4. used as given sheen (glaze) for giving finishing to the cooked food,
5. in preparation of sauces. For example, Béchamel sauce, and
6. as a roux, which acts as a thickening agent.

PACKING & STORAGE

The butter is finally patted into a shape, wrapped in waxed paper and then, stored in a cool place. As it cools, the butterfat crystallizes and the butter becomes firm. Whipped butter, made by whipping air or nitrogen gas into soft butter, is intended to spread more easily at refrigeration temperatures. Separate the cream from the milk. Let your raw milk set in a clear container for at least a day in the refrigerator, until you can easily see a distinct cream line on the top. Two days is enough for the cream to separate from the milk.

Depending on what kind of cow's milk, as well as the season during which the milk was harvested, the cream content of the milk changes. For example, during winter, the cream content in the milk increases, whereas it generally decreases during the summers.

Using a dipper, skim the cream off the top. From one whole gallon of raw milk, you can expect about 2-4 cups of cream – sometimes more, sometimes less. Pour the cream into a glass jar with an accompanying lid.

Let your cream ripen or culture (optional). You do not have to let your butter culture, but if you do, you will get richer, more flavourful butter. Set out on the counter for about 12 hours or until the cream is between 70 and 75 °F (21 and 24 °C) and smells slightly sour.

This is a natural way to let the cream culture and develop a slight acidity in the butter. Hasten the process by adding some culture. The live cultures in the yogurt or buttermilk work great for speeding up the process. For every two cups of cream, add one tablespoon of yogurt or buttermilk. Stir to incorporate. In a warm environment, the cream should be cultured in about 5-6 hours instead of 12. Agitate the cream until butter separate from the buttermilk. If your butter is in a sealed mason jar, agitating is as simple as shaking the jar back and forth, for anywhere from 5 to 15 minutes. You will feel the weight of the jar changing, as the butter solids coagulate. When the cream starts sloshing against the jar and you feel the weight of the solids, start agitating slower.

A quick way of agitating is to use a mixer or blender. Fill it up to half full with cream. Mix on medium low to begin with, until either the motor pulls down or you see lumps floating on top, and then, use the slowest setting to finish the churn. Pour off the buttermilk separated from the butter. You can use the buttermilk in cooking or baking.

Wrap the butter in cheesecloth or butter muslin. When covered completely with cheesecloth, run the butter through a bowl of ice-water. This process "cleanse" the butter, further separating any cream from the butter solids to achieve a richer butter.

When the ice-water bowl becomes milky, dump it out and fill it with more ice and water. Repeat the cleaning process until the water no longer becomes milky after running the butter through it. Knead the butter with a wooden spoon or another slightly rounded implement. Ditch the cheesecloth (you can reuse it, if you want) and dump the butter into a bowl. With a wooden spoon, knead the butter.

Add salt, herbs, or other flavourings to the butter at this point (optional). While you are still kneading the butter, add salt if you like your butter salted (butter without salt is much sweeter). If salting, try 1/2 teaspoon of salt per 1/2 lb of butter and work your way up from there. If you wish to add herbs or spices to your butter, try experimenting with any of the following for just the tip of the iceberg:

- Chives
- Orange, lemon, or lime rind
- Rosemary or thyme
- Garlic or ginger
- Parsley

Press the butter firmly into the container. A nice little butter mould will add a dainty touch to your butter while allowing you to serve it in individual portions. Refrigerate or freeze the butter you are not serving immediately.

BUTTER MAKING PROCESS

1. Raw cream
   - Pasteurisation
   - Starter culture inoculation and cream ripening
2. Aging
   - Butterfat crystallising
3. Churning
   - Butter granules
4. Draining & washing
   - Raw butter
5. Working & salting
   - Finished butter
6. Packaging, storage, etc.

   Buttermilk
   - Pasteurisation, processing packaging

   Raw skim milk
   - Pasteurisation, processing, packaging

Troubleshooting of Problems

1. If your butter tastes a little sour or not fresh, there is a good chance that the milk was allowed to rest too long before the cream was skimmed.
2. If the raw milk is from a farmer, ask for fresh milk.
3. Collect butter that is either too soft or too warm. The butter should be slightly cooled.
4. Getting butter to this consistency is not difficult, but problems do arise sometimes if the butter is too soft; the cream may have been warmer than 75° F (24 °C) when it was agitated or it was not agitated long enough. It may take at least 5-10 minutes to agitate by hand, but not longer than 30 minutes.

5. If you get butter before you hit 5 minutes of agitation, chances are that you started off with cream that was too warm.
6. If the butter is too hard; either the cream was too cold when it was agitated or it was agitated for too long.
7. Again, butter should be agitated when it is 70-75 °F (21-24 °C) and not take longer than 30 minutes to agitate by hand.
8. Collect waxy butter that does not melt in your mouth. This kind of butter is usually overworked during the final stages of kneading.
9. Collect butter that sweats too readily. If you see moisture forming bit too easily on the surface of your butter after all is said and done, it either means it was not rinsed properly or the salt was not incorporated evenly.
10. Making butter is easy with a food processor, and it produces a light fresh taste. You will need:1-2 cups heavy whipping cream or double cream (1/3 litre), food processor with plastic blade, whisk, or normal chopping blade. Fill food processor about 1/4-1/2 full. Blend the cream and it will go through the following stages: sloshy, frothy, soft whipped cream, firm whipped cream and coarse whipped cream. Then, suddenly the cream will seize, its smooth shape will collapse and the whirring will change to sloshing. The butter is now fine grained bits of butter in buttermilk, and a few seconds later, a glob of yellowish butter will separate from milky buttermilk. Drain the buttermilk, you can eat the butter now –it has a light taste – it will store better if you wash and work it. Add 1/2 cup (100 mL) of ice-cold water, and blend further. Discard wash water and repeat until the wash water is clear. Now, work butter to remove the suspended water. Either place damp butter into a cool bowl and knead with a potato masher or forks, or put in large covered jar and shake or tumble. Continue working and pouring

out the water occasionally, until most of the water is removed. The butter is now ready. Put butter in a butter crock; ramekins, or roll in a waxy or freezer paper.

Yield: About half as much butter as the amount of cream you started with.

Various Options

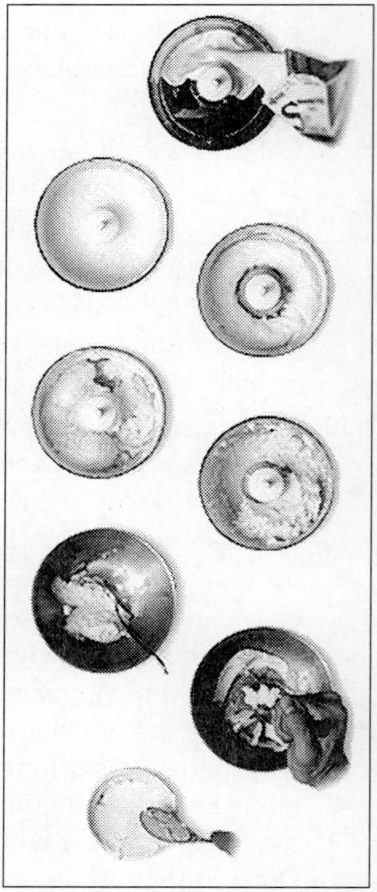

Stages of buttermaking in the food processor, and bowl

- Add salt to taste before working.
- Have the cream around 60 °F/15 °C before churning. (55 °F/13 °C for goat milk).
- Obtain the freshest cream you can. So-called "vat pasteurised cream" tastes better than ultra-heat treated (UHT) or HTST-pasteurised.
- Shake in a jar instead of a food processor. Shake about once a second. Add a marble to speed things up. Do it for 5-30 minutes, depending on the shaking.
- Culture the cream before churning. Add a few tablespoons (50 mL) store-bought cultured yogurt, buttermilk, sour cream, clabbered cream, or crème fraiche, and let it sit about 12 hours at room temperature (75 °F/24 °C is ideal) to thicken and ferment before churning. It should taste delicious, slightly sour, with no aftertaste. If it is bubbly or smells yeasty or gassy, discard it.

- Use some butter making tools, such as a churn, paddle for working, or moulds for forming the finished butter.

TYPES OF BUTTER

Blended Butter

It is the blend of butter which can be taken off from various breeds of animals, which are mixed together to obtain a uniformly acceptable butter at a low price.

Clarified Butter

It is obtained by gently heating the butter and separating solid component, i.e., protein. For example, ghee.

Unsalted Butter

In simple terms, this is a traditional butter without salt. It is ideal for baking or cooking because the lack of salt means that the cook can add his/her own salt, as required by the recipe. They do not need to worry about the extra salt in the butter that can disturb the flavouring.

Salted Butter

Think of salted butter as almost a condiment style of butter. It is commonly used to spread on toast or to season vegetables. The salt in this butter adds flavour, which makes it ideal for eating directly when spread on top of a food. Salted butter can be a problem when baking because you have to account for the salt in the butter in addition to the salt required for the recipe. This is why many recipes call for unsalted butter. Salted butter lasts longer than the unsalted butter because the salt preserves it.

Raw Butter

Raw butter is unpasteurised and unprocessed butter that is made from raw cream. It is believed that raw butter is superior to pasteurised butter because its nutrients are not killed during the pasteurisation process. Of course, there is the debate on whether unpasteurised products are safe or not. Raw butter tends to be pricey.

Dripping

An animal cooking fat, this is separated fat produced from cooking meat.

Lard

This is melted and clarified pork fat. Softer than butter and margarine, it can be used for baking and frying.

Margarine

A butter substitute, made from animal or vegetable fats, margarine can be bought in blocks or tubs.

Suet

Often used in puddings, suet is the fat surrounding the kidneys of certain animals. It is grated and ready for use.

Soft Margarine

Soft margarine (vegetable) fat spreads, high in polyunsaturated fats, which are made from sunflower, soybean and olive oil. It is easier to spread.

Ghee

A type of clarified butter made by heating ordinary butter to rid its impurities, ghee is the yellow liquid left when the sediments have been removed. It has a higher burning point than most other oils, which makes it perfect for frying and sautéing.

Organic Butter

Organic butter comes in unsalted and salted form. Organic here means that it is produced from organic milk. The cows are purportedly pesticide-free, antibiotic-free, and growth hormone-free. The cows are allowed to graze in the pasture for several months during the year, unlike most non-organic producing cows. In theory, this creates a healthier cow and a healthier butter product.

SHORTENINGS

All baked goods use fat as shortening, the amount varying from 5 to 10 % in biscuits and cookies, 10 to 20 % in cakes, and 15 to 30 % in pound cakes.

Fats impact flavour, texture, and tenderness of the bakery product.

Pound Cakes

- Air is incorporated by creaming of fat.
- Each little air is bubbled and is surrounded by the gluten of flour, which stretches and sets to form a rigid structure when the cake is baked.
- The extent of creaming the fat affects the texture of the cake.
- The tenderness of the product is also due to fats.
- Fat lubricates the tough and hard gluten and starch, so that they slide over one another and the walls crumble (tenderness) when the cake is bitten.

Butter Cakes

- Leavening depends on air and steam as well as on carbon dioxide produced from baking powder. The air bubbles serve as the nucleus for CO_2 gas.

  Fats have different shortening abilities.

MARGARINE

Margarine is made from partially hydrogenated (infused with hydrogen) or refined plant oils, which may also contain small amount of milk. It was created as a substitute for butter.

CHECK YOUR PROGRESS

1. What is organic butter? Why is it different from other flavoured butter?
2. What is the role of ripping in the process of butter?
3. What is the use of butter in bakery products?
4. Write a short note on the storage of butter.
5. Describe troubleshooting problems faced at the time of handling butter.
6. What is aging?
7. Identify five key factors to consider while storing butter products.
8. Write a note on unsalted butter.

Unit 5

Flour

COMPOSITION OF FLOUR

Approximate values vary from grain to grain and flour to flour.

Starch	70.5 to 74.5 %
Water	13.5 to 14.0 %
Gluten	7.0 to 10.0 %
Soluble protein	1.0 to 2 %
Sugar	2.0 to 2.5 %
Fat	1.0 %
Ash	0.5 %

MILLING

Milling is the process of breaking open the grain and releasing the starchy centre.

The flour grain has to be milled in order to extract all the components of the grain and to make it ready for the bread making process. There are two main methods employed to do this job, which are:

(a) Stone milling

(b) Roller milling

Stone milled flour is the more primitive method of milling flour and it consists of two heavy stones, on top of each other. The bottom one remains stationary while the top one moves in a circular fashion. There is a small opening on top of the stone, through which the grain is poured in. Heat is generated by friction during milling, part of which is absorbed by the stone. A part of heat goes to the germ and melts the germ oil and mixes it throughout the endosperm. This method is mainly used to make whole wheat flour and when refined flour is to be produced, the flour is sieved through silk bolting cloths to remove the coarse bran particles. However, all the particles are not removed by this method.

Some of the aleurone cells also pass into the flour which causes a slight softening of the flour/gluten. Roller milling is a more modern method of milling, where there is a gradual reduction in the size of the grain from coarse meal to fine flour. The mill consists of two horizontal rollers, one rotating faster than the other. This rolling has a tearing effect on the grain which is ripped open. Here, the germ is separated from the endosperm before milling and hence, the germ oil is not released into the flour. Also the aleurone cells are released into the flour to such a large extent, giving stronger flour.

TYPES OF FLOUR AND THEIR USE

Stone-Ground Wheat Flour

It is the flour that is ground between two roller stones. It has a good flavour and higher-fat content and hence, cannot be stored for long.

Organic Flour

Flours that are grown in field and fertilized by naturally occurring substances—composted materials, aged animal manure, and green manure. The soil as a result becomes more loose and this allows the roots to grow deeper, and the plant structure is strong. When the grain is harvested and cleaned, it is stored without fumigants or synthetic agents. The result is a full-bodied wholesome taste, like a tomato or a carrot grown in your own garden.

Commercial fields are on the other hand treated with pesticides, to fight bugs, herbicides to combat weeds, fungicides to combat fungi and other synthetic fertilizers. The young crop is sprayed repeatedly during the growing season and prayed again after it is harvested and stored. The flour is rather flat tasting and characterless in flavour.

Strong Flour

It is the best type of flour for making breads. If the flour is too hard, then we get bread that is course-textured.

Wheat Germ

This little seed is rich in vitamins B and E, proteins and salt and is present in the whole meal flour but partially removed in brown flour.

Barley Flour

Grown across Europe and was used to make breads when wheat became expensive. Now used more commonly for brewing. This flour can be found in baby foods and malted milks. In some countries, large quantities of barley flour are used for bread making.

Buck Wheat

It comes from the family of rhubarb and dock and therefore not a cereal but buckwheat flour provides a distinctively flavoured pancake and breakfast food ingredient.

Wheat Germ Flour

It is flour that has 10 % added wheat germ. It is very healthy and has a very nutty flavour.

Semolina

The wheat kernel or endosperm milled after removing the bran and the wheat germ.

From bread to biscuits, cookies to cakes, baking is the art of turning flour into (delicious) food. Flour, finely milled wheat or other grains, lends structure to baked goods, but different baked goods demand different structural supports. Choose the right flour for the right task and you are a long way towards baking success.

High-protein wheat varieties (10-14 % protein) are classed as "hard wheat." Low-protein wheat variety (5-10 %) is known as "soft wheat." Simply put: more protein equals more gluten equals more strength. And more strength translates into more volume and a chewier texture. Dough made from high-protein flours is both, more elastic (stretch further) and more extensible (hold their shape better) — desirable qualities in bread and many other yeasted products, where a firm structure is paramount, but undesirable in pastries and cakes, where the goal is flakiness or tenderness.

Unless labelled "whole-wheat," all flour is white flour, that is, milled from the starchy, innermost part of the wheat kernel, known as the endosperm.

All-Purpose Flour

If a recipe calls simply for "flour," it is calling for all-purpose flour. Milled from a mixture of soft and hard wheat, with moderate protein content (10-12 %), all-purpose flour is a staple among staples. While not necessarily good for all purposes, it is the most versatile of all flours, capable of producing flaky pie crusts, fluffy biscuits and chewy breads. All-purpose flour is sold bleached or unbleached; the two are largely interchangeable, but it is always best to match your flour with your recipe.

Cake Flour

This flour with the lowest protein content (5-8 %). The relative lack of gluten-forming proteins makes cake flour ideal for tender baked goods, such as cakes (of course), biscuits, muffins and scones. Cake flour is generally chlorinated, a bleaching process that further weakens the gluten proteins and, just as important, alters the flour's starch to increase its capacity to absorb more liquid and sugar, and thus, ensure a moist cake.

Pastry Flour

It is unbleached flour made from soft wheat, with protein levels somewhere between cake flour and all-purpose flour (8-9 %). Pastry flour strikes the ideal balance between flakiness and tenderness, making it is perfect for pies, tarts and many cookies. To make your own pastry flour, mix together $1^1/_3$ cups A-P flour and $^2/_3$ cup cake flour.

Bread Flour

With protein content of 12-14 %, bread flour is the strongest of all flours, providing the most structural support. This is especially important in yeasted breads, where a strong gluten network is required to contain the CO_2 gas produced during fermentation. The extra protein does not just make for better volume and a chewier crumb; it also results in more browning of the crust. Bread flour can be found in white or whole wheat, bleached or unbleached. Unbleached all-purpose flour can generally be substituted for bread flour with good results.

Self-Rising Flour

It is flour to which baking powder and salt have been added during milling. A southern staple, self-rising flour is generally made from the low-protein wheat, traditionally grown in the South India. It is best for tender biscuits, muffins, pancakes and some cakes. Self-rising flour is best stored as tightly wrapped in its original box and used within six months of purchase—longer than that and the baking powder begins to lose its oomph.

To make your own self-rising flour, combine 1 cup pastry flour with 1½ teaspoon baking powder and 1/4 teaspoon salt.

Whole-Wheat Flour

During milling, the wheat kernel is separated into its three components: the endosperm, the germ (the embryo) and the bran (the outer coating). In whole-wheat flours, varying amounts of the germ and bran are added back into the flour. Whole-wheat flour tends to be high in protein, but its gluten-forming ability is compromised by the bran and germ—just one of the reasons why whole-wheat flour tends to produce heavier, denser baked goods.

In most recipes, whole-wheat flour can be substituted for up to half of the all-purpose flour. Because wheat germ is high in oils and prone to rancidity, you may store whole-wheat flour for up to three months at cool room temperature, and then transfer it to the freezer.

Gluten-Free Flours

There is a wide variety of gluten-free flours available, made from all sorts of grains, nuts and starches. Some of the most widely available ones are based on rice flour, blended with tapioca and potato starch. A small proportion of xanthan gum is sometimes added to help simulate the chewiness normally associated with gluten. Consult the specific recipe or packaging for information on how to substitute gluten-free flour for wheat flour in your favourite baking recipes.

Bleached and Unbleached Flours

Unbleached flour is ground wheat flour with the bran sifted out, but with all germs remaining. As the sifted flour is stored and aged, it naturally starts bleaching and lightens in colour. It was found that the aged bleached flour was easier to manipulate into the dough, so commercial bakeries began to demand the whitened flour. To accommodate this need without the lengthy aging period, chemical methods of bleaching were developed.

Rye Flour

It contains a small amount of gluten protein and may be used to produce dark rye breads. It is often blended with wheat flour to produce finer textured, light rye breads. The distinctive flavour of rye flour makes it a common inclusion in such items as snack foods and pre-packaged toasts.

Corn Flour and Corn Meal

It is used in the production of crusty corn breads and muffins. Corn has no gluten but does have a distinctive flavour and a pleasant yellow colour that is desirable in many products.

Oat Flour and Oat Meal

It is used primarily in breakfast foods and granola-type products. Oat flour is the most nutritionally complete of all flours.

Sorghum and Millet Flours

They are utilized in the making of flat bread, tortillas, and pancakes. They are popular in India, Central America, and Ethiopia.

Rice

Rice has long been the staple food of Asia. It is normally eaten as a whole grain, so rice mills remove either the hull to produce brown rice or both the hull and the bran coat for the production of white rice. A small percentage of rice is converted to flour and is used in baby foods and sauces.

Wheat Flour

The most commonly used grain in flour manufacture is the wheat grain or the Triticum group. Though there are thousands of varieties of wheat, there are three main groups under which wheat can be classified. These are:

1. Triticum vulgare
2. Triticum durum (high sugar, starch susceptible to diastase)
3. Triticum compactum (too soft for bread making)

THE WHEAT PLANT

Wheat is an annual plant made up of roots, a stem, leaves, and the head, which is also called a "SPIKE". The roots can grow about 3-6 feet (90-180 cm) deep. The hollow stem has about six segments joined by nodes, each with an attached leaf. Wheat leaves may be short and wide or narrow and long. They are made up of a sheath, which surrounds the stem, and the leaf blade, which lies out flat so it can gather light. Each leaf is on the opposite side of the stem, from the leaf above or below it. Some wheat varieties grow only 2-3 feet (61-91 cm) tall, while others may grow 5 feet (152 cm) tall. The shorter varieties are more suitable food crops.

The head or spike is that part of the plant where the grain forms. The head is usually made up of a zigzag central axis along which are alternating spikelets, each containing several flowers. The flowers are enclosed by protective structures called glumes. In some bearded varieties of wheat, the glumes have a long, slender bristle called an awn.

Fertilisation begins about two days after the spike emerges from the sheath of the flag leaf. As the flowers open up, the antlers shed pollen that sticks to the stamen and germinates to grow into the ovary and fertilize the egg cell. Wheat is self-pollinating, which means that it is fertilized by its own pollen. The grain starts to grow after fertilisation. The time needed for the grain to grow and mature depends on such factors as, temperature and rainfall. In much of the United States, this takes about one month.

The Wheat Kernel

The wheat kernel consists of a tiny plant called the embryo or germ, which makes up about 3 % of the weight of the kernel; the starchy endosperm; and the protective seed coat, or bran. The endosperm makes up about 83 % of the weight of the kernel and is the food supply for the seedling, when a seed germinates. When wheat is milled into flour, the bran and germ are removed. Flour is produced by grinding or rolling the endosperm into powder.

Hard wheat used to make bread has 12-15 % protein, while soft wheat has only 7-11 % protein. This extra protein in hard wheat makes bread dough sticky, so that it rises better during baking. The rest of the wheat kernel is 2 % fat, 2 % mineral, 65-70 % carbohydrate, 3 % fibre, and 13 % water. Wheat grain also contains some vitamin E and several B vitamins, especially niacin. Since the bran contains more proteins and vitamins than does the starchy endosperm, whole wheat flour is more nutritious than white flour. In addition to being one of the oldest grains grown, wheat is the world's most widely grown cereal. It is believed to have been milled into meal 9000 years ago. In modern times, wheat is used to produce meal, breakfast cereals, and flour for bakery products. It can be cultivated in a wide range of soils but thrives in temperate climates. There are essentially two kinds of wheat; hard wheat, which is grown mainly in the United States and Canada, and soft wheat, which is raised mainly in Europe and Australia. The hard wheat is better for bread making, the soft wheat for cakes and biscuits. There are also differences between the varieties of wheat planted in the spring and those in winter. Spring wheat grows quickly and is harvested in late spring or early summer, whereas winter wheat is planted in late autumn and is not harvested until spring or early summer.

Structure of Wheat

Wheat is the backbone of most yeast breads. A wheat berry (the actual seed that is clustered on the stalk) is an edible power package. Within just one wheat berry, there is the near perfect balance of nutrients that so efficiently sustained our ancestors. Up to 19 % of the grain is composed of protein and the rest being nutritionally valuable complex carbohydrates.

There are three main parts of the grain: the bran, the germ, and the endosperm.

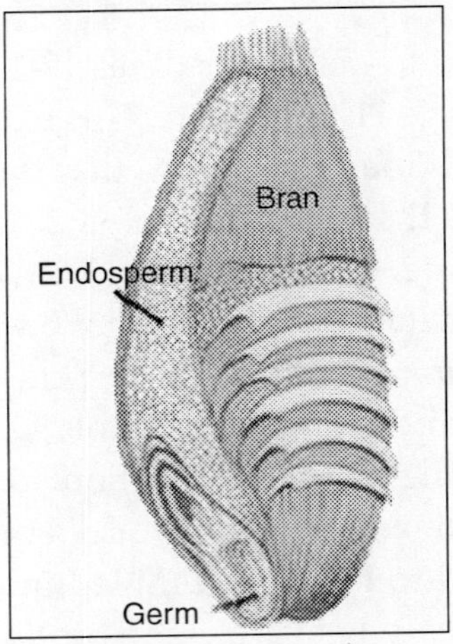

Wheat structure

Bran: The bran is the outermost layer and is the protective covering of the grain. It has five layers which are epidermis, epicarp, endocarp, episperm or testa and aleurone cells or cerealin. It protects the grain against pest, illnesses, etc. It is removed during milling and contains:

- Vitamin B and minerals.
- Insoluble fibres.

Germ: The germ is the smallest part of the grain and contains most of the oil content and hence, has a tendency to go rancid. It also contains the cellulose and other valuable components which are removed during the milling of refined flour.

It contains:

- All rudimentary tissues for growth (germination).
- Vitamins B and E.
- No starch.
- It has high protein (25 % enzymes).
- It has high sugar content (18 % sucrose + raffinose).
- It has high lipids (removed during flour milling to avoid rancidity during storage).

Endosperm: The endosperm is the portion from where refined flour is milled. It consists of 85 % of the grain and is made up of a number of small compartments of cellulose. These are tightly packed with starch cells, in spaces between them are found other substances, like insoluble protein, fats, moisture and sugar. Endosperm is used to make white flour and it contains mostly starch.

Types of Wheat

There are two basic types of wheat: winter and spring. Winter wheat is seeded in the fall, grows slowly during the winter months, accelerates in growth as spring arrives, and is ready for harvest in early summer. Where winters are harsh, spring wheat is planted in the spring and harvested in late summer. It can also be sown in the fall where winters are mild.

There are winters and spring varieties of both hard and soft wheat. Hard wheat grains are rich in gluten and make fine bread flour. Soft wheat is generally grown in areas with high levels of rainfall. They tend to be rich in starch and low in gluten. Soft wheat lacks stickiness for bread making but is used in pastries and is often mixed with bread wheat. White wheat is usually soft winter wheat.

1. **Hard red winter:** This wheat is grown in large quantities. It has moderately high-protein content and is used primarily for bread flours. The term red in the name refers to the dark colour of the bran and husk (layers of the wheat berry), not to the interior of the grain, which is white.
2. **Hard red spring:** This wheat has the highest protein content among North American wheat and it is an important component of strong bread flours.
3. **Hard white:** This high-protein wheat is grown in small quantities for bread flours. One interesting use for this wheat is for making whole-wheat flours that are lighter in colour and not as strong in flavour as whole-wheat flours from red wheat.

4. **Soft white:** This is a low-protein wheat, useful for pastries, cakes, crackers and other products in which a softer wheat is required.
5. **Soft red winter:** This is another low-protein wheat, used for cake and pastry flours.
6. **Durum:** This is the hardest of the six wheat classes. It is used primarily for spaghetti and other macaroni products.

Growing Conditions

Weather that is comfortable for humans is also good for wheat. Wheat needs 12-15 inches (31-38 cm) of water to produce a good crop. It grows best when temperatures are warm, from 70 to 75 °F (21 to 24 °C), but not too hot. Wheat also needs a lot of sunshine, especially when the grains are filling. Areas with low humidity are better since many wheat diseases thrive in damp weather.

Biological Control of Insects/Pests in Wheat

Wherever wheat grows there are many enemies that attack it, reducing yields or even destroying the crop. The worst enemies are diseases caused by fungi, bacteria, viruses, insects, and weeds. In most regions, fungal diseases are the greatest threat to wheat crops. Many problems are controlled by using resistant varieties or by using herbicides and pesticides to destroy or deter the invading enemy.

Wheat Crops Around the World

Most of the world's wheat is grown in temperate areas of the Northern Hemisphere. Spring wheat is grown in the mild winters of North Africa, Pakistan, India, Mexico, South America, and Australia. Winter wheat is planted in the fall in most of the United States, Europe, and China. Only spring wheat is grown in areas where winters are extremely cold, as in Canada and the northern United States.

Wheat is harvested somewhere in the world every month of the year. More than 80 % of the world crop is harvested from June to August. Much of this harvested crop must be stored. Some wheat is stored on the farm where it is produced; the rest is either stored in large bins or silos or is exported to other countries. In the United States, most of the wheat that is not kept by farmers is sold to private companies for processing or to export.

Since wheat harvest usually takes place during warm, dry weather, grain that is combined often contains only about 12 % water. Such dry grain stores well. Damp grain is dried by fans. Wheat stored wet can mould and become unusable. Insects that eat stored wheat eat more grain when it is wet.

PROCESSING OF WHEAT FLOUR

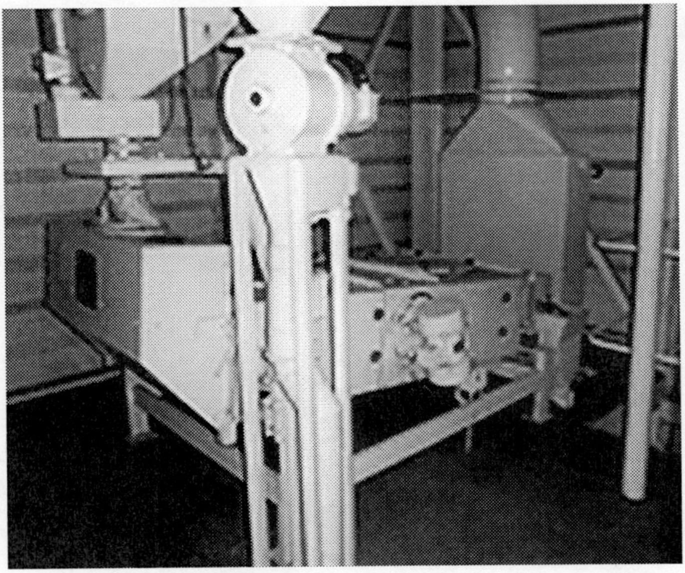

Cleaning: The wheat is cleaned to remove stones, dust, grit, metal and any other impurities. This is done using: magnets to remove metal, aspirators (uses air to remove light dust) and scourers (equipment that rubs dust from the grain).

Conditioning: Water is added to soften the wheat and make it easier to process.

Breaking: The wheat passes through rollers which break or crack open the grain.

Sieving: A series of sieves separate the grain into its three component parts, endosperm, bran and germ. The starchy endosperm passes through more sieves and rollers, getting finer as it goes.

Protein in Wheat Flour

The five constituents of protein in the wheat grain are albumin, globulin, proteose, glutenin, and gliadin. These are either water soluble, salt soluble or completely insoluble. The first three proteins are soluble and act as nitrogenous matter for yeast food. Glutenin and gliadin are insoluble in water and get hydrated when the water is added to form the insoluble protein "gluten". Gliadin gives elasticity to the gluten while acting as a binding agent to the tough protein. Glutenin gives stability and tenacity. Gluten provides the means whereby gas generated by the yeast is captured in the structure of fine strands of the gluten, which will stretch as the gas is formed, making the dough to rise. These proteins coagulate when heated and set firmly to give a firm structure to the bread. The art of bread making centres on having the gluten at an oven-ready stage, so that it gives in easily to the expanding gases, at the same time retaining them without breaking down.

Gluten can be conditioned as a result of combination of many factors such as:

- Amount of yeast and its activity
- Dough temperature
- Acidity of the dough
- Manipulation of the dough
- Effects of the additions in the dough

Salt increases the stability of the gluten in small quantities. Yeast controls the rate of gas production and this affects the gluten quality. Fermentation time has an appreciable effect on the gluten, as this gives the water to have a softening effect on the gluten. Casein of milk has a tightening effect on the gluten, while fat has a lubricating effect on the gluten fibres, allowing them to slip on top of each other. Whole wheat flours have lesser concentration of gluten as the bran content is increased. This causes a weaker structure in the bread. Also, the bran particles being slightly abrasive, they cut the gluten fibres resulting in a loaf with a smaller crumb. The presence of the bran particles also allows for high-moisture absorption, resulting in a short fermentation time.

When the germ is present in the flour, there is a higher enzyme activity, as a result of which the gluten develops faster and the breads are made with a shorter fermentation time.

BAKING PROCESS

The basic process of baking yeast bread starts with measuring and mixing the various ingredients to make the dough and adding yeast, so that it rises. The dough is then kneaded to develop the gluten and is again allowed to rise. The kneading and rising steps may be repeated several times. Next, the dough is shaped into a loaf and baked. Baking cooks the dough, firms the loaf and forms a crust on it, and improves the flavour. Finally, the loaf of bread may be sliced before being wrapped. Commercial bakeries have machines that do the work of measuring, mixing, kneading, baking, slicing, and wrapping. Skilled bakers run the machines, and nothing is left to chance. The ingredients are weighed precisely, the temperature and humidity are closely monitored, and the individual steps of the baking process are carefully timed.

Every bakery uses a special blend of flour, produced by mixing the wheat, before or after it has been milled. In most large bakeries, the manufacturing process begins in bins on a high floor, so that gravity can draw the flour or dough from one machine down to the next. After a final sifting, the flour is put into the scale that automatically weighs the required amount and pours it into a mixer on the floor below. Water or another liquid is poured in to form dough, and yeast and other ingredients are added. The amount of flour used to make the dough can be affected by the temperature and humidity in the bakery. In addition, the temperature of the water must be exactly correct to dissolve the yeast. The yeast will be killed if the water is even slightly overheated. On the other hand, its growth will be stunted by water that is too cold. In the next step of the manufacturing process, the dough flows into huge troughs that are taken into a fermentation room. It is left there to rise for a set amount of time, usually for several hours. Next, a divider scales the dough into pieces of just the right weight for the baking pans. The rounder shapes the pieces into balls, which then move through the overhead proofer. There, the dough rests for a few minutes to recover from the rough dividing and rounding processes, thus ensuring tender loaves.

The balls of dough drop from overhead proofer into a moulder, which moulds them to fit the baking pans exactly. The filled pans are placed in the proof box, where the final rising takes place. The proof box has a slightly warmer and moister atmosphere than that of the fermentation room. The pans then go into an oven, where they are baked at a temperature of more than 400 °F (204 °C) for about 30 minutes. Low-pressure steam is injected into the oven to prevent the crust from forming too quickly. Most large bakeries use reel ovens or travelling ovens. A reel oven looks like an enclosed Ferris wheel, with the pans of bread on rolling racks. In a travelling oven, the pans move slowly on a conveyor belt through a long baking chamber, and the bread comes out of the other end. Some travelling ovens measure more than 100 feet (30 metres) in length, and they can bake more than 5,000 loaves of bread per hour.

After the loaves have been slowly cooled, a slicer cuts them into uniform slices. Finally, a wrapping machine places moisture-proof paper around each loaf and seals the paper to keep the bread fresh and protect its flavour. The loaves are then packed into trucks and taken to stores. The process of making unleavened bread, which is sometimes called no-yeast bread or quick bread, is much simpler than that used for yeast bread. Since the dough contains no yeast, kneading and rising are not involved. The procedure consists merely of measuring and mixing the ingredients and then, shaping the dough and baking it.

CHECK YOUR PROGRESS

1. Explain the milling of wheat and the role of bran and germ.
2. Describe the structure of a wheat grain.
3. What is bread flour?
4. What is whole wheat flour?
5. Explain the role of gluten in flour. How does it work?
6. What are the different types of flour used for making various products?
7. Describe the process of flour making.
8. Write any five products which are made with high-gluten flour.

Unit 6

Shortenings (Fats & Oils)

Fats have a relatively high melting point and are solid at room temperature, whereas those having lower melting points and are liquid at room temperature, are called oils. Fat is present naturally in many foods, this fat is often referred to as invisible fat. Examples of foods containing appreciable quantities of invisible fat include meat, poultry, fish, dairy products, eggs, nuts and seeds. Visible fats are made from these products; they are lard, cooking oils, salad oils, margarine and butter. Fats play a variety of roles in both, food preparation and nutrition.

Fats and oil come under lipids; lipids are insoluble in water but soluble in chloroform, benzene, and acetone. Lipids which are solid at normal temperature are called fat and those which are liquid, are called oil. Actually, fats and oil are ester of fatty acid and glycerol. Ester is a salt, derived from alcohol and acid.

Chemically, fats are made up of glycerine molecules and three fatty acids. This is why they are sometimes called triglycerides or even triacylglycerols. The key to learning about this often puzzling part of our foods is the fatty acids. These are, for the most part, made up of two types of molecules: carbon and hydrogen. These molecules are joined in specific configurations, which determine their types as fatty acids. A fatty acid is simply a chain of carbon atoms.

The basic function of fats and oil in cookery is to add richness and flavour to the food and as a cooking medium, to fry and cook food. They improve the texture of various preparations such as cakes, pastries, and biscuits.

Fats and oil is found in plants, animals and in marine foods. The property of fats and oil depends on their source as well as number of other factors. The quality of food products depends largely on fats or oil, which are used while preparing it. The storage condition of fat as well as preparation, temperature and time, influence the quality of final products.

Vegetable fats, sometimes referred to as butter or tropical oils, are derived from tropical plants or fruits such as cocoa, coconut and palm. Saturated fats melt within a very narrow temperature range. These are good for use in confectionery.

Classification based on degree of saturation

Lipids
Fats and oil
Glycerol + fatty acids

- Saturated
- unSaturated
  - Monounsaturated (One double bond)
  - Polyunsaturated (Two or more double bond)

Characteristics of Fats

1. Fats are insoluble in water and soluble in fat solvents like ether, acetone, etc.
2. They are greasy to touch.
3. They have a specific gravity, less than one.
4. At room temperature, fats are solid due to high percentage of saturated fatty acids.
5. Oils are liquid because of the higher percentage of unsaturated fatty acids.

6. Fats do not melt sharply but soften over a range of temperature. This is because fats are generally mixed triglycerides, each one having its own melting point.
7. The spreading quality of fat is due to its plastic nature. Solid fats which can spread over, are composed of a mass of tiny crystals in a matrix of liquid fats. The crystals slide over one another as they are not trapped in the liquid oil and merits the fat to be deformed.
8. Fats and oil are heated to the temperature, at which a thin bluish smoke is released and it is called a smoke point. Fats used for deep frying should have a high smoke point.
9. When fats and oil are heated to high temperature, the fat is decomposed into glycerol and free fatty acids. Glycerol is further broken down by high temperature and acrolein is formed. Acrolein has a sharp odour and irritates the nose, throat, and eyes.
10. Iodine value is a measure of the extent of unsaturated fatty acids present in fats and oil.

Composition

Fatty acids composition of commonly used oils (in percentage)

Oil	Saturated	Mono-unsaturated	Poly-unsaturated
Coconut	91	8	1
Cotton seed	34	26	40
Groundnut	20	54	26
Mustard	6	73	21
Niger	12	35	55
Palm	80	13	7
Safflower	11	13	76
Sesame	14	46	40
Soyabean	15	25	60
Sunflower	8	34	58

When fats contain high proportion of saturated fatty acids, such as palmitic and stearic acids, they have relatively high melting points, whereas fats containing high proportion of unsaturated fatty acids, such as the monounsaturated oleic acid and polyunsaturated linoleic acid, have relatively low melting points and are oils at room temperature.

Shortenings

- Regular shortenings have a tough, waxy texture and they hold together the particles within a dough or batter.
- Emulsified shortenings are soft and they spread easily and are used to make cake batters. They are used when there is more sugar than flour in a recipe and are sometimes called high-ratio shortenings.
- Puff pastry shortening is very firm and is used for making rolled-in doughs, when it is important that the fat stays in distinct layers of the dough.

Role of Shortenings (Fats/Oils)

- Shortening, margarine, butter (solid fats) or vegetable oils contribute to the tenderisation of baked products by inhibiting gluten development and starch gelatinisation.
- Fats coat the flour proteins to water-proof them and reduce their contact with the liquid ingredients in a recipe. This prevents from gluten formation and contributes to tender baking.
- Fats can help leaven a product to incorporate air. When solid fats are creamed with crystalline sugar, tiny air cells are incorporated into the batter, so that the baked goods will have a fine, aerated texture.
- Butterfat contributes flavour to a recipe. Margarine does not.

Role of Fat/Oil in Cookery

Fat/oil used as medium of cooking: Fat is used in shallow and deep frying. Pan-frying is used to cook dosas, chapatis, omelettes, cutlets and tikkis. Deep frying method is used in preparing pooris, vadas, cutlets, bhajis and pakodas.

Fat improves the texture of foods: Fat plays an important role in the development of texture in cakes, biscuits and cookies. Its function is particularly important in a pastry which has no sugar to contribute to its tenderness.

(a) **Fats help in leavening:** The role of fat in the leavening process is its ability to trap air during the mixing process. So the fat is indirectly responsible for the tenderness of the cake. Thus, fats contribute to the grain and volume of baked products. Though all packed products use fat, amounts used are different.

(b) **Fat as a shortening agent:** One of the most important functions of fat is to shorten baked products, which otherwise are solid masses firmly held together by strands of gluten. The usual fat used, if any, in yeast bread is butter or margarine. In biscuits, a hard fat must be used so that fat can be distributed in small pieces to give the desired flakiness to the biscuits. Shortened cakes are made using a plastic fat, which combines readily with the ingredients in the flour mixture. Butter is used in puff pastries.

(c) **Fats for smoothness:** They limit the size of water crystals and help in maintaining a smooth texture. They affect the smoothness of crystalline candies through retarding of crystallisation and the gelatinisation of starch in starch-thickened mixtures. Fats prevent lump formation and bring smoothness.

Fats improve palatability: Fat gives taste and flavour to the food. Some fats, like ghee, are used in the kitchen to improve flavour. Ghee and butter, when used in the recipe, improve the flavour. The ability of fats to take up or dissolve certain aromatic flavour substances is frequently used in food preparation. Onion, ginger, garlic, pepper and other flavourful foods are cooked in oil, so flavours can be incorporated initially into other foods. Aromatic fruits and other flavours are also dissolved by fat. Colouring agents, like turmeric, when added to oil helps in the distribution of colour throughout the food.

Plasticity

Most fats that appear to be solid at room temperature actually contain both solid fat crystals and liquid oil. The liquid part is held in a network of small crystals. Because of this unique combination of liquid and solid, the fat can be moulded or pressed into various shapes without breaking. This property of fat is called plasticity.

Nutritional Importance of Fats

1. They are concentrated sources of energy. They furnish 2.25 times more energy than proteins and carbohydrates. All oils and fats, except butter, give 900 kilocalories per hundred grams.
2. They reduce bulk in the diet.
3. They are excellent sources of fat-soluble vitamins A, D, E and K. Butter contains 15,000 I.U of vitamin A. Refined vegetable oils and hydrogenated shortenings contain little or no vitamin A but vegetable oils are good sources of vitamin E.
4. They play a part in the biosynthesis of several long chain fatty acids.
5. They provide essential fatty acids, which are components of membranes of living cells.
6. Fats are slow in leaving the stomach and hence, retard digestion.

THE CULINARY FRUIT OILS AND THEIR CHARACTERISTICS

Apricot Kernel Oil

It is derived from dried kernels of the apricot tree. It is usually cold or expeller pressed, is high in monounsaturated fats (64 %) and contains no trans-fatty acids. The oil is suitable for high-heat cooking such as pan-frying and sautéing and the mild flavour makes it excellent when used in salad dressing. Apricot kernel oil is a popular massage oil, and a carrier for aromatherapy oils.

Avocado Oil

The light and unique taste makes it a popular choice for salad dressings, as well as for seasoning, and for roasting vegetables. Refined avocado oil has the highest smoke point among the plant oils and is therefore,useful for high heat cooking. This oil is a good source of monounsaturated fats (70 %), and vitamin E, making it nutritionally beneficial.

Coconut Oil

It is extracted from the dried meat of the coconut. This oil is very popular in Indian, Southeast Asian, and Caribbean cuisine. Coconut oil has a high level of saturated fats (92 %) and was previously thought best to be avoided. However, several studies have shown that the saturated fat in this oil metabolizes in the body in a way that is similar to an unsaturated fat. As a result, LDL (low-density lipoprotein, the bad cholesterol) does not increase. This oil is also widely used in baked goods, candies, and as a cooking oil. It is also used in soaps and cosmetics.

Grapeseed Oil

It is a by-product of the wine-making industry; most of the oil is extracted from grape seeds in Italy, France, and Switzerland. The subtle flavour makes it suitable for many types of salad. Refined grapeseed oil has a high smoke point, making it an excellent choice for frying or sautéing.

Olive Oil

It is obtained from the olive tree, *Olea europaea.* It is considered healthy because of its high monoun saturated fat (69 %) content. There are three basic types available: **extra virgin, virgin,** and **plain.** The **extra virgin** olive oil means the acidity level can be not more than 1 %. This oil is best used in salads, spreads, or dips and should not be heated. Virgin olive oil has a maximum acidity level of 2 %, and can be used in cooking as well as in salads. Products labelled 'olive oil' or 'pure olive oil' are usually 85 % refined, and 15 % virgin or extra virgin. It has less flavour, is less expensive but has the same health benefits of the higher grades. It also has a higher smoke point, making it an excellent choice for cooking. Olive oil is also used in cosmetics, soaps, and pharmaceuticals.

THE CULINARY SEED OILS AND THEIR CHARACTERISTICS

Almond Oil

Pale oil made from sweet almonds, this nut oil is used in baking and confectionery. It is used to coat cake pans or cookie sheets when preparing delicate baked goods, or heat gently with slivered almonds and serve with fish or cooked green vegetables.

Avocado Oil

Avocado oil is from the avocado pits, and sometimes from blemished fruits. This oil is colourless with a faint aniseed flavour. It is used mainly in North America.

Corn Oil

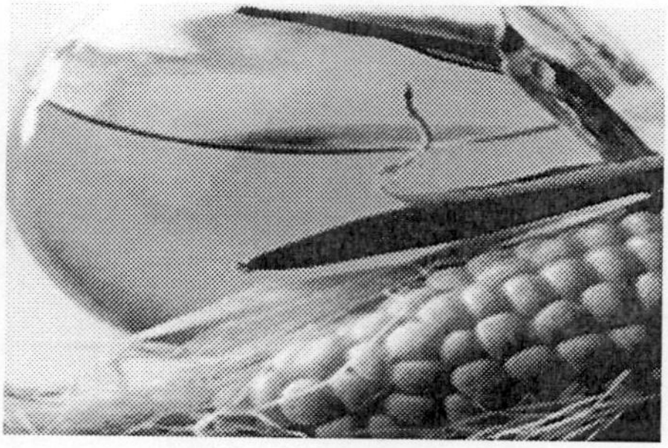

One of the most economically and widely used all-purpose oil, this is deep yellow in colour and heavy in texture. Corn oil is high in polyunsaturated fats and has a high smoke point, so it is both healthy and ideal for most culinary preparations.

Palm Oil

Also known as palm nut oil, this is extracted from the pulp of the fruit of oil palms. Orange-gold in colour, it has a pleasant nutty flavour. Although it is all-purpose oil, light in colour and taste and good for frying and making salad dressings, it turns rancid rapidly.

Peanut Oil

This is a very fine, almost tasteless oil for general use in salads, cooking, and frying. The cold-pressed variety has a mild peanut flavour, that is good with fruit-flavoured vinegars for salad dressings. Peanut oil is moderately high in monounsaturated fats and low in saturates.

Pumpkin Seed Oil

It is a dark brown oil with a pleasant flavour of toasted pumpkin seeds. It is popular in Austria, where most of it is produced. It is also used as a last-minute seasoning for steamed vegetables or fish.

Sesame Oil

There are many types of this oil. European, or cold-pressed sesame oil, is light in colour and nutty in flavour with a high smoke point, making it a good cooking oil. Asian sesame oil is made from toasted sesame seeds, giving it a darker colour and more pronounced taste. Middle Eastern sesame oils are lighter in flavour than Asian ones, with a deep golden colour. All are aromatic and capable of being heated to a high temperature.

Sunflower Oil

This is one of the best all- purpose oils. It is high in polyunsaturated fats, tasteless, pale, light in texture, and inexpensive. It can be used for frying, cooking and salad dressings.

Walnut Oil

This is a delicious topaz-coloured oil, with a rich, nutty flavour. Walnuts from the Perigord and Dordogne in France are said to produce the best oil. In these regions, walnuts are strictly graded for quality; it is even possible for one tree to have two separate grades of walnut. Production is small and therefore, this oil is expensive. Walnut oil cannot be kept for long, either opened or unopened, so keep it in a cool place, but not in the refrigerator. It makes a delicious salad dressing, and in baking, it adds flavour to cakes, especially those that contain walnuts. It is also good with fish, poultry, and vegetables, or to use wherever a walnut taste goes well with the ingredients.

Using Nut and Seed Oils to Add Flavour

Nut and seed oils are generally used as a flavouring for cold food, or added to hot dishes at the last minute. Pumpkin seed, walnut and hazelnut oils, Asian sesame oil, cold-pressed peanut and pine seed oils all make superb salad dressings, vegetable seasonings, and marinades. Because they are quite flavourful, often to the point of being overpowering. They should always be used sparingly and in combination with neutral oil, such as sunflower. They can also be used as a pat of butter and to flavour cooked foods; toss steam or boil green beans with walnut oil just before serving.

TYPES OF FATS AND OILS

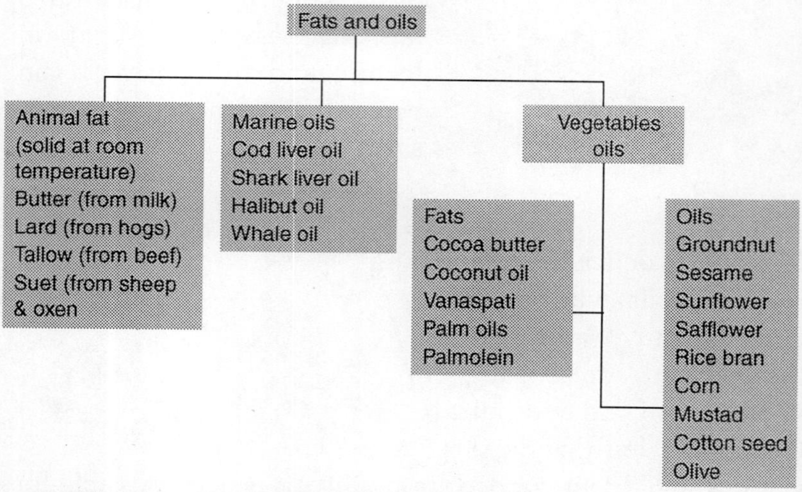

PROCESSING AND REFINING OF FATS

Fats and oils commonly used in food preparation are separated from various materials and refined. Many oils come from seeds or fruits, lard comes from pork tissue and butter comes from cream. Further processing produces fats, such as margarine and hydrogenated shortening.

REFINED OILS

Vegetable oils are removed from oil-containing seed fruits or nuts by various pressing processes, by solvent extraction and by combination of these. After extraction, the crude oils are refined.

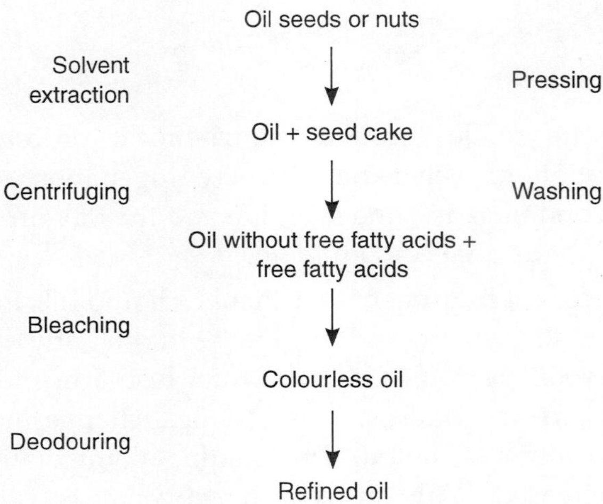

SPECIFIC FATS

Lard

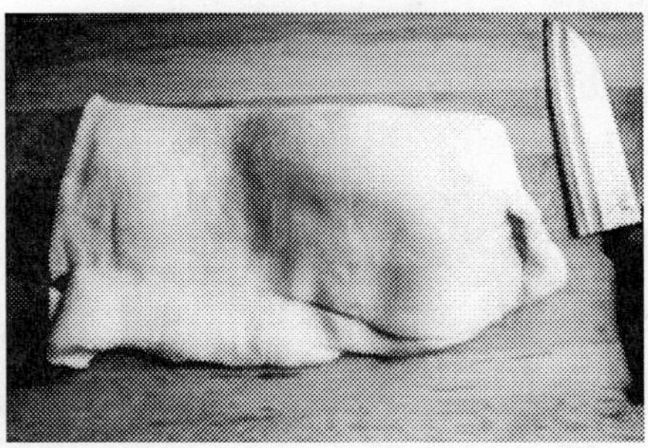

To make lard, fatty tissues of the hog are chopped into small pieces and heated, with or without the addition of water, to remove fat from the cells, a so-called rendering process. The quality of the lard depends on the location of the fatty tissue in the animal and on the method of heating. An antioxidant is added to delay the onset of rancidity. To improve its quality, it may be hydrogenated, bleached or emulsifier is added.

Hydrogenation

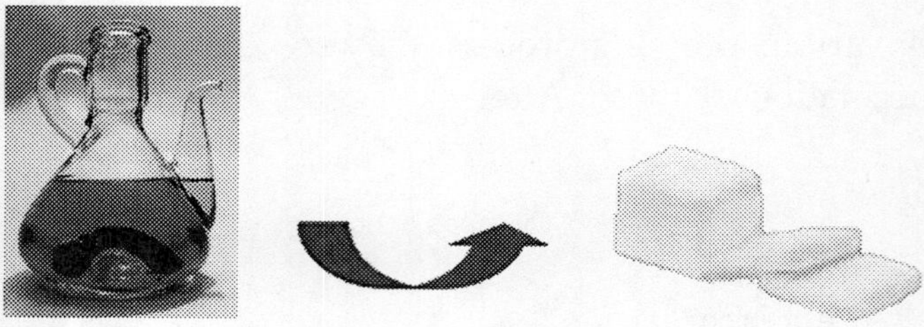

Transfats are made through the chemical process called hydrogenation of vegetable oils. Hydrogenation solidifies liquid oils and increases the shelf life and the flavour stability of oils and foods that contain them.

The process of hydrogenation changes liquid oils into more solid plastic shortenings and to increase the stability of the oils to prevent spoilage from oxidation, which results in undesirable rancid flavour and odours. This chemical change makes the fatty acids more saturated. The melting point of the fat is thereby increased. With sufficient hydrogenation, it becomes solid at room temperature. Soybean oil, cotton seed and palm oil are used for hydrogenation.

Winterisation

In this process, the temperature of the oil is lowered to a point at which the higher-melting triglycerides crystallise. Then the oil is filtered to remove these crystals. The remaining oil has a lower melting point and does not crystallise at refrigerator temperatures. It is referred to as salad oil.

Butter

Butter is the fat of cream that is separated more or less completely from other milk constituents by agitating or churning. Butter formation is an example of the breaking of an oil-in-water emulsion by agitation. The resulting emulsion that forms in butter itself is a water-in-oil emulsion with about 18 % water being dispersed in about 80 % fat and a small amount of protein acting as the emulsifier. Many volatile fatty acids and substances called diacetyl, formed from bacterial action is an important flavour component of butter. Butter is highly valued for its flavour.

Margarine

Margarine is made from one or more optional fat ingredients churned with cultured pasteurised skimmed milk or whey. Other ingredients added to margarine are vitamins A and D for nutritive purposes; diacetyl as a flavour constituents; lecithin, monoglycerides and/or diglycerides of fat-forming fatty acids as emulsifying agents, artificial colours, salt, and citric acid or certain citrates and sodium benzoate as preservative to the extent of 0.1 %.

FLAVOUR REVERSION

Flavour reversion is defined as a change in edible fats that is characterized by the development, in the refined material, of an objectionable flavour prior to the onset of true rancidity. It may develop during the exposure of the fat to ultraviolet or visible light or by heating. A small amount of oxygen seems to be necessary for the reaction that is catalysed by the presence of small amount of metals, such as iron and copper. Selective hydrogenation decreases the amount of linolenic acid and aids in preventing flavour reversion. Soya bean oil is most susceptible for flavour reversion.

RANCIDITY

Spoilage of fats may occur on storage, particularly if the fats are highly unsaturated and the conditions of storage are conducive to chemical change in fats. Rancidity is of two types, hydrolytic and oxidative.

1. **Hydrolysis:** Hydrolysis is brought about by enzymes that decompose fats into free fatty acids and glycerol. Heating thoroughly to destroy the lipase enzyme, that catalyses the hydrolysis of triglycerides, should prevent hydrolytic rancidity. Contaminating microorganisms may also produce lipase and these can similarly be destroyed with sufficient heating.
2. **Oxidation:** Only unsaturated fats and foods which have lipoxygenase are susceptible to oxidative changes. Highly hydrogenated and saturated fatty acids are relatively resistant to oxidation.

Prevention of Rancidity

1. Storage at refrigerator temperature prevents rancidity.
2. Light rays catalyse oxidation of fats by the use of coloured glass containers that absorb the active rays, fats can be protected against spoilage. Certain shades of green bottles and wrappers and yellow transparent cellophane wrappers are effective in preventing rancidity.
3. Vacuum packaging also helps to retard the development of rancidity by excluding oxygen.
4. Antioxidants naturally present in food such as vitamin C, beta carotene and vitamin E protect against rancidity.

SMOKING POINT

Smoke point of a fat is the temperature at which smoke comes continuously from the surface of the fat. Development of free fatty acids by some hydrolysis of the fat during frying causes a decrease in the smoke point. Suspended matter, such as flour or batter particles, also lowers the smoke point. And the greater the surface of the fat exposed, the lower is the smoke point.

Smoking temperature of fats

Fat/Oil	Smoking temperature (°C)
Butterfat	208
Cotton seed oil	230
Coconut oil	138
Groundnut oil	149-162
Hydrogenated fat	221-232
Lard	194
Olive oil crude	176
Olive oil refined	234
Soya bean oil	230

CHANGES IN FAT ON HEATING

There are four main ways in which the oil decomposes and all of these pathways lead to a diminution of smoke point and operating temperature. Cooking oil is chemically decomposed in the cooking process and this decomposition leads to deterioration in cooking quality if the oil is kept in use for a long time.

Pyrolysis (thermal breakdown): The action of heating the oil, whether or not it is in contact with food, causes a breakdown in its molecular structure.

Oxidation: Reaction of the hot oil surface with oxygen in air causes molecular breakdown and ultimately, the development of rancidity. This change occurs whenever the oil is heated.

Hydrolysis: As water is boiled in large quantities from food during frying, some of this water tends to decompose the oil.

Reaction with food residues: Any food fragments left in the oil after cooking undergo chemical reaction, particularly if the oil is heated again without the residues being removed. Straining the oil after use can help to prevent this decomposition.

Animal fats	**Marine oil**	**Vegetable oil**	
↓	↓	↓	
(Solid at room temperature)	cod- liver oil	(Mainly liquid at room temperature)	
		Fats	**Oil**
Butter- from milk	shark- liver oil	cocoa butter	Groundnut
Lard- from hog's	halibut oil	coconut oil	Sesame
Tallow- from beef	whale oil	vanaspati	Sunflower
Suet- from ox and sheep			Mustard

CHECK YOUR PROGRESS

1. What changes take place in fats while heating?
2. 'Fats improve palatability', describe this statement.
3. Explain how shortenings perform an important role in terms of nutritional value.
4. Give some examples of animal fat.
5. Describe in detail the role of fat/oil in cookery.
6. What is oxidation?
7. Write a short note on hydrogenation.
8. Explain the processing and refining of fats.

Unit 7

Raising Agents

Any process by which dough or batter is filled with gas holes, which are retained upon baking, is the leavening process. The major function of leavening agents is to aerate the dough or batter to make it light and porous. This porosity of the batter or dough is responsible for imparting good volume to the finished product.

In terms of goods production, leavening is the production of gases in baked goods which increases their volume. For example, bread dough rises when proofed because of the CO_2.

Some of the advantages of leavening of bakery products are:

- It increases the volume of the bakery products.
- The leavened products being light and porous are easily chewed and digested.
- Leavened bakery products are more palatable and appetizing than those made without leavening; which may be due to uniformity of cell structure, brightness of crumb colour, softness of texture, etc.
- Microorganisms are useful in two chief ways in bread making. First, they may produce gas to leaven or rise the dough, giving bread the desired loose, porous texture and second, they may produce desirable flavouring substances. They may also function in the conditioning of the dough.

CLASSIFICATION OF LEAVENING AGENTS

Leavening agent-producing gas by chemical or biological methods:

- **Chemically** – gives CO_2 during baking, e.g., bicarbonate of soda (baking soda) and baking powder.
- **Biologically** – CO_2 from fermentation of yeast.

  Certain yeasts are actually represented in two different genera based on whether they reproduce sexually.

  The principal bases for the identification and classification of genera of yeast are as follows:

1. Whether ascospores are formed.
2. If they are spore-forming:

   The method of production of ascospores:

   - Produced without conjugation of yeast cells (parthenogenetically). Spore formation may be followed by
     (i) conjugation of ascospores; and
     (ii) conjugation of small daughter cells.
   - Produced after isogamic conjugation (conjugating cells appear similar).
   - Produced by heterogamic conjugation (conjugating cells differ in appearance).
3. Appearance of vegetative cells: shape, size, colour, inclusions.
4. Physiological characteristics (used primarily to differentiate species or strains within a species):
   - Nitrogen and carbon sources
   - Vitamin requirements
   - Oxidative or fermentative: film yeasts are oxidative; other yeasts may be fermentative and oxidative.

METHODS OF LEAVENING

The leavening of bakery products could be brought about by following four general ways:

1. Mechanical (aeration)
2. Biological (fermentation by yeast)
3. Water vapour
4. Chemical

1. **Leavening by Mechanical Way**
   - (a) **Creaming:** During this process, the air is entrapped into the shortening, which expands when heated during process, thus giving volume to the bakery products.
   - (b) **Beating / whipping:** When eggs are beaten or whipped, they become fluffy and foamy because of the whipping in air; that's basically air circulating process. This air, thus incorporated during whipping of eggs, expands while the batter is being baked and causes the cake to rise. The sponges and mouse or cake rise are examples of products leaven through this manner.
   - (c) **Leavening by biological way:** A simplified equation describing this alcohol by fermentation reaction could be written as

$$\underset{\text{Glucose/fructose}}{C_6H_{12}O_6} \longrightarrow \underset{\text{Ethyl alcohol}}{2\,C_2H_5OH} + \underset{\text{Carbon dioxide}}{2\,CO_2}$$

The carbon dioxide is responsible for leavening of bakery products. The advantages of yeast leavening, as opposed to chemical leavening, are that it can contribute a characteristic taste and aroma and the evolution of gas can continue over a much longer period of time. The disadvantage of that is it is difficult to control. The yeast leavening process is a little calculating process, if it is used more in the product it becomes difficult to handle it.

Yeast is microscopic plant which ferments, which means it converts carbohydrates into CO_2 and alcohol when it gets warmth and moisture.

Yeasts may be useful or harmful in foods. Yeast fermentation is involved in the manufacturing of foods such as bread, beer, wines, vinegar, and surface-ripened cheese, and yeasts are grown for enzymes and foods. Yeasts are undesirable when they cause spoilage of sauerkraut, fruit juice, syrups, molasses, honey, jellies, meats, wine, beer, and other foods.

2. **Leavening by Biological Way (by Yeast)**

   The yeast used in preparation of the fermentation of bakery products (like breads, bread rolls, and other bakery products) is leavening in biological way.

$$\underset{\text{Simple sugar}}{C_6H_{12}O_6} \longrightarrow \underset{\text{Carbon dioxide}}{2CO_2} + \underset{\text{Alcohol}}{2C_2H_5OH}$$

Yeast is a living organism, which is sensitive to temperature

34 °F (1 °C)	inactive (storage temperature)
60-70 °F (15-20 °C)	slow action
70-90 °F (20-32 °C)	best growth (fermentation and proofing temperature for breads)
Above 100 °F (38 °C)	slow reaction
140 °F (60 °C)	yeast is killed

Yeast is available in three forms:

1. **Fresh Yeast**

Fresh yeast, also called compressed yeast, is moist and perishable and is preferred by professional bakers.

- Fresh yeast or wet yeast
- Short life
- Storage – 1 week of storage in the refrigerator

2. **Dry Yeast**

- It's in granular form
- Longer shelf life
- Storage – up to six months at room temperature

- *Active dry yeast* is a dry, granular form of yeast. Active dry yeast must be rehydrated 4 times its weight of warm water (about 110 °F) before use. When using active dry yeast in a bread formula, use a part of the liquid in the formula to dissolve yeasts. Do not add additional water.
- *Instant dry yeast* is also a dry granular form of yeast, but it does not have to be dissolved in water before use. It can be added in its form because it absorbs water much more quickly than regular yeast. It also produces water more than gas as compared to regular dry yeast. Instant dry yeast is also known as rapid-rise or quick-rise yeast.

3. **Leavening by Water Vapour**

   All leavened products rely, to some extent, on water vapour pressure to expand the vesicles or gas bubbles during the later stages of baking, but some items also utilize the leavening action produced by the rapid build-up of steam as the interior of the product reaches the boiling point. These foods include puff pastries, used for patty shells and napoleons, and choux pastes, often used for cream-puff and éclair cases.

4. **Leavening by Chemical Way**

   Leavening of dough may be accomplished by chemical agents instead by microorganisms, but the product so obtained cannot be called bread, according to the standards of identity, which specify yeast leavening. Carbon dioxide gas, which may be incorporated directly into the dough, or baking powder, which is a combination of chemical compounds that release gas, are mixed into the dough and may be employed for leavening. The addition of ammonium bicarbonate can be used since the heat from baking results in the release of carbon dioxide and ammonium gas. Self-rising flour contains both, acid and basic components of baking powder, which react upon moisture.

   (a) Baking soda

   The chemical reaction of gas formation is as follows:

   $$2NaHCO_3\,(s) \xrightarrow{\text{heating}} Na_2CO_3\,(s) + CO_2\,(g) + H_2O\,(g)$$

   (b) Ammonium bicarbonate

   The chemical leavening reaction of this salt could be written as:

   $$NH_4HCO_3 \longrightarrow NH_3 + CO_2 + H_2O$$

USE OF FILLER IN BAKING POWDER

Various types of fillers such as edible starches like maize starch, topicca, rice starch, wheat starch, arrowroot starch, potato starch, sorghum starch or other neutral materials such as calcium lactate, sodium sulphate, calcium carbonate, hydrated silicate work as neutral medium and thereby, do the below stated functions:

- To keep the soda particles and the acid particles from intimate contact (partition effect) and thereby, minimising the possibility of premature action (minimises gas evolution during storage).
- Act as an absorptive medium for free moisture incorporated into the powder during manufacture on assimilation in the course of storage.
- To facilitate handling and measuring in actual use, as it keeps it into powdered form (lump formation avoided).

TYPES AND USES OF RAISING AGENTS

Baking Soda

Baking soda (sodium bicarbonate) acts as a leavening agent when mixed with an acid such as sour cream, sour milk, buttermilk, molasses or citrus juices. If the moisture and acid are present, soda releases carbon dioxide gas, which leavens the product.

Heat is not necessary for the reaction (though the gas is released faster at high temperature). For this reason, product leavened with soda must be baked, once gases will escape and leavening powder will be lost.

The amount of soda used in a formula is generally the amount needed to balance the acid. If more leavening powder is needed, use baking powder, however, the large amount of baking soda is not good for end-product.

Yeast

Yeast is the most popular and simple of all leavening agents.

Continuous bread making: Continuous bread making processes usually involve growth and fermentation by the yeast in parts of the ingredients to get a large yield of active yeast or at least the addition of more yeast than usual before the final dough is formed. Leavening may take place in the pan just before baking.

Flavour production: Yeasts are reported to contribute to the flavour of bread through products released during fermentation of sugar, although most workers believe that yeasts add little or no flavour, especially in bread made by rapid methods now employed. Alcohol, acids, and aldehydes are products that may add desirable flavours. Most experts maintain, however, that bacteria growing in the dough can contribute the most to flavour. Too little time is allowed in the usual industrial leavening, but the longer time available during the older method of making it in the home permits enough bacterial growth for a considerable production of desirable flavours.

The primary key for effective use of yeast is temperature control. Dry yeast should be dissolved in 110-115 °F milk or water. When using the newer types of instant yeasts, follow the manufacturer's direction.

Baking Powder

This is made of an acid and an alkali when they come in contact with water. It carbonates and forms air pockets.

Bicarbonate of Soda

This is leavening in the Irish soda bread. This is an alkali when mixed with water and an acid releases carbon dioxide gas.

Brewer's Yeast

Till the end of the last century, this was the only leavening agent that was commonly used. It was famous due to the mineral contents present in it.

Cream of Tartar

Powder extracted from the wine casks.

Citric Acid

Powdered substance extracted from citrus juices.

Natural Leaveners

They are made with a medium of flour or grown on potatoes, yoghurt and treacle.

Sour dough is also based on natural leavening. It depends wholly on the wild yeast in atmosphere. In France, it is called leva in, used for baguettes. In local language, it is called a starter. It can take up to a week to ferment.

ACTION AND REACTIONS

Leavening/raising is the production of gases in baked goods, which increases volume. Yeast is a microscopic plant.

Thermophilic Bacteria or Thermophiles

These bacteria, with an optimal temperature at least above 45 °C but usually 55 °C or above, are important in foods held at high temperature.

Thermoduric Bacteria

Thermoduric bacteria are usally defined as those which can survive heat treatment, like pasteurisation. Bacillus species, micrococci, and enterococci can survive pasteurisation of liquid egg. Some thermoduric bacteria, such as bacillus and enterococci, can also be psychrotrophic. In milk, where higher pasteurisation and longer refrigeration times are significant, these heat-resistant or thermoduric psychrotrophs can be found often.

Osmophilic or Saccharophilic Bacteria

Most frequently encountered osmophilic microorganisms in food are various species of yeasts. Osmophilic bacteria are those which grow in high concentrations of sugar; however, most bacteria called osmophiles are merely sugar-tolerant.

Pigmented Bacteria

Colour produced by pigmented bacteria growing on or in food, range through the visible spectrum and also includes black and white. There are numerous examples in the subsequent discussion of spoilage of foods.

Gas-Forming Bacteria

Many kinds of bacteria produce a small amount of gas and yield it so slowly that it cannot be detected ordinarily. This is sometimes true for the heterofermentative lactic, although under other conditions, gas evolution is evident. Among the genera that contain gas-forming bacteria are Leuconostoc, Lactobacillus (heterofermentative), and Clostridium. Bacteria of the first three genera produce only carbon dioxide and those of the other genera, yield both carbon dioxide and hydrogen.

CHECK YOUR PROGRESS

1. Discuss briefly the different types of leavening agents used in bakery products.
2. What are biological leavening agents?
3. What are leavening agents?

4. Write a short note on compressed yeast and bread improver.
5. Discuss the use of baking powder in cake products.
6. Which raising agent is best for bread? Give an appropriate reason.
7. Explain the use of filler in baking powder.

Unit 8

Thickening Agents

Thickening agents, or thickeners, is the term applied to substances which increase the viscosity of a solution or liquid/ solid mixture without substantially modifying its other properties; although most frequently applied to foods where the target property is taste. Thickeners may also improve the suspension of other ingredients or emulsions which increases the stability of the product. Thickening agents are often regarded as food additives. Some thickening agents are gelling agents, forming a gel, dissolving in the liquid phase as a colloid mixture that forms a weakly cohesive internal structure.

Food thickeners are frequently based on either polysaccharides (starches, vegetable gums, and pectin), or proteins. A flavour-less powdered starch used for this purpose is a fecula (from the Latin faecula, diminutive of faex meaning "dregs"). This category includes starches as arrowroot, cornstarch, katakuri starch, potato starch, sago, tapioca and their derivatives. Vegetable gums used as food thickeners include alginin, guar gum, locust bean gum, and xanthan gum. Proteins used as food thickeners include collagen, egg whites, furcellaran, and gelatin. Sugars include agar and carrageenan. Other thickening agents act on the proteins already present in food. One example is sodium pyrophosphate, which acts on casein in milk during the preparation of instant pudding.

Different thickeners may be more or less suitable in a given application, due to differences in taste, clarity, and their responses to chemical and physical conditions. For example, for acidic foods, arrowroot is a better choice than cornstarch, which loses thickening potency in acidic mixtures. At (acidic) pH levels below 4.5, guar gum sharply reduces aqueous solubility, thus, also reducing its thickening capability. If the food is to be frozen, tapioca or arrowroot is preferable over cornstarch, which becomes spongy when frozen.

Many other food ingredients are used as thickeners, usually in the final stages of preparation of specific foods. These thickeners have a flavour and are not markedly stable and thus, are not suitable for general use. However, they are convenient and effective, and hence, are widely used.

Functional flours are produced from specific cereal variety (wheat, maize, rice or other) conjugated to specific heat treatment, that is able to increase stability, consistency and general functionalities. These functional flours are resistant to industrial stresses such as acidic pH, sterilisation, freeze conditions, and can help food industries to formulate with natural ingredients. For the final consumer, these ingredients are more accepted because they are shown as "flour" in the ingredient list.

Flour is often used for thickening gravies, gumbos, and stews. It must be cooked in thoroughly to avoid the taste of uncooked flour. Roux, a mixture of flour and fat (usually butter) cooked into a paste, is used for gravies, sauces and stews. Cereal grains (oatmeal, couscous, farina, etc.) are used to thicken soups. Yogurt is popular in Eastern Europe and Middle East for thickening soups. Soups can also be thickened by adding grated starchy vegetables before cooking, though these add their own flavour. Tomato puree also adds thickness as well as flavour. Egg yolks are a traditional sauce thickener in professional cooking; they have rich flavour and offer a velvety smooth texture but achieve the desired thickening effect only in a narrow temperature range. Overheating easily ruins such sauce, which can make egg yolk difficult to use as a thickener for amateur cooks. Other thickeners used by cooks are nuts (including rehan) or glaces made of meat or fish.

Many thickening agents require extra care in cooking. Some starches lose their thickening quality when cooked for too long or at too high temperature; on the other hand, cooking starches too short or not hot enough might lead to an unpleasant starchy taste or cause water to seep out of the finished product after cooling. Also, higher viscosity causes foods to burn more easily during cooking. As an alternative to adding more thickener, recipes may call for reduction of the foods' water content by lengthy simmering. When cooking, it is generally better to add thickener cautiously; if over-thickened, more water may be added but loss of flavour and texture may result.

Gelling agents are food additives used to thicken and stabilize jellies, desserts, candies, etc. The agents provide the foods with texture through formation of a gel. Some stabilizers and thickening agents are gelling agents.

Typical gelling agents include natural gums, starches, pectins, agar-agar and gelatin. Often they are based on polysaccharides or proteins.

A food product used to provide thickness to a liquid or a food dish. Some thickeners are used for medical purposes, e.g., to enable the swallowing of food without choking. Thickeners are also used to improve the texture or flavour of a dish. A variety of common thickeners are available, such as agar, arrowroot, roux, and browned flour pasta, cornstarch, potato starch, split peas, and egg yolks.

CLASSIFICATION OF THICKENING AGENTS

Most natural food thickeners are chemical composition of poly-saccharide and polysaccharide derivatives (except gelatine, which is composed of amino acids) widely distributed in nature. More than 40 species, however, can be divided into two major kinds: natural and synthetic (including semi-synthetic).

Based on the source of a thickening agent, thickeners can be roughly divided into four categories:

1. By preparing plants exudate: Arabic gum, peach gum.
2. Seeds from plants: guar gum, carrageenan.
3. By preparing protein of plants and animals: gelatin, chitin.
4. Made of natural materials on the basis of semi-synthetic: xanthan gum and CMC.

Thickening agents involved in industrial classification

1. Natural thickeners: Starch and xanthan gum, gelatin, guar gum, natural rubber, AGAR, carrageenan, chitin, and so on.
2. Cellulose thickeners: Methyl cellulose, hydroxyethyl cellulose, hydroxypropyl methyl cellulose, sodium carboxymethyl cellulose, etc.
3. Inorganic thickeners: Organic bentonite, diatomite, fumed silica, sodium base bentonite, silica gel and so on.
4. Synthetic polymer thickeners: Polyurethane thickener, sodium polyacrylate, polyvinyl alcohol, polypropylene amide, and so on.

ROLE OF THICKENING AGENTS

Most sauces and gravies are thickened with some kind of starch. Thickening agents increase the viscosity of a liquid, mixed without interfering with its other properties. Each thickening agent has properties best suited for specific recipes. One of the most commonly used methods for thickening sauces and other recipes is through the gelatinisation of starches like cornstarch, arrowroot, and wheat flour. Leavening agents, like baking soda and yeast, expand in recipes to give dough that light, fluffy texture.

Preparing Your Thickener

If you attempt to thicken a sauce by simply stirring flour into the simmering liquid, you will end up with lumps. The starch around each lump of powder expands and forms a gel that prevents granules from separating. Luckily, there are methods to help prevent lumpy sauces! They also help eliminate any unpleasant raw-flour taste that can occur if sauce is not simmered long enough. The following are methods commonly used to prepare flour or starch before you use it as a thickener.

Roux

The most common method to prepare flour or starch for thickening is to create a roux. Roux thickens sauces, soups, and stews, and lends a unique flavour to these dishes (for example, a dark roux is a key ingredient in Creole and Cajun gumbos and stews). Made from a mixture of fat (generally pan drippings or butter) and flour, a roux is slowly cooked on its own before it is added to sauces. The fat helps the starch expand and separate, lubricating it so it can be smoothly incorporated into the liquid. A roux should be cooked, cooled slightly, and then whisked into the sauce when you are ready to thicken it.

Prep Note: When preparing a roux, add cold liquid to a hot roux, and add hot liquid to a cold roux.

Remember this Thumb Rule: The darker the roux, the less thickening power it has. However, you will get a deeper flavour from a darker roux (both the flavour and colour of the roux becomes deeper the longer the roux cooks). White roux has more thickening power than a darker roux, because the browning process causes some of the starch in the flour to break down, making it unavailable for thickening.

Slurry

The easiest and quickest thickening method, slurry thickens almost immediately and creates a glossy appearance. To create slurry, corn starch is stirred into a small amount of cold water or stock, and then whisked into a simmering sauce. The same method can be used for nearly any starch; however, it is important not to overestimate the amount of starch you need, or to overheat the sauce. Too much heat can cause the starch to break down and the sauce to thin.

Prep Note: Slurries can be prepared in advance; just be sure to stir right before use to mix starch that has settled to the bottom of the container.

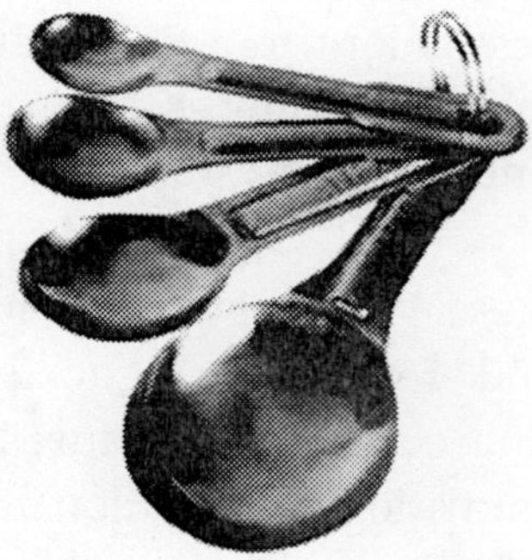

Beurre Manié

Essentially, the same as a roux, beurre manié (or kneaded butter) is a quicker method commonly used to thicken soups and sauces. It is also used as a finishing step for sauces to give a smooth, shiny texture to sauces prior to serving. To create this mix, flour is worked into the butter by hand or with a fork, then formed into small balls and added (uncooked) to a sauce. When the beurre manié is whisked into a warm liquid, the butter melts to release the flour without creating lumps.

Prep Note: Beurre manié works as a last-minute thickener, but note that it should be used sparingly. Too much can leave a floury taste behind.

Cooking Precautions

Thickening agents require extra care when cooking. Some starches lose their thickening quality when cooked for too long or at too high temperature; on the other hand, cooking starches for too short of a time or too low of a temperature can result in an unpleasant, starchy taste or cause water to seep out of the finished product after cooling. Also, note that higher viscosity can cause foods to burn more easily during cooking. When cooking, add thickener cautiously. If over-thickened, more water may be added but it may result in loss of flavour and texture.

TYPES OF LEAVENING AGENTS

Here, we break down the difference between pure starches versus common leavening agents. In short, pure starches have greater thickening power and add less colour to a final dish, making them ideal for sauces, puddings, and fillings. Common leavening agents, on the other hand, are best for recipes requiring dough or batter to rise.

Gluten-free thickeners have become an emerging trend for food allergy-conscious bakeries and restaurants. Luckily, many pure starch and leavening ingredients are naturally gluten free! Just be sure to check nutrition information for ingredients containing these variations of wheat: barley, durum, faro, malt, matzo, oats, rye, semolina, spelt, and wheat (bran, flour, germ, starch, and hydrolyzed protein).

Pure Starches

Pure starches have greater thickening power, ounce for ounce, than flour and do not require extended simmering time. They also add much less, colour to a final dish,

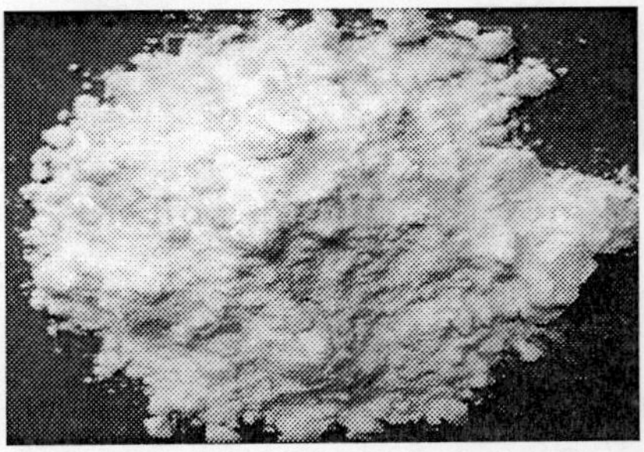

making them ideal for thickening sauces, puddings, and fillings, where a translucent effect is desired. Keep in mind, however, that pure starches break down more quickly over time than roux.

To avoid lumps, never add dry starch to a product. Instead, dilute these thickeners using the methods described above in 'Preparing Your Thickener' (roux, slurry, or beurre manié).

Storage: If not promptly used, most thickeners (especially powder) can deteriorate. They should always be kept tightly covered; if they absorb moisture from the air, they can lose their effectiveness. Store in a cool, dry place, as heat deteriorates them. Be sure to check individual labels for storage instructions.

Arrowroot Powder

This thickening powder is roughly equivalent to cornstarch, but more translucent. It will not gel or weep when cooled. This is the popular choice for mixing with acidic liquids, as corn starch loses potency when mixed with acids.

Cornstarch

This translucent powder is the popular choice for fruit sauces or Asian dishes that need high-gloss sheen. Cornstarch thickens when heated, but gels and weeps upon cooling. Its thickening power diminishes with excessive heating.

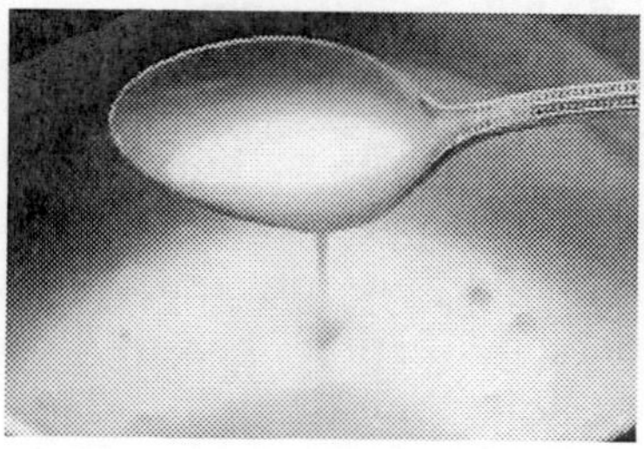

Tapioca Granules

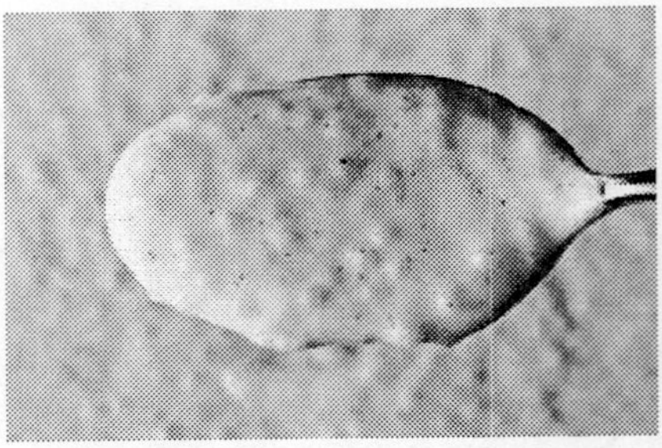

These translucent, pearly granules have a thickening power slightly greater than cornstarch. They are commonly used to thicken pie fillings, and can also be used for creamy puddings, custards, and thickening soups and gravies. Starch thickens quickly, and at a relatively low temperature. It is a good choice if you want to correct a sauce just before serving it.

Baking Soda and Baking Powder

These are principal chemical leavening agents. They release gases (primarily carbon dioxide) through chemical reactions between acids and bases in your recipe. These gases form air pockets throughout the dough or batter. As the product bakes, the gases expand and cause the product to rise. The proteins in the dough or batter then set around the air pockets to give products their rise and texture.

Storage: If not promptly used, most thickeners (especially powder) can deteriorate. They should always be kept tightly covered; if they absorb moisture from the air, they can lose their effectiveness. Store in a cool, dry place, as heat deteriorates them. Active dry yeast should be kept refrigerated in an airtight container after opening. Be sure to check individual labels for storage instructions.

Baking Soda (Sodium *Bicarbonate*)

This alkaline compound (base) releases carbon dioxide gas if both an acid and moisture are present. When heated during baking, the carbon dioxide expands to give baked goods their characteristic texture known as "crumb." Heat is not necessary for this reaction to occur; therefore, products made with baking soda must be baked at once to prevent carbon dioxide escaping from batter or dough.

Acids commonly used with baking soda are buttermilk, sour cream, lemon juice, honey, molasses, and fruits high in acid such as citrus.

Prep Note: If more leavening action is needed, add baking powder instead of baking soda. Too much baking soda results in a soapy or bitter taste, and yellow and brown colouring.

Baking Powder

This is a mixture of baking soda and an added acid, such as cream of tartar and/or sodium aluminium sulphate. Baking powder also contains a starch to prevent lumping and to balance chemical reactions. Once baking powder is in contact with liquid, it reacts quickly; therefore, products made with baking powder must be baked soon after the powder is added to prevent carbon dioxide escaping from batter or dough.

Yeast

This living organism feeds on sugars, producing alcohol and carbon dioxide, the gas that lightens dough to give it the proper texture. This organic leavening agent takes a substantial amount of time to rise, so temperature must be controlled carefully. These are less common thickening agents to add unique flavour and texture to your baked goods and puddings. Some of them even double as both thickeners and bakery toppings.

Storage: If not promptly used, most thickeners (especially powder) can deteriorate. They should always be kept tightly covered; if they absorb moisture from the air, they can lose their effectiveness. Store in a cool, dry place, as heat deteriorates them. Be sure to check individual labels for storage instructions.

Cocoa Powder

Popular in desserts, cocoa powder is actually a starch (although it is not commonly referred to as one) made from the brown powder left after fat (cocoa butter) is removed from cocoa beans, cocoa powder does not contain sweetener or flavouring and is used primarily in baked goods.

Cream of Tartar (Potassium Hydrogen Tartrate)

This fine white powder is a by-product from the wine-making process (it forms inside barrels during grape fermentation). It is commonly used when beating egg whites to increase heat tolerance and volume, making it ideal for meringues and soufflés. It also helps prevent crystallisation of sugar syrups, resulting in creamier candy and frostings.

Malted Milk Powder

A dry mix of malted barley flour, wheat flour and powdered milk, this powder is commonly used to thicken milk shakes and baked goods. It also doubles as a topping for these products.

CHECK YOUR PROGRESS

1. Describe the role of thickening agents.
2. Describe the classification of thickening agents as per their uses.

3. Write a short note on baking soda.
4. Write a note on cornstarch.
5. If a product requires more leavening action, then what should we use and how?
6. Classify thickening agents in terms of their industrial uses.
7. Discuss different uses of thickening agents.
8. Name any five natural thickeners.

Unit 9

Sugar

The word sugar derives from the Arabic word "sukkurs", which itself has evolved from the Sanskrit word "sakara" in India, used famously for jaggery, which is also known as Indian sugar. However, the refined white grain sugar was introduced by 'chini' and that is why, grain is known as chini in Hindi. Generally, when we say just sugar, it refers to white grain sugar, i.e., surcouse. Simple carbohydrates are called sugar.

Carbohydrates, also called carbs, are defined as aldehydic or ketonic compounds with some number of oxydrilic groups (poly-hydroxy aldehydes or ketones as well).

Many of them, but not all, have general formula $(CH_2O)_n$ (only molecules with $n > 4$ are considered carbohydrates); some, in addition to carbon (C), oxygen (O) and hydrogen (H), include nitrogen or sulphur.

On the basis of the number of forming units, three major classes of carbohydrates can be defined: monosaccharides, oligosaccharides and polysaccharides.

Sugars are classified under the group carbohydrates – monosa-ccharides, oligosaccharides and polysaccharides.

- Monosaccharides or simply sugars are formed by only one polyhydroxy aldehydeidic or ketonic unit. The most abundant monosaccharide is D-glucose, also called dextrose.
- Oligosaccharides are formed by short chains of monosaccharidic units (2-20), linked one to the next by chemical bonds, called glycosidic bonds.

The most abundant oligosaccharides are disaccharides, formed by two monosaccharides, and especially in human diet, the most important are sucrose (common table sugar), lactose and maltose. Within cells, many oligosaccharides formed by three or more units do not find themselves as free molecules but linked to other ones, lipids or proteins, to form glycoconjugates.

- Polysaccharides are polymers consisting of 20 to 107 monosaccharidic units; they differ from each other for the mono-saccharides recurring in the structure, for the length and the degree of branching of chains or for the type of links between units.

  In the plant kingdom, several types of polysaccharides are present, while in vertebrates, there is only a small number. Polysaccharides having more starch, cellulose, gums are difficult to digest.

  The primary sugar, glucose, is a product of photosynthesis and occurs in all green plants. In most plants, the sugars occur as a mixture that cannot readily be separated into the components. In the sap of some plants, the sugar mixtures are condensed into syrup. Juices of sugarcane (*Saccharum officinarum*) and sugar beet (*beta vulgaris*) are rich in pure sucrose, although beet sugar is generally much less sweet than cane sugar. These two sugar crops are the main sources of commercial sucrose.

- The sugarcane is a thick, tall, perennial grass that flourishes in tropical or subtropical regions. Sugar synthesized in the leaves is used as a source of energy for growth or is sent to the stalks for storage. It is the sweet sap in the stalks that is the source of sugar as we know it. The reed accumulates sugar to about 15% of its weight.

VARIOUS STAGES OF COOKING SUGAR

There are seven stages of cooking sugar:

Name	Temperature	Description	Usage
Thread	223-235 °F	The syrup drips from spoon and forms thin threads in water.	Glace and candied fruits
Soft ball	235-245 °F	The syrup easily forms a ball while in the cold water, but flattens once removed.	Fudge and fondant
Firm ball	245-250 °F	The syrup is formed into a stable ball, but loses its round shape once pressed.	Caramel candies
Hard ball	250-266 °F	The syrup holds its ball, but loses its round shape once pressed.	Divinity and marshmallows
Soft crack	270-290 °F	The syrup will form firm but pliable threads.	Nougat and taffy
Hard crack	300-310 °F	The syrup forms brittle threads and easily crack and shaps.	Brittles and lollipops
Caramel	320-350 °F	The sugar syrup will turn golden brown and have a fragrant caramel smell.	Caramel syrup, pralines

IMPORTANCE OF SUGAR

Sugar is disaccharide sucrose ($C_{12} H_{22} O_{11}$), a carbohydrate found in every fruit and vegetable. It has various advantages, which are as follows:

- Sugars create sweetness
- Sugars also create tenderness because they weaken gluten
- Sugars add colour to the crust when they bake
- Sugars improve keeping qualities because sugar is hydroscopic, meaning it absorbs water
- Sugars act as creaming agents with fat

TYPES OF SUGAR

Refined Sugar

1. Granulated sugar is the most commonly used.
2. Very fine sugars are used in cakes and cookies.
3. Coarse sugars are called sanding sugars, for topping baked goods.
4. Icing sugar is very fine and is used in icings or for dusting finished products.

Molasses and Brown Sugar

1. Molasses is concentrated sugar cane syrup, with the sugar removed.
2. Brown sugar is simple white sugar with some of the molasses left in. You can make it by mixing molasses with sugar.

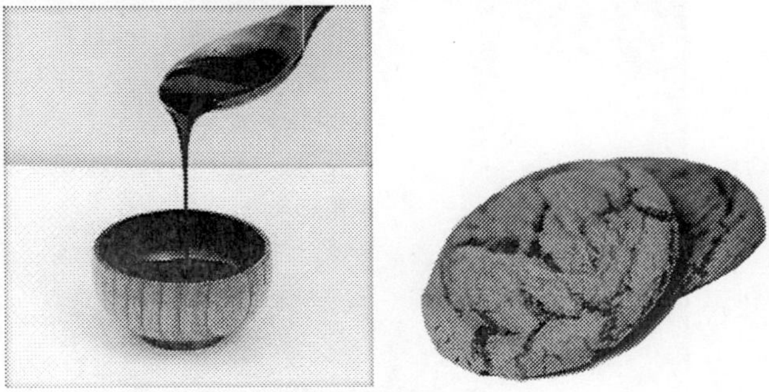

Molasses

Grain Sugar

Castor Sugar/Breakfast Sugar

Icing Sugar

Brown Sugar

Golden Syrup

Corn Syrup

Date Sugar

Jaggery

SUGAR SUBSTITUTES

Honey

Honey is 25 to 50 % sweeter than sugar, and has a distinctive flavour. The flavours and colours of honey can vary depending upon the bees' diet–buckwheat honey, for example, is darker and stronger than clover honey. Baked goods made with honey are moist and dense, and tend to brown faster than those made with granulated sugar.

Honey is a flavour powerhouse. It is rich, intense, and syrupy-sweet. The different types of honey are endless, from mild clover to dark, deep buckwheat. You can't use honey in any recipe that requires creaming (the process of beating together softened butter and sugar). Granulated sugar crystals contain sharp edges that slice through the butter, creating air pockets that expand when heated, contributing to a lofty, risen pastry. Honey doesn't create those air pockets, and it results in a denser baked good. It makes a softer product, but dries out more quickly than baked goods made with sugar. It is also more expensive than refined white sugar.

Best for: Soft, moist cakes and quick breads, puddings, ice creams and gelato.

Tip: Use honey in recipes that have a soft, cake-like texture (like coffee cakes).

Maple Syrup

Maple syrup has a beautiful thick consistency and an earthy sweetness.

Honey, maple does not "cream" into a recipe the way granulated sugar does. It is also expensive.

Best for: Caramels, candies, ice creams, and puddings.

Tips: Maple is sweeter than sugar, which means you can use less (this helps soften the price tag). Use maple in recipes that do not require a creaming step, and try combining it with other sweeteners, like barley malt syrup or molasses. You can also

Sugar substitutes chart

	Honey	Maple Syrup	Agave Nectar	Stevia
1 cup sugar (8 oz/240 gm)	¾ cup	¾ cup	⅔ cup	1 tsp.
1 tbsp. Sugar	¾ tbsp.	¾ tbsp.	¾ tbsp.	⅛ tsp.
1 tsp. Sugar	¾ tsp.	¾ tsp.	¾ tsp.	Just a pinch
Notes	Decrease liquid by 2-4 tbsp.	Decrease liquid by 3 tbsp.	Decrease liquid by ¼ cup	To replace bulk, add applesauce, apple butter, or yogurt

find evaporated maple syrup, which comes in golden-brown granules and has a texture similar to muscovado sugar. Maple sugar can be substituted 1:1 for refined sugar.

The benefits of maple syrup are: It comes directly from a plant's sap and contains over 50 antioxidants. Make sure to grab the real stuff (sorry, Aunt Jemima) and spread it over waffles or use it in homemade granola.

Barley Malt Syrup

Barley malt syrup is made by sprouting, drying and then, roasting barley grains, while molasses is produced by boiling juice extracted from sugarcane or, less commonly, beets. Both barley malt syrup and molasses are intensely flavoured and super rich—they can add a deep, satisfying note to baked goods and pastries. Molasses is also very acidic, which makes for light and airy cakes when combined with baking soda.

Some may find the flavour of molasses and barley malt syrup too intense. It can bully other, more subtle flavours into submission.

Best for: Gingerbreads, cookies, as additions to other sweeteners.

Tips: Combining barley malt and molasses with another ingredient (molasses pairs particularly well with maple) makes for a more palatable baked good.

Lemon

Fans of gin can skip the extra sugar in a Tom Collins and add an extra lemon squeeze.

Applesauce

Instead of a half-cup white sugar in a batch of oatmeal cookies, swap in an equal amount of apple sauce. The natural sweetness from a Golden Delicious or Fuji apple is perfect in an after dinner treat. Purchase the no sugar-added kind.

Erythritol

This sugar alcohol is practically a guilt-free sweet solution. At 0.2 calories per gram, the white powder from a plant occurs naturally in many fruits. Plus, it does not lead to tooth decay and other not-so-sweet effects of sugar consumption. It is not quite as sweet as natural sugar, so try it in chocolate baked goods, like brownies.

Raisins

For a creative spin on things, blend a cup of raisins in a food processer. With antioxidants and fiber, these little dried grapes add a kick to any baked good.

Cinnamon

Spice up a morning cup of coffee with cinnamon. This super spice adds subtle sweetness, while boosting immunity, no calories included.

Unsweetened Cocoa Powder

For a warm winter treat, mix some unsweetened cocoa powder in a glass of hot water or skim milk. It will satisfy that sweet tooth without all the extra sugar the sweetened version includes. Add a splash of vanilla extract for extra flavour.

Cranberries

Skip the cup of sugar and add cranberries to a batch of muffins or scones. These little tart treats add a dose of antioxidants refined sugar can't offer.

Processed Dates

Grab a bunch of dates for an extra boost of antioxidants in the next baking experiment. With a low glycemic index and some subtle sweetness, it may be perfect for brownie batter or the base of homemade granola bars. Substitute two-thirds cup for one cup of regular sugar.

Grapefruit

For a daily dose of vitamin C, opt for grapefruit juice in a cocktail over soda or tonic water. It will add a sweet and sour kick to any beverage.

Coconut Sugar

Get a little tropical and use coconut sugar in a fruit smoothie. Made from the sap of coconut flowers, this natural sugar comes in block, paste, or granulated form. Plus, it's loaded with potassium, which helps keep our bones strong.

Brown Rice Syrup

Brown rice syrup comes from brown rice. More nutritious than its high-fructose alternative, this buttery and nutty flavoured syrup is perfect in granola bars and baked breads.

Lime

Make juice boxes a thing of the past and spice up a glass of sparkling water with a squeeze of lime. The tart and tang will keep taste buds satisfied without the extra sugar rush.

Puréed Banana

In the next loaf of banana bread, try using extra-ripe banana, eliminating the sugar. The fruit naturally becomes sweeter as it ripens, so there is no need for extra sugar.

Milk

The natural sugar in milk adds a touch of sweetness to that morning cup of Joe, so think twice before adding a teaspoon or two of sugar. The lactose in milk may do the trick.

Frozen Juice Concentrate

Use apple juice. With additional fibre and antioxidants, the pie will be a sweet solution for a nutritious dessert!

Sucanat

Introducing sugar in its most natural state. Sucanat is a sneaky acronym that stands for sugar cane natural. This sweetener is made from organic cane sugar and packs in some nutrients white sugar lacks.

Apricot Puree

Apricots are a nutritional A+ with vitamin C, fiber, and iron. Make some of the sweet stuff and mix it in plain Greek yogurt or enjoy it with hearty whole-grain bread.

Fresh-Squeezed Orange Juice

In a batch of homemade bread, swap out the sugar for fresh orange juice. Looking for a cool treat? Freeze some juice in an ice-pop mould rather than buying what is in the freezer section.

Rum

Alcohol is not just for drinking—caramelize a few slices of pineapple in rum and add them to pancakes or unsweetened yogurt. Now that is a fancy way to stay sweet!

Molasses

Molasses is a by-product of refined sugar production. It contains small amounts of B vitamins, calcium, and iron. Molasses imparts a dark colour and strong flavour to baked foods, but is not as sweet as sugar. When substituting molasses for sugar, use $1^1/_3$ cups molasses for 1 cup sugar, and reduce the amount of liquid in the recipe by 5 tablespoons. Molasses is also more acidic than sugar; add ½ teaspoon baking soda for each cup of molasses used. Replace no more than half the sugar called for in a recipe with molasses.

Corn Syrup

Corn syrup is known as an "invert sugar;" it is useful in cooking and candy-making because, unlike other sugars, it does not crystallize. Corn syrup is less sweet than sugar, and does not add flavour like molasses or honey. "Golden Syrup," common in the United Kingdom, is refinery syrup made from sugar. It is used in place of corn syrup. Some cooks believe sugar syrups have alivelier flavour than corn syrups and add more character to dishes such as pecan pie.

OTHER NATURAL SWEETENERS

Refined Fructose

It is sweeter than granulated sugar. It can be easily substituted in baking recipes–simply add one-third less. Some tasters find that, although products made with fructose taste sweet, they also taste a little flat. Fructose attracts more water than sucrose, so fructose-sweetened products tend to be moist. Baked products made with fructose will be darker than if they were made with white sugar. Fructose is available in health-food stores.

Brown Rice Malt Syrup

It consists of maltose, glucose and complex carbohydrates. It is an amber-hued syrup resembling honey, but it is not as sweet as honey. It can be substituted cup per cup for granulated sugar, but the liquid ingredients should be reduced by ¼ cup per cup of rice syrup. Enzyme-treated syrup, as opposed to malted syrup, tends to liquefy the batter of a baked product. Use the malted syrup for best results.

Fruit Juice Concentrates

Fruit juice concentrates, such as apple juice concentrate, orange juice concentrate, or white grape juice concentrate, are wonderful substitutes for sugar and add interesting flavours as well. Juice concentrates are made up of fructose and glucose. Use ¾ cup for every cup of white sugar, and decrease the amount of liquid by 3 tablespoons.

Stevia

Stevia is a naturally sweet herb that has been used for hundreds of years in South America. Since neither the herb nor its powdered form has been approved as a food additive by the FDA, it is available only as a dietary supplement.

Saccharine

Saccharine is 200-700 times sweeter than sugar. It can be used in baked goods. However, the manufacturer recommends substituting it for only half of the sugar in a recipe. Substitute 6 (1 gram) packets for each ¼ cup sugar. It is sold under the brand name "Sweet and Low".

Aspartame

Aspartame is 160-220 times sweeter than granulated sugar. This sweetener is heat-sensitive: it loses its sweetening power when heated, and cannot be used for cookies or cakes. The manufacturer does recommend trying it in no-bake pies and in puddings after they have been removed from the heat. Substitute 6 (1 gram) packets for each ¼ cup of sugar. It is sold under the brand names "Equal and NutraSweet".

Acesulfame Potassium

Acesulfame potassium is 200 times sweeter than sugar. It is heat-stable, so it can be used in baking and cooking. Use acesulfame K in combination with granulated sugar when baking. Substitute 6 (1gram) packets for each ¼ cup sugar. It is sold under the brand names "Sunette and Sweet One".

Sucralose

Sucralose is made from sugar, but is not metabolized by the body like sugar. It is 600 times sweeter than granulated sugar. Granular sucralose is the form used when baking. Substitute 1 cup granular sucralose for each cup of sugar called for in the recipe. Recipes made with this product tend to bake faster than usual, so check for doneness.

CHECK YOUR PROGRESS

1. Describe the cooking temperature test.
2. Explain types of sugar.

3. Discuss the role of honey in cooking process.
4. Write a note on sucralose.
5. Draw sugar substitute's chart.
6. What is the difference between molasses and brown sugar?
7. Discuss the different uses of corn syrup.
8. Describe the natural sugar ingredients which we use in cooking.

PART 2

BAKERY AND CONFECTIONERY

Unit 10

Pastry Creams

Pastry cream is defined as the custard which can thicken the flour or starch. Sometimes, it may be used for toppings and for icing desserts or any other preparation. Egg yolks in the custard may be used as thickening agents.

It is a basic component in every French and Italian dessert. It can be used as icing and filling and as toppings. It sometimes completes your dish by giving flavours, garnishes and visual appeal to your product.

It is made from butter, shortening, sugar, egg white, lemon juice, vanilla essence, water and some kinds of flavouring agents, e.g., chocolate, coffee, and buttercream recipes.

Care should be taken while preparing pastry cream

1. Don't use an aluminium pot while making it; it may change the flavour or colour.
2. It can curdle sometimes.
3. As soon as it thickens, transfer it to a pot or a bowl or it will continue to cook even when you switch off the heat. Sometimes, there may be some congealed or some stuff visible in the bottom pan. Do not try to pick that layer, leave as it is.
4. If you strain through the strainer. You never see lumps in it.
5. Let cool and cover with parchment paper, so that a skin does not form on top.
6. Beat only after it is chilled, so as to make it silky smooth.

7. Always follow the ingredients according to your recipe.
8. Never let it boil. Always follow your recipe.

BASIC PASTRY CREAMS

Fondant

Fondant is sugar syrup that is crystallized to a smooth, creamy white mass. It is familiar as the icing for napoleons, éclairs, petits fours, and some cakes. When applied, it sets up into a shiny, non-sticky coating.

As it is difficult to make it in a bakery, it is mostly purchased either in ready-to-use moist form or in a dry form that requires only the addition of water.

Buttercream

Buttercream icings are light, smooth mixtures of fat and confectionery sugar. They may also contain eggs to increase their smoothness or lightness. These popular icings are used for cakes. They can be easily flavoured and coloured.

Three basic kinds of buttercream:

1. Simple buttercreams are made by creaming together fat and sugar to a desired consistency and lightness. A small quantity of egg whites may be whipped in.
2. Decorator's buttercream is a simple buttercream used for making flowers and other cake decorations. It is creamed only a little because if too much air is beaten in, it would not be able to hold delicate shapes.
3. Meringue type buttercreams are prepared by first beating egg whites and adding a boiling syrup or just sugar. Soft butter is then mixed into the meringue. This is a very light, smooth icing.

French butter creams are similar to the meringue-type, but the foam is made with egg yolks (sometimes, whole eggs) and boiling syrup. This is a very rich, light icing.

Meringues

Meringues are beaten egg whites sweetened with sugar. Their most frequent use in North America is for pie toppings and cake icings (known as boiled icing). They are also used to give volume and lightness to buttercream icings and to such preparation as dessert soufflés.

Another excellent use for meringues is to bake them in a oven until crisp. In this form, they can be used in place of cake layers or pastry shells to make light, elegant desserts. Chopped nuts may be folded into meringue before forming and baking, to make these desserts flavourful.

When beating egg whites, make sure that all equipment are free of any trace of fat or grease, and that the egg whites have no trace of yolk in them. Even a small trace of fat will prevent the whites from foaming properly.

Soft meringues, used for pie topping, may be made with as little as 500 gm sugar of 500 egg whites. *Hard maringues,* baked until crisp, are made with twice as much sugar as egg white.

Basic Meringues

The stiffness to which meringues are beaten may vary, as long as they are not beaten until they are too stiff and dry. For most purposes, they are beaten until they form stiff, or nearly stiff, moist peaks.

1. *Common meringues* are made from egg whites at room temperature, beaten with sugar. It is easier to make and is reasonably stable due to the high amount of sugar.
2. *Swiss meringues* are made from egg whites and sugar warmed over a double boiler while beating. Warming gives meringues better volume and stability.
3. *Italian meringues* are made by beating hot sugar syrup into the egg whites. These are the most stable of the three, because the egg whites are actually cooked by the heat of the syrup. When flavoured with vanilla, the meringue is also known as boiled icing. It is also used in meringue-type buttercream icings.

PREPARATION AND CARE

Care for Making Buttercream

Butter, especially sweet, unsalted butter, is the preferred fat buttercream because of its flavour and melt-in-the-mouth quality. Icings made with shortening only can be unpleasant because the fat congeals and coats the inside of the mouth and does not melt. However, butter makes a less stable icing because it melts so easily. There are two ways around this problem.

- Use buttercreams in cool weather only.
- Blend a small quantity of emulsified shortening with the butter to stabilise it.

Simple Buttercream

S. No.	Ingredients	Metric
1.	Butter	500 gm
2.	Shortening	250 gm
3.	Confectioners	1 kg
4.	Egg white (pasteurised)	75 gm
5.	Lemon juice	5 mL
6.	Vanilla	15 mL
Procedure		
1. Cream together the butter, shortening, and sugar until blended well, using the paddle attachment. 2. Add the egg whites, lemon juice, and vanilla. Blend in all medium speed. Then mix at high speed until light and fluffy.		
Variations		
Decorator's buttercream Use 750 gm regular shortening, no butter, lemon juice and vanilla. Reduce egg whites to 60 gm blend at low speed until smooth. Do not whip. **Cream cheese icing** Substitute cream cheese for the butter and shortening. If necessary, thin the icing with cream or milk. If desired, flavour it with grated lemon or orange zest instead of vanilla.		

Meringue-Type Buttercream

S. No.	Ingredients	Metric
1.	Sugar	1 kg
2.	Water	250 mL
3.	Egg whites	500 gm
4.	Butter, soft	1 kg
5.	Emulsified shortening	250 gm
6.	Lemon juice	10 mL
7.	Vanilla	15 mL

Procedure

1. Combine the sugar and water in a saucepan. Bring to a boil, stir to dissolve the sugar.
2. Continue to boil until the syrup reaches a temperature of 115 °C.
3. While the syrup is boiling, beat the egg in a clean, grease-free bowl, using the whip attachment, until they form firm, moist peaks. Do not overbeat.
4. As soon as the syrup reaches 115 °C, pour it slowly into the egg white while the mixer is running at medium speed.
5. Continue to beat until the meringue is cool and forms stiff peaks.
6. With the mixer still running at medium speed, begin adding the butter, a little at a time. Add it just as fast as it can be absorbed by the meringue.
7. When all the butter is beaten in, add the shortening in the same way.
8. Beat in the lemon juice and vanilla.

Meringue

S. No.	Ingredients	Metric		
		Common	Swiss	Italian
1.	Egg white	500 gm	500 gm	500 gm
2.	Sugar	1 kg	1 kg	1 kg
3.	Water	-	-	250 mL

Note: For soft meringue to top pies, use half the amount of sugar.

Procedure

Common Meringue

1. With the whip attachment, beat the egg whites at high speed until they form soft peaks.
2. Gradually add the sugar with the machine.
3. Continue to beat until the meringue forms stiff but moist peaks.

(Contd...)

Swiss Meringue

1. Place the egg whites and sugar in a stainless steel bowl or on the top of a double boiler. Beat with a wire whip over hot water until the mixture is warm (50 °C).
2. Transfer the mixture to the bowl of a mixing machine and whip at high speed until stiff peaks form.

Italian Meringue

1. Heat the sugar and water in a saucepan until the sugar dissolves and the mixture boils. Boil until a candy thermometer placed in registers 115 °C.
2. While the syrup is cooking, beat the egg whites in a mixing machine until they form soft peaks.
3. With the machine running, slowly beat the hot syrup into the egg whites.
4. Continue beating until the meringue forms firm peaks.

Meringue Desserts

1. Pie toppings
2. Baked meringue shells
3. Japonaise meringue
4. Baked Alaska

French Buttercream

S. No.	Ingredients	Metric
1.	Sugar	1 kg
2.	Water	250 mL
3.	Egg yolks	375 gm
4.	Butter, soft	1.25 kg
5.	Vanilla	15 mL

Procedure

1. Combine the sugar and water in a saucepan. Bring to a boil, stir to dissolve the sugar.
2. Continue to boil until the syrup reaches a temperature of 115 °C.
3. While the syrup is boiling, beat the yolks with the whip attachment until they are thick and light.
4. As soon as the syrup reaches 115 °C, pour it slowly into the beaten yolks while the mixer is running at medium speed.

(Contd...)

5. Continue to beat until the mixture is cool and the yolks are light and thick.
6. With the mixer still running, add the butter, a little at a time. Add it just as fast as it can be absorbed by the mixture.
7. Beat in the vanilla. If the icing is too soft, refrigerate until it is firm enough to spread.

Variation

Flavoured buttercreams are made by adding the desired flavouring to any of the basic buttercream recipes. In addition to the variation, extracts and emulsions such as lemon, orange, and almonds may be used.

Chocolate buttercream

Add 125-150 gm sweet chocolate, melted and cooled, to each 500 gm buttercream.

Coffee buttercream

For each 500 gm buttercream, add 22 mL instant coffee dissolved in 10 mL hot water.

CHECK YOUR PROGRESS

1. Write three basic kinds of buttercream.
2. Write a detailed note on meringues.
3. Describe two desserts which are prepared by meringue.
4. Describe the recipe of simple buttercream.
5. Write a note on Italian meringues.
6. Write about care should be taken while preparing buttercream.
7. Describe the use of fondant in pastries section.
8. Write five best uses of buttercream.

Unit 11

Pastry

Pastries are made from a variety of doughs and special batters. Most individual pastry servings are made with base or shell of short dough, puff pastry dough, pie crust dough or cream puff or éclair shells. There are variety of shapes and fillings for pastry variations. Reference is made to application of fruits, glaze preparation and whipped cream topping and garnish of various nuts and chocolates.

SHORT DOUGH

Short dough is a form of cookie dough. It is used for cookies as well as tarts. The most important factor in making and handling short dough is careful addition of flour. Overmixing or using straight high-gluten flour, makes the dough hard.

Pie Crust

This blend is usually 50% short dough and 50% pie crust dough. These doughs are blended until smooth. Chocolate or cocoa may be added, and then used to make special crust and chocolate cream rolls.

Fruit Tart and Fruit Cake

Fruit tart and fruit cake require a short dough, pie dough or a combination of both. This dough serves as a shell or support of fruit.

Hamentashen (Triangular Cookies)

Hamentashen are made from short dough or cookie dough. These are also made from rich yeast dough.

PUFF PASTRY

Puff pastry dough is laminated pastry dough. Puff pastry serves as the source for the finishing of many custards, whipped cream, cream toppings, and fruit filled pastries. These are delicate, flaky and tender products.

PRINCIPLES OF PASTRY MAKING

1. Good mixing technique is the basic principle of good pastries. All the pastry dough should be mixed directly on a marble slab or smooth stone slab. Majority of the pastry dough need cool conditions. Strudel and hot water paste require warm conditions.
2. The flour-to-fat ratio depends on the type of pastry. Dry ingredients must be mixed thoroughly, especially for short pastes.
3. It is important to have the correct amount of liquid for mixing. The amount of water should be adjusted according to the different types of flour. Too much liquid leads to rough dough and liquid leads to crumbly structure and that is difficult to handle.
4. Doughs need resting and they should be allowed to set after rolling.
5. Do not turn the pastry over but turn the pastry around.
6. When baking, oven must always be pre-heated to the correct temperature before placing any pastry in the oven.
7. Rolling out
   (a) Sprinkle just enough flour to prevent dough from sticking to the slab.
   (b) Roll with short forward strokes.
   (c) Do not roll over the edges, especially when rolling puff pastry, as the layers will break and force air out of the dough.

TYPES OF PASTRY

Non-Laminate Pastry

- Short crust pastries (pies & tarts)
- Choux pastry
- Brioche

Laminate Pastry

- Crossiant
- Danish
- Phyllo / filo
- Puff Pastry
- Strudel

SOME IMPORTANT INSTRUCTIONS

Baking Measurements

1 ounce	30 gm
2 ounces	55 gm
3 ounces	85 gm
4 ounces (1/4 pound)	115 gm
8 ounces (1/2 pound)	225 gm
16 ounces (1 pound)	455 gm
1 cup	250 mL
1 quart	1 litre
1 and 1/2 quarts	1.5 litres
2 quarts	2 litres
2 and 1/2 quarts	2.5 litres
3 quarts	3 litres
4 quarts	4 litres

TYPES OF PASTRIES

Short Crust Pastry

Short crust pastry is a mixture of flour, fat, sugar and sometimes, egg and milk. The flour should have low gluten content, one that is milled from soft wheat flour. The fat reduces the extensibility of the gluten, that is, it makes the gluten strands shorter. Hence, the term **shortening** for the fat is used in a bakery and the term **short crust pastry**. The usual method of making short crust pastry is by rub-in method. Chilled fat or butter is rubbed into the sieved flour, so that it is finely dispersed and resembles a sandy or bread crumb-like texture. The fat forms a thin layer or coating on the glutenin and gliadin molecules, without turning the fat into a continuous paste. Cold water is sprinkled over the mixture to form smooth dough. The fat-to-flour ratio is normally 1:2, but the fat can be increased to equal the flour to obtain rich dough. This dough is difficult to work with. Pate Sucre is a sweet version of this pastry and sugar is creamed with butter before the flour and the moisture is added. The ratio of sugar, fat and flour is 1:2:4. Various sweet and savoury products are made with short crust pastry. It forms the base of several pies, tarts, flans and also products like cheese straws and turnovers. Some precautions must be taken when making short crust pastry. It is important not to work the dough too much as it will get tough due to the development of gluten. This can also happen when scrapings and trimmings are added to the dough and are worked. The use of too much flour for dusting also alters the ratio of the mixture and causes toughening as the extra flour proteins – glutenin and gliadin – do not have a coating of fat around it, and thus come together to form gluten.

Some faults in short crust pastry:

1. Hard or tough pastry is due to too much liquid or too little fat. It is also probably due to overmixing.
2. A soft and crumbly pastry is due to too little water for the binding, too much fat or the use of self raising flour instead of plain flour.
3. A shrunken pastry is due to excess stretching during rolling.
4. A soggy pastry is a result of the filling in the product being too moist.

Recipes and methods of preparation with their baking standards

Short Crust Pastry (Basic Recipe)

Refined flour — 60 gm
Salt — 1/8 t
Butter — 30 gm
Cold water

Place the flour, butter and salt into a large clean bowl. Rub the butter into the flour with your fingertips until the mixture resembles fine breadcrumbs, working as quickly as possible to prevent the dough becoming warm. Add water to the mixture and using a cold knife stir until the dough binds together; add more cold water, a teaspoon at a time if the mixture is too dry. Wrap the dough for a minimum of 15 minutes.

Put down the knife and quickly bind the mixture into a smooth dough with the hand in a circular motion, leaving the bowl clean. Do not knead. Place the dough on a lightly floured board or table top and to remove cracks press lightly if needed. Flour the pastry roller/ rolling pin lightly using short sharp strokes. Roll the pastry to the shape and size required. Roll in one direction only and turn as necessary, taking care not to stretch it. Bake as directed in individual recipes.

{Preparation of various pies, tarts, etc.}

Laminated Pastry

This category of pastry includes puff, flaky, rough puff and Danish pastry.

Puff and flaky are two of the most remarkable products of a bakery. Although they are similar, they are made differently and it is almost impossible to tell which is what. Puff is referred to as the French method, whereas the English refer to it as flaky pastry. The Scots have their own version and call it rough puff pastry. The flour used for laminated pastry must be of high gluten content, so that it stands up to the manipulation involved in building up the laminated structure. Butter is the preferred fat because of its flavour and melt-in-the-mouth quality. Special pastry margarine is also available. It has a low moisture content and good creaming value, ideal for this kind of pastry. This product is easy to work with as it does not get too hard in the refrigerator. A weak acid solution such as lemon juice or cream of tartar is added to the dough, as it confers greater extensibility to the gluten.

Puff pastry has equal amounts of fat and flour. Dough is made with flour, salt, and lemon juice. After allowing it to rest, the dough is rolled out into a square and the creamed block of fat is placed in the centre. The dough is then folded around the fat and is refrigerated for a while. Then, it is rolled into a rectangle about ½ thick. Fold the two ends to the centre and then into half (book fold). Make sure that the edges/corners are even. Refrigerate/rest the dough to relax the gluten. Do not refrigerate for too long as the fat will harden. Now turn the dough 90 °C on the table so that the length now becomes the breadth. This step must be repeated before subsequent rolling so that it helps to stretch the gluten in all directions, not just lengthwise. Failure to do this will result in the product that shrinks unevenly when they are baked. Repeat the rolling and folding a total of four times. The dough is now ready to be rolled out for the final shaping and cutting.

Flaky pastry is a similar product. The dough is similar but the amount of fat is only two-thirds of the flour. The fat is creamed into a homogenous mass and divided into three parts. The dough is rolled out into a rectangle of about half inch thick. One-third of the fat is then spread onto two-thirds of the dough surface. The dough is then folded into three so that there are alternate layers of fat and dough. The dough is then rested/ refrigerated to relax the gluten. The process is repeated twice more to use up all the fat and then once again without fat (blind fold). Remember to rest the dough between each rolling. The pastry is now ready for the final make up.

Khari biscuits, vol-au-vents, cream horns, cheese straws, meat and vegetable puffs are some of the sweet and savoury products made with puff and flaky pastry.

Rough puff pastry is the Scottish answer to puff and flaky pastry. This is the quickest method of making a laminated pastry. Old books describe it as the "Blitz method", the term being derived from the German *Blitzen,* meaning lightening. In this method, the fat is mixed into the sieved flour in pieces, the size of walnuts. Dough is made using water and a little lemon juice, without using too much pressure so that the fat does not completely blend into the dough. The dough is then rolled out like the flaky pastry method and the process is repeated two more times. The dough is now ready for rolling or cutting into the desired shape.

When laminated pastries are baked, the fat melts and forms oil layers between the layers of dough, preventing them from sticking to each other. As the heat penetrates the product, the water in the dough layers changes into steam and pushes the lubricated leaves of dough apart. This produces an increase in the volume of the dough. Later, the gluten in the flour coagulates while the water is dried out so that by the time the pastry is properly cooked, it is able to retain its distended puffy volume. The temperature of the oven has an important role to play in the success of this product. The temperature must be high enough to generate the steam required.

Danish pastry is rich, sweet and fermented dough. The fat is laminated into the dough and therefore, Danish is also considered a laminated pastry. A ferment of yeast, sugar, eggs and milk is added to the flour to make a soft dough. After resting and knocking back the dough, it is then rolled into a rectangle and the fat spreads evenly. The dough is then cut into three uneven sizes and a spool is made, that is, rolling the smallest into the medium and then that into the largest piece of dough. The dough is wrapped into a moist cloth and refrigerated for 15 to 20 minutes. It is then rolled and cut into the desired shapes. Egg wash is applied and the product is allowed the second proofing and then, is baked at 200 °C for 20 minutes. The pastry is brushed with sugar syrup after baking. Croissants, windmills, turnovers, napoleons, and breakfast Danish are examples.

Recipes and methods of preparation with their baking standards

Flaky/Puff Pastry

Cold fat — 37 gm
Refined flour — 50 gm
Salt — a pinch
Cold water — 20 mL

1. Sieve the flour with salt. Divide the fat into three equal portions. Rub one portion into the flour to get a bread crumb texture and make dough of rolling consistency with iced water.
2. On a lightly floured marble top roll out the dough [about ½ cm thickness] into an oblong shape. Take the second portion of fat & cut it into small pieces, place them on ⅔ rd of rolled dough. Leave the remaining ⅓ rd portion without fat.
3. Bring up the bottom third of the pastry dough and fold like an envelope with its flap open. Then bring up the folded portion over again so as to close the envelope.
4. Turn pastry at right angle, seal its open ends. This means to depress it with a rolling pin at intervals to give a corrugated effect and equalizing pressure cover and cool in the fridge for about 5-10 minutes, if it feels sticky and is difficult to handle.
5. Repeat step 2 with the third portion of the fat, cool it for 30 minutes. It is because the cold pastry when exposed to the heat of the oven rises better.

   Now the pastry is ready to be rolled for different uses like vol-an-vent, pies, patties, etc.

Flan Pastry

Butter	–	30 mg
Sugar	–	5 gm
Refined flour	–	60 gm
Salt	–	a pinch
Egg yolk	–	¼
Cold water	–	for binding

Cream the fat and sugar in a mixing bowl until fluffy and light in colour. Sieve the flour and salt together and add the creamed fat, mixing lightly with a palette knife. Add the egg yolk and sprinkle enough water to make firm dough of a rolling consistency.

Use the fingertips to feel the pastry. A pastry is light in texture when it rolls into a large ball with very little handling.

Choux Pastry

The French term for this pastry "Pate a choux" literally means cabbage paste, because the profiteroles and cream puffs made from this pastry resemble little cabbages. These are hollow shells which have a crisp and brittle texture. They are then filled with a variety of fillings both sweet and savoury – including creamed cheese, fresh cream, crème patissiere, fish, and meat pate. Water, butter and salt are boiled together and then the flour is added to form a partly gelatinised paste. It is mixed vigorously with a wooden spoon and then cooked once more till the mixture has a shiny appearance and leaves the sides of the pan. Beaten eggs are added gradually to the paste, beating continuously to form a smooth pliable and piping consistency mass. It is then piped into the desired shapes – rosettes, fingers or balls. Choux paste is baked at 200 °C so as to achieve maximum rise. The temperature is then reduced to 150 °C to dry out the shells and to obtain the crisp and brittle texture. During baking, the products should not be subjected to unnecessary movements, otherwise the structure will collapse. Shells can be stored in airtight containers and used as and when required. Éclairs, Duchesses, profiteroles and cream puffs are all choux pastry based items.

Recipes and Methods of Preparation with their Baking Standards

Choux Pastry

Refined wheat flour	—	75-115 gm
Salt	—	a pinch
Butter	—	60-115 gm
Water	—	150-180 mL
Castor sugar	—	5-10 gm
Eggs	—	2-3 large

Sift the flour and salt together. Put the butter, water and sugar into a saucepan and heat gently until the butter melts, then raise the heat and rapidly bring mixture to a boil. Draw the pan off the heat and tip the flour in all at once. Stir quickly with a wooden spoon until the flour absorbs all the liquid. Return to heat until the dough is smooth and comes away from the sides of pan.

Allow it to cool until the pan is hand warm. Lightly mix the egg and beat in gradually. The pastry should be shiny and thick enough to hold its shape but not stiff.

Use this pastry dough for making choux swans, éclairs, buns, etc.

Hot Water Pastry

This is also known as the cooked pastry and is seldom used these days. It is lean dough made by cooking the flour, salt and a little fat in water to a paste. This paste is then used to line the sides of pie tins, using the hands to apply the mixture; the filling is then placed inside the tin and then covered with more paste. After baking, the dough is often discarded and it is more like a protective layer over the filling. At lunch time, the pastry was broken open and the filling, meat or fish, was consumed. Cornish pastries, traditional Welsh favourite, was originally made with hot water pastry.

Sweet and Short Pastry

The main ingredients for sweet and short pastry are flour, fat and sugar usually in the ratio of 1 part sugar, 2 parts fat and 3 parts flour (1:2:3).

Flour

The flour should be soft. The fat / butter or commercial short paste margarine gives the paste butter handling properties.

Fat

Preferably butter should be used, as it gives flavour.

Sugar

Castor sugar or icing sugar is recommended. They are more readily soluble which has a softening effect on the gluten in the flour, in turn, influencing the shortening properties in the paste. Other ingredients for short pastry are: cheese, paprika, herbs, caraway, poppy seeds and many others.

Methods to Prepare Pastries

Creaming

- Mixing fat and sugar.
- Aim is to make the mixture lighter by incorporating air.
- Fat should be soft and not oily.

Rubbing in

- Fat and flour are rubbed together.
- Fat is reduced to breadcrumb-sized particles.

- Fat particles melt during baking, giving off steam which makes the pastry expand and rise.

Folding in

- Dry ingredients are added to a creamed or whisked mixture.
- Add gradually and turn gently.
- Disturb the air bubbles as little as possible.

Docking

- Small holes are made in pastry.
- Aim is to allow steam to escape during baking to avoid distorting the pastry.

Blind Baking

Pastry without fillings is baked with beans to keep the shape and prevent it from shrinking or rising during baking.

CHECK YOUR PROGRESS

1. What is blind baking?
2. Write a detailed note on pastry.
3. What is hot water pastry?
4. Give an example of choux pastry.
5. Write faults in short crust pastry.
6. What factors control the volume of choux pastry?
7. Why is puff pastry allowed to stand for half an hour before baking?
8. Why is an acidic medium like lemon juice or cream of tartar added to flour while making a puff pastry?

Unit 12

Icings & Toppings

Fillings and toppings not only make a cake attractive, they also have a practical use. Cakes, which have been filled and iced, stay moist longer. There are four basic types of toppings: buttercream, cooked-fudge frosting, fluffy cooked frosting and soft sugar icing.

Icings can be classified into three major types:

- Flat icing
- Fluffy or creamed icing
- Combination icing

Flat icing is made with icing sugar, water, corn syrup and flavour, a small amount of fat may be used in addition. With this, a thick paste is made and icing warmed to about 110 °F. Cooking method may use double boiling to avoid extra heat contact with icing. Overheating is the most common problem faced, which causes loss of the icing's gloss or shine when it cools. Do not add water to soften or chilling icing, it will always cause running and stickiness.

Creamed icing/fluffy icing is made with fat, icing sugar, milk powder, eggs, water, salt, flavour, and perhaps a stabilizer commonly used in standard recipes, in addition can be used other more ingredients. The procedure starts with creaming of fat and sugar, then, gradually add egg and cream it well. The water and flavours are blended in the last stage. In the fudge-type of creamed icing, an emulsified fat is used and blending, rather than creaming method, is used.

Icings, also called frostings, are sweet coatings for cakes and other baked goods.

Icings have three main functions:

- Contribute flavour and richness.
- Improve appearance.
- Improve keeping qualities by forming protective coatings around cakes.

Use top quality flavourings for icings, so that they can enhance the cake. Use moderation when adding flavours and colours. Flavours should be light and delicate. Colours should be delicate pastel shades, except chocolate, of course.

SIX TYPES OF ICINGS

1. **Buttercream** icings are light, smooth mixtures of fat and sugar. They may also contain eggs to increase their smoothness or lightness. Through these popular icings, any kind of cake can be easily flavoured and coloured to suit a variety of purposes. There are many variations of buttercream formulas.

   (a) **Italian buttercream** is made with Italian meringue (cooked), butter, and flavourings. The use of egg whites in Italian buttercream results in a relatively white coloured product that is very light in texture. The light colour and texture of a finished Italian buttercream make it a common choice in wedding cakes or for any pastry requiring white frosting.

   (b) **Swiss buttercream** is aerated through whipping, and stabilized by the dissolving sugar, creating a meringue (uncooked), successfully incorporated with other ingredients. The combination of the fluffy consistency and the paleness of the Swiss buttercream make it ideal for use in wedding cakes and any pastry where white buttercream is desired.

(c) **German buttercream** is a combination of pastry cream, butter, and flavourings. The pastry cream also contributes to the cream's yellow colour. Because it is yellow in colour, it is unsuitable for some purposes where white icing is desired. German buttercream has a richer texture than meringue-based buttercreams due to the whole eggs present in the pastry cream.

(d) **French buttercream** is made either with whole eggs or egg yolks, butter, cooked sugar syrup, and flavourings. It is similar to meringue-based Italian buttercream in technique, but the egg yolks make it richer and give it a yellow colour.

2. **Fudge-Type Icings** are rich and heavy. Many of them are made somewhat like candy. They may be flavoured with a variety of ingredients and are used on cupcakes, layer cakes, loaf cakes, and sheet cakes. Fudge icings are stable and hold up well on cakes and in storage. Stored icings must be covered tightly to prevent drying and crusting. To use stored fudge icing, warm it in a double boiler until it is soft enough to spread.
3. **Foam Icings,** sometimes called boiled icings, are simply meringues made with boiling syrup. Some also contain stabilizing ingredients like gelatine. Foam icings should be applied thickly to cakes and left in peaks and swirls. These icings are not stable. Regular boiled icing should be used the day it is prepared.
4. **Glazes** are thin, glossy, transparent coatings that give a shine to baked products and help prevent drying. The simplest glaze is a sugar syrup or diluted corn syrup brushed onto coffee cakes or Danish pastries while it is hot.
5. **Fondant** is a sugar syrup that is crystallized to a smooth, creamy white mass. It is familiar as the icing for napoleons, éclairs, petits fours, and some cakes. When applied, it sets up into a shiny, non-sticky coating.

6. **Royal Icing,** also called decorating or decorator's icing, is similar to flat icings except that it is much thicker and made with egg whites, which make it hard and brittle when dry. It is used almost exclusively for decorative work.

DECORATING EQUIPMENT

With a few simple tools, it is possible to create the most stunning cake decorations. Thick swirls of butter icing formed with a palette knife or stark-white icing sugar dusted over a contrasting dark chocolate icing, instantly provide an impressive effect. As your skills develop, you will probably want to invest in some specialized icing equipment, such as:

1. Flower nail
2. Small rolling pin
3. Paper
4. Cutter
5. Nozzlebrush
6. Plastic paper
7. Frill cutters
8. Piping bag
9. Cocktail cutter
10. Shaped cutters

Cakes require a specific appearance for special occasions. Ideas range from quick-mix icings, such as butter icing and chocolate icing, which may be instantly poured, spread, or piped and other ideas like sugar paste icing, royal icing, glace icing and many more.

POINTS TO BE CONSIDERED WHILE USING FILLINGS AND TOPPINGS

1. Always cool the cake thoroughly before filing and icing, and brush off any loose crumbs which could stick to the icing.
2. Cut surfaces, such as those produced when a slab cake is cut up into a smaller cake, are often covered with thin layers of almond glace or fondant icing.
3. Never put a firm-textured frosting or filling on a soft-crumbled surface. For crumbly sponge cakes, use a light cream filling, which spreads easily.
4. Make sure the top of the cake is completely flat if it is to be iced. The cake can be turned upside down.
5. To sandwich two layers of cake, place one layer, topside down, on a plate or flat surface and spread the filling to the edge. Allow the filling to set for a few minutes, then place the second layer, topside up, on the filling and lightly press the two together.
6. Before coating a cake with soft icing, put the cake on a wire rack over a plate. Pour the icing over the centre of the plain or filled cake, and gradually work the icing over the top and downside with a palate knife.
7. For a professional touch, spread the icing evenly around the sides of the cakes before rolling it in chopped nuts or chocolate vermicelli. Spread the icing evenly over the top of the cake, then pipe on colour icing in thin lines, ½ to ¾ inch apart, using a plain writing tube. Before the icing has set, draw lines, at right angles, over the colour icing with the blunt edge of a knife blade. Turn the cake 180 °C and draw the knife between the intersections.
8. Piped decorations should be applied after the covered icing sets, but shaped decorations, such as rose buds, etc., should be applied while the icing is still soft.

TYPES OF ICINGS

1. Buttercream

Butter — 125 gm
Icing sugar — 225 gm
Vanilla essence (optional)
Milk — 1-2 tablespoon

Method

Beat to soften the butter with a wooden spoon or in an electric mixture, until creamy. Gradually, beat in the sifted icing sugar, a spoon full at a time, adding a few drops of vanilla essence (if used) and the milk for more liquid consistency. This amount is sufficient to coat the sides and top of a 7-inch cake.

To this basic butter cream, a number of different flavours can be added:

1. **Almonds:** Add 2 level tablespoons of finely chopped, toasted almonds. Substitute almond essence for vanilla essence.
2. **Chocolate:** Add 22-35 gm melted chocolate and omit 1 tablespoon milk; alternatively blend 1 level tablespoon cocoa with 1 tablespoon hot water, cool and add, omitting the milk.
3. **Coffee:** Omit vanilla essence and milk; flavour with 2 level tablespoons instant coffee, blend with 1 teaspoon water; or use 2-3 tablespoons coffee essence.
4. **Ginger:** Omit vanilla essence; add 50 gm finely chopped stem ginger.
5. **Liqueur:** Omit milk and vanilla essence; add 2-3 tablespoons of liqueur.
6. **Mocca:** Omit vanilla essence, mix 2 level tablespoons cocoa with 2 level tablespoons instant coffee powder to a smooth paste with hot water, cool before adding and omit milk.

7. **Orange:** Omit vanilla essence and milk; beat in 2 tablespoons fresh orange juice, the finely grated rinds of 1 small orange and if needed, 1 tablespoons orange bitter.

   Storing: The icing will keep for up to three days, in an airtight container stored in the refrigerator.

2. Honey Butter Frosting

Butter	—	75 gm
Icing sugar	—	175 gm
Clear honey	—	1 level tablespoon
Lemon juice	—	1 T

Method

Beat the butter which should be at room temperature, until soft but not oily. Gradually sift in the icing sugar beating well. Half way through, beat in the honey and lemon juice.

3. Caramel Icing

Top of the milk	—	5 T
Butter	—	75 gm
Castor sugar	—	2 T
Icing sugar	—	325-350 gm

Method

Warm the milk and butter in a small saucepan. In another pan, heat the castor sugar over a medium heat until it turns to a golden caramel. Remove both pans from the heat, pour the milk mixture over the caramel and return to low heat. Continue heating it until the caramel is dissolved. Stir continuously. Gradually stir in the sifted icing sugar and beat until the icing sugar is smooth and of a spreading consistency.

4. American Frosting

Castor sugar — 450 gm
Pinch cream of tartar
Egg whites — 2
Vanilla essence (optional)

Method

- A sugar boiling thermometer is necessary for this frosting; if this is not available, then it is difficult to make it best in texture.
- American frosting makes a light, fluffy yet crisp topping. Its soft white, contrasting well with chocolate caraque.

5. Chocolate Buttercream Frosting

Squares unsweetened chocolate — 4 (1 oz)
Butter or margerine — ¼ c
Powdered sugar — 3 ½ c
Milk — ½ c
Vanilla — 1 t
Salt — ¼ t

Method

- Melt butter and chocolate until smooth.
- Beat in the remaining ingredients.
- Beat just until spreading consistency.
- You may need to add more milk to make frosting thinner.

6. Chocolate Cream Cheese Frosting

Semisweet chocolate pieces — ½ c
Cream cheese, softened — 3 oz
Powdered sugar — 4 T

Method

- Melt chocolate over low heat, stirring constantly.
- Remove from heat; cool.
- In a bowl, beat cream cheese with powdered sugar.
- Stir into melted chocolate and beat till smooth.

7. Chocolate Fudge Frosting

Cocoa — 3 T
Sugar — 1 c
Evaporated milk — ⅓ c
Safflower oil — 3 T
Salt — ¼ t
Vanilla — 1 t

Method

- In a medium saucepan, combine all ingredients except vanilla.
- Bring to a boil, reduce heat and simmer for 1 minute.
- Remove from heat.
- Add vanilla; beat for 5 minutes with electric mixer.
- Spread over cake.

Storing: Not suitable for storing. Use immediately after making.

8. Chocolate Icing

Cocoa — 6 T
Butter, melted — 3 T
Powdered sugar — 2 c
Hot water — 4-6 T

Combine all ingredients in a bowl and beat by hand until smooth.

Chocolate Mint Frosting

Mint chocolate chips — ½ c
Butter — ¼ c
Vanilla — 1 t
Salt — ¼ t
Powdered sugar — 3 c
Milk — 6 T

Method

- Combine the mint chocolate chips and butter in hot water.
- Stir until chips are melted and mixture is smooth.
- Stir in vanilla and salt.
- Transfer to a large bowl.
- Gradually beat in powdered sugar alternately with milk; beat until smooth.

Storing: Not suitable for storing, icing must be used immediately after making.

9. Chocolate Mocha Cream Cheese Icing

Butter, softened — ½ c
Heavy cream — ¼ c
Coffee flavoured liqueur — 1 T
Cream cheese, softened — 8 oz
Baking cocoa — ½ c
Instant dry coffee — 1 T
Powdered sugar — 3 ½ c

Method

- Beat butter, whipping cream, liqueur, and cream cheese on medium speed until fluffy. Beat in cocoa, coffee, and powdered sugar on low speed until smooth.
- *Storing:* Not suitable for storing, the icing must be used immediately after making.

10. Ghiradelli Chocolate Frosting

Ghiradelli semi-sweet chocolate — 4 oz
Butter — 4 T
Powdered sugar — 3 c
Hot milk — ⅓ c
Vanilla — 1 t
Salt — ⅛ t

Method

- In a heavy saucepan on low heat, melt broken chocolate with butter, stirring constantly.
- Beat sugar with milk, vanilla, and salt until smooth.
- Add melted chocolate and beat until thick enough to spread.

11. Milk Chocolate Frosting

Heavy cream — ½ c
Pinch salt
Corn syrup — 1 T
Milk chocolate, chopped — 10 oz
Powdered sugar — ½ c
Cold butter, cut into pieces — 8 T

Method

- Heat cream, salt and corn syrup in a microwave-safe measuring cup on high temperature, until simmering, for about 1 minute.
- Place chocolate in a work bowl of food processor fitted with steel blade.
- With machine running, gradually add hot cream mixture through feed tube; process for 1 minute. Add powdered sugar to work bowl and process to combine, about 30 seconds.
- With machine running, add butter through fed tube, one piece at a time, process until incorporated and smooth.
- Transfer frosting to medium bowl and cool at room temperature, stirring frequently until thick and spreadable, for about 1 hour.

12. Perfectly Chocolate Frosting

Butter or margerine, melted — ½ c
Cocoa — ⅔ c
Powdered sugar — 3 c
Milk — ⅓ c
Vanilla — 1 T

Method

- Mix butter and cocoa. Alternately, mix in milk and powdered sugar.
- Beat until spreading consistency. Beat in vanilla.
- You may need to add more milk to make thinner or more powdered sugar to make thicker.

13. Sour Cream Chocolate Frosting

Butter, softened — ¼ c
Unsweetened chocolate, melted — 3 oz
Powdered sugar — 2 c
Sour cream — ½ c
Vanilla — 2 t

Method

- Combine butter, unsweetened melted chocolate, powder sugar and sour cream.
- Mix all ingredients in a bowl until smooth.

14. White Chocolate Frosting

White chocolate, chopped — ¾ c
Flour — 2 ½ T
Milk — 1 c
Unsalted butter, softened — 1 c
Powdered sugar — 1 c
Vanilla — 1 ½ t

Method

- Combine the chocolate and flour in a medium saucepan.
- Blend in the milk.
- Cook over medium heat, stirring constantly, until very thick.
- Remove from heat and cool.
- In a large bowl, cream the butter, sugar and vanilla.
- Beat until light and fluffy, for about 3 minutes. Gradually add the cooled chocolate mixture, beating after each addition.
- Beat at a high speed until frosting is in a whipped cream consistency.

15. White Chocolate Ganache

White chocolate, chopped — 8 oz
Heavy cream — 1 c
Light rum — ¼ c

Method

- Using a double boiler, bring the cream to a very warm, but not quite boiling temperature.
- Slowly add the white chocolate chunks, stirring constantly, allowing the chunks to melt evenly.
- When all the chocolate has been melted and blended, gently add the rum and stir a bit more to incorporate it.

16. Marzipan

Ground almonds — 8 oz
Icing sugar — 4 oz
Castor sugar — 4 oz
Lemon juice — 1 t
Almond essence — 2 drops
Beaten eggs — 4

Method

- Put the ground almonds, icing and castor sugar into a bowl and mix together.
- Add the lemon juice, almonds essence and beaten eggs to mix to soft but firm dough. Gather them together with your fingers to form a ball.
- Knead the marzipan on a work surface, lightly dusted with sifted icing sugar,until smooth.

Storing: The marzipan will keep for up to four days, wrapped in clean film in an airtight container, and stored in the refrigerator.

17. Sugar Paste Icing

Egg whites — 3
Liquid glucose, warmed — 1 T
Icing sugar, sifted — 12 oz

Method

- Put the egg white and glucose in a bowl. Stir together with a wooden spoon to break up the egg white. Add the icing sugar and mix together with a palette knife or a common knife, using a chopping action, until blended well and the icing begins to bind together.
- Knead the mixture with your fingers until it forms a ball.
- Knead the sugar paste on a work surface lightly dusted with sifted icing sugar, for several minutes until smooth, soft and pliable. If the icing is too soft, knead in some more sifted icing sugar until it is firm and pliable.

Storing: The icing can be kept for up to a week, wrapped in clear film or a plastic bag and stored in the refrigerator. Bring to room temperature before using. If a thin crust forms, trim off before using or it will make the icing lumpy. Also, if the icing dries out or hardens, knead in a little boiled water to make it smooth and pliable again.

18. Royal Icing

Makes 675 g royal icing

Egg whites — 3

Icing sugar (Sifted) — 675 g / 1.5 lb / 6 c

Glycerine — 1.5 t

Few drops of lemon juice colouring (optional)

Put the egg white in a bowl and stir lightly with a wooden spoon to break them up.

Add the icing sugar gradually in small quantities, beating well with a wooden spoon between each addition. Add sufficient icing sugar to make a smooth, white, shiny icing with the consistency of very stiff meringue. It should be thin enough to spread, but thick enough to hold its shape.

Beat in the glycerine, lemon juice, and food colouring, if using. It is best to let the icing sit for about 1 hour before using. Cover the surface with a piece of damp clear film or a lid so the icing to burst any air bubbles. Even when working with royal icing, always keep it covered.

Storing: Royal icing can be kept for up to three days in an airtight container, stored in the refrigerator. Stir the icing well before use.

BALANCING CAKE RECIPES

It refers to the proper combination of various ingredients used in baking to achieve a desired product. Bakers try to improve their recipe by trial and error method. Knowledge of balancing in understanding special cake falls and helps in correcting them for getting best result.

All the basic ingredients used in a recipe serve the special purpose. The basic ingredients are classified as:

Tougheners provide the structure and toughen and bind the cake. Binding ingredients include flour, milk, solids, egg whites, etc.

Tenderizers provide shortness and softness to the cake, e.g., sugar, shortening, egg yolks and other fat containing ingredients.

Moisteners provide moisture and maintain the quality. These liquids include milk, water, eggs, and syrups.

Driers absorb and retain the moisture and provide structure to the cake, e.g., flour, milk, solids and starches.

Flavourers provide natural flavours like coca, chocolate, butter, egg, and other natural ingredients.

Balancing pound cakes and other creamed-cake mixes

The first type of cake, that was accepted, was made by mixing equal amounts of butter, sugar, eggs and flour, which led to the formation of a pound cake. This also helps to develop your actual calculation of pound cake.

MIXING METHODS

The selection of high quality ingredients is necessary to produce a good quality cake. However, good ingredients alone do not guarantee a fine cake. A thorough understanding of mixing procedures is essential. Slight errors in mixing can result in cakes with poor texture and volume.

The mixing methods presented in this chapter are the ones used for most types of cakes prepared in the modern bakeshop. Each of these methods is used for particular types of formulas.

The goal of mixing cake batter is to combine ingredients uniformly, incorporate air cells and develop a proper texture.

High Fat Cakes

1. **Creaming method:** First, the fat and sugar are "creamed" or blended until smooth and light. Then, eggs are added, and finally, the sifted dry ingredients are added in two or three additions. If there is any liquid, the dry ingredients and liquid are added alternately, starting and ending with the dry ingredients. It is important that ingredients for a creamed batter or dough are at room temperature and the fat is soft before beginning to mix.

2. **Two-stage mixing method:** This method was designed to be used when making high-ratio cakes; containing a higher proportion of sugar and emulsifiers than other cakes. A high-ratio cake is one in which the weight of the sugar is equal to or greater than the weight of the flour, and the weight of the eggs is equal to or greater than the weight of the fat.

   The first step in making high-ratio cakes is blending the flour and other dry ingredients with shortening. Then this mixture becomes smooth and the liquids (including eggs) are added in the following stages.

3. **Flour batter cakes:** It is used only for a few specialty items. It produces a fine textured cake, but there may be some toughening due to the development of gluten. Flour batter cakes include those made with either emulsified shortening or butter or both.

   Sift the flour and other dry ingredients except sugar into the mixing bowl. Add fat. Blend together until smooth and light. Whip the sugar and eggs together until thick and light. Add liquid flavouring ingredients, such as vanilla. Combine the flour-fat mixture and the sugar-egg mixture and mix until smooth. Gradually add water or milk (if any) and mix smooth.

Foam Cakes / Unshorten Cakes

Most egg-foam cakes contain little or no shortening and depend on the air trapped in beaten eggs for most or all of their leavening. Egg-foam cakes have a springy texture and are tougher than shortened cakes. This makes them valuable for many kinds of desserts that require much handling to assemble. Flour for egg-foam cakes must be weak in order to avoid making the cake tougher than necessary.

1. **Sponge method:** Sponge cake batter is made in two basic steps: (1) eggs and sugar are whipped to a thick foam, and (2) sifted flour is folded in. Additional ingredients, such as butter or liquid, complicate the procedure slightly.

2. **Angel food method:** Angel food cakes are based on egg white foams and contain no fat. Egg whites for angel food cakes should be whipped until they form soft, not stiff, peaks. Overwhipped whites lose their ability to expand and to leaven the cake. A dry flour-sugar mixture is folded into the egg whites.
3. **Chiffon method:** Chiffon cakes are based on egg white foams. In chiffon cakes, a batter containing flour, egg yolks, vegetable oil, and water is folded into the whites. Egg whites should be whipped until they are a little firmer than those for angel food cakes, but do not whip them until they are dry. Chiffon cakes contain baking powder, so they do not depend on the egg foam for all their leavening.

VARIOUS TYPES OF CAKES AND THEIR RECIPES

Genoise Sponge

S. No.	Ingredients	Quantity
1.	Flour	85 gm
2.	Sugar	85 gm
3.	Eggs	3 no.
4.	Vanilla essence	½ t
5.	Melted butter / fat	30 mL

Preparation

1. Before starting this Génoise Sponge recipe, make sure you have organised all the necessary ingredients.

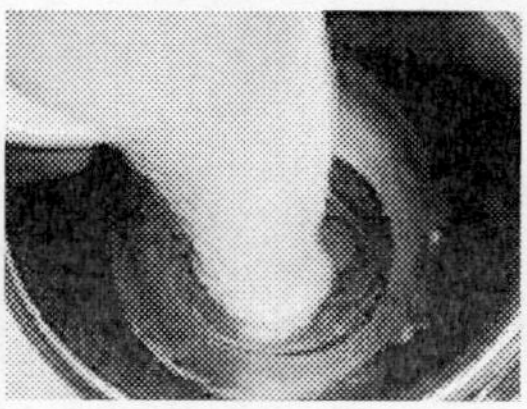

2. Combine the eggs and sugar in a mixing bowl or in the stand mixer recipient.

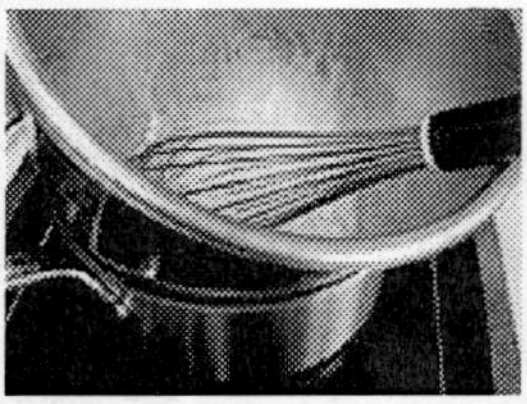

3. Using a hand whisk beat the preparation over a bain-marie.

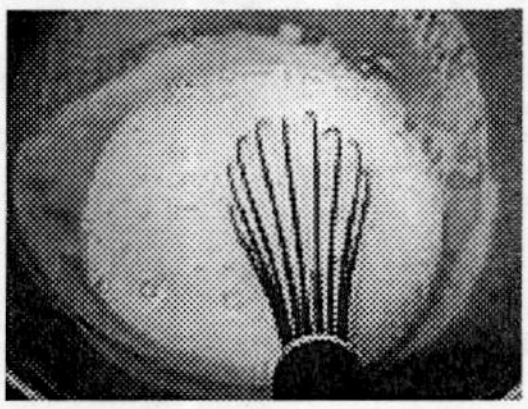

4. The temperature should roughly be 40 °C.

5. Finish beating with an electric whisk until cooled down completely. If you do not have an electric whisk, you can finish beating manually. The preparation is ready when doubled in volume.

6. Add the sifted flour.

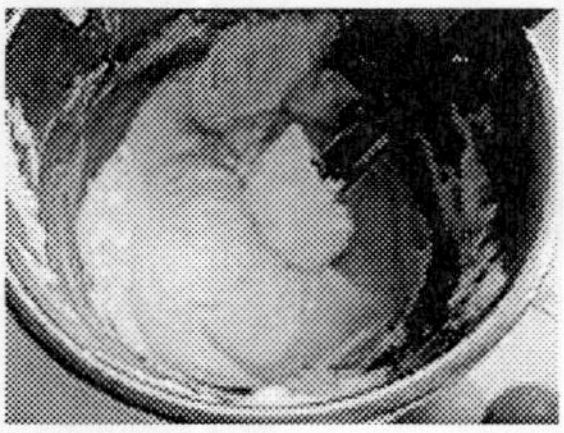

7. Stir gently with a rubber spatula or a skimmer in rotating motions.

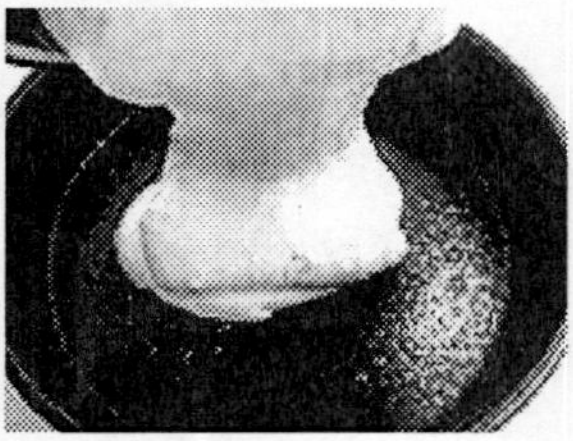

8. Butter and flour around the cake tin. Pour the mixture.

9. Bake at 180 °C.

10. The Génoise sponge is ready when golden. To check whether the génoise is cooked, insert the knife in the cake. If nothing sticks to the knife, you can remove the dish from the oven.

11. Remove from the mould. Leave it to cool on a rack.

Butterscotch Sponge

S. No.	Ingredients	Quantity
1.	Flour	85 gm
2.	Golden castor sugar	85 gm
3.	Eggs	3 nos.
4.	Yellow colour	Few drops
5.	Melted butter / fat	30 mL
6.	Milk	1 T
7.	Cream cheese	40 gm
8.	Butterscotch essence	Few drops

Preparation

Combine the eggs and sugar in a mixing bowl or in the stand-mixer recipient. Using a hand whisk, beat the preparation over a bain-marie.Temperature should roughly be 40 °C. Finish beating with an electric whisk until cooled down completely. If you do not have an electric whisk, you can finish beating manually. The preparation is ready when doubled in volume. Sift flour in the mixture and stir gently with a rubber spatula or a skimmer in rotating motions. Add all the ingredients and then mould it.

Butter and flour a round-cake tin. Pour the mixture. Bake at 180 °C. Génoise sponge is ready when golden. To check whether the Génoise is cooked, insert the knife in the cake. If nothing sticks to the blade, you can remove the dish from the oven. Remove it from the mould. Leave to cool on a rack.

Fat-Less Sponge

S. No.	Ingredients	Quantity
1.	Flour	60 gm
2.	Castor sugar	170 gm
3.	Eggs	4 nos.
4.	Vanilla essence	Few drops
5.	Cornflour	35 gm
6.	Baking powder	1 t

Preparation

Separate eggs. Whisk egg whites and sugar. Whisk yolks. Whisk all.

Fold in flour, corn flour and baking powder. Divide between two 20 cm (8″) tins.

Bake at 180-190 °C / Gas 4-5 for 20 minutes.

Rich-Butter Cake

S. No.	Ingredients	Quantity
1.	Butter	250 gm
2.	Breakfast sugar	200 gm
3.	Eggs	3 nos.
4.	Refined flour	313 gm
5.	Milk	160 mL
6.	Essence	Few drops
7.	Icing sugar mixture	To serve

Preparation

Preheat oven to 180 °C /160 °C fan-forced. Grease and line an 8 cm deep, 19 cm(base) square-cake pan with baking paper. Using an electric mixer cream butter, castor sugar and vanilla in a medium bowl on medium-high speed, until light and fluffy. Add eggs, 1 at a time, beat them to combine. Add half the flour and stir to combine. Add half the milk and stir to combine. Repeat with the remaining flour and milk to mix it well. Spread the mixture into prepared pan. Bake for 1 hour or until a skewer inserted into the centre comes out clean. Stand in pan for 10 minutes. Turn out onto a wire rack to cool. Dust with icing sugar. Serve.

CHECK YOUR PROGRESS

1. Write three preparations with royal icing.
2. Write a short note on chocolate base icings.
3. Write the steps involved in milk chocolate frosting preparation.
4. Explain the use of marzipan.
5. Describe decorative equipment involved in cake preparation.
6. Write in detail the recipe of royal icing.
7. Describe the different types of icing.
8. Discuss the points to be considered while using fillings and toppings over cakes.

Unit 13

Frozen Desserts

Frozen dessert is the generic term for desserts made by freezing liquids, semisolids, and sometimes even solids. They may be based on flavoured water (shave ice, sorbet, snow cones, etc.), on fruit purées, on milk and cream (mostly ice creams), on custard (frozen custard and some ice creams), on mousse, etc. In the UK and Ireland, where the term "dessert" is uncommon, frozen desserts are referred to as "ices".

In some countries including Canada, the term is often used on products which are similar in taste and texture to ice cream, but which do not meet the legal definition of that term (often being made primarily with vegetable oils, i.e., mellorine, as opposed to milk or cream).

The two main categories are still frozen and churned frozen. Still frozen desserts have the air incorporated into, before they are frozen, this would include frozen mousses and things of similar nature. Churned frozen desserts have air incorporated into them while they are being frozen, things like ice cream.

TYPES OF FROZEN DESSERTS

Ice Cream

Ice cream is the most popular frozen dessert. Ice cream mixtures can be as simple as pureed fruit, sugar and cream, known as Philadelphia style, or based on more complicated cooked custards, French-style. Both are delicious, though French versions are slightly richer.

To qualify as "ice cream", it usually consists of a mixture of dairy ingredients such as milk and non-fat milk, and ingredients for sweetening and flavouring, such as fruits, nuts and chocolate chips. Functional ingredients, such as stabilizers and emulsifiers, are often included in the product to promote proper texture and enhance the eating experience. By federal law, ice cream from the supermarket must contain at least 10 % milkfat, before the addition of bulky ingredients.

Freezies / Smoothies / Whips: Generally speaking, these are made from whole frozen fruits (frozen bananas, strawberries, peaches, etc.), which are then whipped in a blender or food processor till smooth.

Frozen Custard or French Ice Cream

This is something of a misnomer, since many ice cream recipes are virtually custards anyway, although frozen crème caramel, surely qualifies as a distinctly different dessert. Supermarket brands must also contain a minimum of 10 % milkfat, as well as at least 1.4 % egg yolk solids.

Frozen Soufflé

This airy mixture of fruit pure egg yolk sauce and stiffly-beaten egg whites is less fragile when frozen (compared to baked soufflé, which is very delicate).

Frozen Yogurt

Supermarket brands contain 10-20 % real cultured yogurt. Yogurt can replace the ice cream, giving a smooth and creamy, although not as rich result. As with the ice creams, you can add myriad chunked flavourings to frozen yogurts, including chopped fruits, or nuts, or healthy sprinkling of wheat germ. It has become very popular and competes head-to-head with ice cream. The health benefits of yogurt have long been touted. It is certainly a good source of vitamin B, protein and calcium and is much more digestible than fresh milk. It is also said to keep the intestinal system populated with good bacteria. These benefits, however, are thought to be lost when yogurt is frozen, which destroys most of the beneficial bacteria.

Fruit Ice

Similar to granita, this is usually made from fruit juices, frozen and then chopped in a blender to form coarse granules.

Gelato/Gelati

Also known in the singular as "gelato", this Italian version of ice cream contains less air than its North American counterpart and therefore has a denser texture. It is also characterized by an intense flavour and is served in a semi-frozen state. Gelato contains sweeteners, milk, cream, egg yolks and flavourings.

Granita (also Granité) or Ice

Something like a sorbet, this dessert-cum-beverage is usually more granular in nature and often made from whole fruits rather than just the juices.

Ice Cream Roulade (Rolls)

Ice milk can mean low-fat, light or both. Ice milk is made in much the same way as ice cream, except for the fact that it contains less milk fat and milk solids. This is a frozen dessert with less than 10 % butterfat, if a supermarket brand. The result, other than a lowered calorie count, is a lighter, less creamy texture. The more butterfat, generally, the smaller the ice crystals formed, and the smoother the taste, so ice milk must be beaten more than ice cream for smoothness.

ITALIAN ICE

Mousse

Frozen mousse is usually fortified with gelatin to make it stand well to the strenuous beating, required to give it its characteristic frothiness. It's a rich, airy dessert usually containing fruit puree or syrup, plus some egg.

Novelties: Novelties are separately packaged single servings of a frozen dessert – such as ice cream sandwiches, fudge sticks and juice bars – that may or may not contain dairy ingredients.

Parfait: Real French parfait is frozen custard with egg yolks, sugar, whipped cream and flavourings, such as fruit puree. In the U.S., a parfait is known as ice cream layered with fruit or flavoured syrup and whipped cream – not the same thing at all!

Popsickles: Popsickles have been around for nearly a hundred years. Ever since a cold night in 1905, when 11-year-old Frank Epperson left a cup of soda pop with a stirring stick in it outside. Popsicles have been a cool and flavourful treat for young and old alike. While the trademarked popsickle brand is the most popular, the industry sells more than a billion of the various flavoured ice on a stick treats every year.

Sherbet: Its "SHUR-bet", never pronounced as "sherbet". Sherbets are ices based on sweetened fruit juice or puree. Similar to sorbets (sometimes the words are used interchangeably) but sherbets usually have more ingredients, such as milk, egg whites or gelatine. Supermarket brands must have a milkfat content between 1 % and 2 %, and a slightly higher sweetener content than ice cream. Sherbet weighs a minimum of 6 pounds to the gallon and is flavoured either with fruit or other characterizing ingredients. Recipes can be varied in infinite ways by changing the fruits used. Sorbets can be turned into sherbets if you add a beaten egg white to the mixture after it is partially frozen.

Sorbet: Light dessert, generally made of puréed fruits, water and sugar; is frozen before serving. Similar to sherbets, sorbets contain no dairy ingredients. Sorbets freeze quicker than ice cream, and melt quicker. They need to have a balance of sugar and /or alcohol as these two items lower the freezing point of the sorbet, making it hard to set and affect the frozen texture. A squeeze of lemon juice is good in sorbets to give balance to sweet fruit. Sorbet's consistency is also often softer than sherbet.

It is usually made from a fruit purees liquor or wine, and is often served as a "palate cleanser" between courses in a big meal. Champagne sorbet is a classic form; margarita sorbet is a 21st century innovation.

Tofulati: This is a frozen tofu confection's name registered to Mario's Gelati, a Vancouver-based company, making ice cream and sorbet treats the old-fashioned, old world way.

Tofuti: Originally invented in New York just a few years ago, this is a frozen dessert made with tofu substituted for cream or milk.

Tofutti: Tofutti is dairy-free ice cream made from tofu (soybean curd).

Quiescently frozen confection: It is a frozen novelty, such as a water-ice novelty on a stick.

ICE CREAM MANUFACTURE

Raw Materials

Ice cream is made from a blend of dairy products (cream, condensed milk, and butterfat), sugar, flavourings, and federally approved additives. Eggs are added for some flavouring, particularly French vanilla. The broad guidelines allow producers to use ingredients ranging from sweet cream to non-fatdry milk, cane sugar to corn-syrup solids, fresh eggs to powdered eggs. Federal regulations do stipulate that each package of ice cream must contain at least 10 % butterfat.

The additives, which act as emulsifiers and stabilizers, are used to prevent heat shock and the formation of ice crystals during the production process. The most common additives are guar gum, extracted from the guar bush, and carrageenan, derived from sea kelp or Irish moss.

Ice cream flavours have come a long way from the standard vanilla, strawberry, and chocolate. By the 1970's, the International Association of ice cream manufacturers recorded over 400 different flavours of ice cream. In an ever-expanding array of combinations, fruit purees and extracts, cocoa powder, nuts, cookie pieces, and cookie dough are blended into the ice cream mixture.

Air is added to ice cream to improve its ability to absorb flavourings and to facilitate serving. Without air, ice cream becomes heavy and soggy. On the other hand, too much air results in ice cream that is snowy and dry. The federal government allows ice cream to contain as much as 100 % of its volume in air, known in the industry as overrun.

Makers of high-quality ice cream (sometimes known as gourmet ice cream) use fresh whole dairy products, a low percentage of air (approximately 20 %), between 16 and 20 % butterfat, and as few additives as possible.

The Body and Texture of Ice Cream

By body, the whole mass of ice cream is referred to its firmness, its resistance; and texture refers to the finer particles of the ice cream.

- **Effect of fat on texture:** High butterfat produces a firm body, for the fat particles chilled are very firm. Too much fat produces a very hard ice cream. Fillers are sometimes used to give a better body. In home-made ice cream when little cream is used, egg may be added to produce a firmer body, and to add flavour.
- **Effect of proteins on texture:** The milk solids not fat and the protein content particularly affect the body of the ice cream. The casein and albumin of milk are found as calcium and magnesium caseinates and albuminates in the milk. As such, they imbibe water and swell. With too little protein, the body has little resistance and with too much protein, its hydration produces a very soggy, heavy ice cream. Mortensen states that high serum solids give a smooth mix as they absorb the water, but their use can be carried to an extreme. He adds that those who do not use a high percentage of serum solids must pay more

attention to the treatment of the mix. Combs and Martin concluded that a certain amount of acidity produces a finished appearance in the mix. They have found that too high acidity causes the ice cream to melt quickly, since the reaction is brought nearer the isoelectric point of casein and at the isoelectric point, very little water is held by casein.

- **Effect of treatment of the mix on texture:** Any treatment of the ingredients of the ice cream or of the mix itself that increases the viscosity affects the body and texture of the ice cream. Pasteurisation, homogenisation, and aging all affect the viscosity and will be discussed later. Though the texture of the ice cream, like the body, is affected by the ingredients used and their proportions, it is also affected to a greater extent than the body by the freezing process. The texture of ice cream depends largely on the size of the crystals and the amount of air incorporated during freezing.
- **Incorporating chocolate or fruit:** Some special problem studies have indicated that the temperature at which the chocolate is combined with other ingredients is the most important factor in obtaining a uniform colour and not a speckled product. The temperature, at which the chocolate is combined, at least with a portion of the ingredients, should be above the melting point of the chocolate. The chocolate may be added to a portion of the milk which has been warmed or made into syrup. Martin advises that the chocolate be made into syrup with the sugar and a portion of the milk.

  Fruits, such as strawberries, raspberries, and peaches, may be put through a sieve before adding to the mix. If larger pieces of fruit are desired, they can be prevented from freezing into chunks of ice by letting them stand for some time or overnight in heavy syrup. The sugar entering the berries or fruit lowers the freezing point of the fruit, so that it does not freeze or is less hard. To keep the fruit as whole as possible, the syrup should be added to the cream mix. Then, the fruit is added after the cream is in a soft-frozen state.

- **The freezing process:** If the ice cream mix has not been cooled before it is put in the freezer, it is better to turn the freezer slowly until the mix is cooled. If the freezer is turned rapidly, while the mix is at a temperature above 4.5 °C or 40 °F, the butterfat is clumped together and a buttery product results. If carried far enough, butter may even be churned in the mix. The mix does not hold the air incorporated in it until its temperature is cooled to about 1 °C or 34 °F, so that rapid turning is of no advantage from this standpoint until the mix is cooled. With a freezer turned by hand, if the freezer is turned rapidly all the time, one's energy is often expended before the freezing is finished, and it is during the latter part of the freezing period that the turning should be rapid. The size of the crystals formed during freezing depends upon the rate of turning of the freezer and the length of time of the freezing process. Stirring the solution during crystallisation increases the number of nuclei formed, and the resulting crystals are smaller than if the mixture is not stirred. If the ice cream is not stirred during freezing, a few nuclei are formed, the water crystals join onto each other, and a product with very coarse, large, spiny crystals is the result. On the other hand, if the ice cream is stirred, the size of the crystals depends upon the rate of turning. Very slow turning, while freezing is in progress, results in larger crystals; rapid turning results in smaller crystals. If the freezer is turned very slowly, the crystals build upon the crystals already formed; with rapid turning, many new crystals are developed. The time of the freezing process also affects the size of the crystals. If the crystals are formed very rapidly, too little air is mixed with the cream, which produces an ice cream without a velvety texture. Since rapid freezing occurs with low temperatures, it is better not to have the temperature of the brine too low, thus 1 part of salt to 8 parts of ice produces good results.

- **Overrun:** The addition of air to the ice cream during freezing causes it to swell so that the ice cream increases in bulk. This increase is known as the swell or overrun.

  This swell or overrun due to the incorporation of air particles gives a smoother, more velvety texture to the ice- cream. Mortensen states that it is preferable to have the air cells in the finished cream small, for the strength of the film of a small air cell is stronger than that of a large one. To obtain small air cells in the ice cream the mix should be viscid. A viscid substance resists incorporation of air, and it will work in finer divided portions. With increased viscosity, the air is held in the mix butter after it is incorporated. Mortensen includes homogenisation as an important factor in increasing the viscosity of the ice cream mix.

  As the swell in freezing improves the texture, it is desirable to obtain it in home-made ice cream. In the home-made ice cream, the freezer is often filled so full that there is no room for overrun and no air is beaten into the ice cream during freezing. Filling the freezer two-thirds to three-fourths gives good results for home-made ice cream. In home, freezing the overrun obtained is seldom as great as with commercial ice creams, for the freezing conditions in the home are not controlled so carefully as in the factory.

  Too great an overrun produces an ice cream of poor body and quality, for it becomes frothy and foamy. An overrun of 50 % is considered to give a desirable texture.

- **Percentage overrun:** The percentage of overrun depends upon the speed of freezing and rate of turning.

Effect of the speed of the machine on overrun (Baer)

Revolutions per minute	Overrun		Time of freezing	
	Lot I	Lot II	Lot I	Lot II
50	25	33	10	11
50	28	33	11	10
50	25	35	9	12
150	48	43	7	7
150	48	39	8	5
150	50	40	7.5	6
175	45	58	7	6
175	50	50	7.5	6.5
175	52	55	8	6

The above table, from Baer's results, shows the effects of the speed of the machine on the overrun. He concluded that 50 revolutions per minute were too slow, as the overrun was too low, the texture of the ice cream was coarse, and the body, weak and spiny.

From the table, it is be noted that increasing the speed of the freezer shortens the freezing time. The first crystals are formed at the edge of the ice cream mix and against the side of the metal container. The faster speed of turning keeps these crystals scraped away and brings warmer portions of the mix against the can to be frozen. In this way, the whole mass is chilled and frozen more rapidly than it would be if the mix was not stirred.

For home freezing it is probably better to over-freeze a little but not too much, if the ice cream is to be served soon after it is frozen. After the stirring is stopped, the rate of cooling is slower. Therefore, it requires a period of standing after the freezing process is completed for the ice cream to harden suitably for serving. Increasing the quantity of salt for packing also increases the rate at which the ice cream hardens.

Basic steps in the manufacturing of ice cream:

- Blending
- Pasteurisation

- Homogenisation
- Aging the mixing
- Freezing
- Packaging
- Hardening

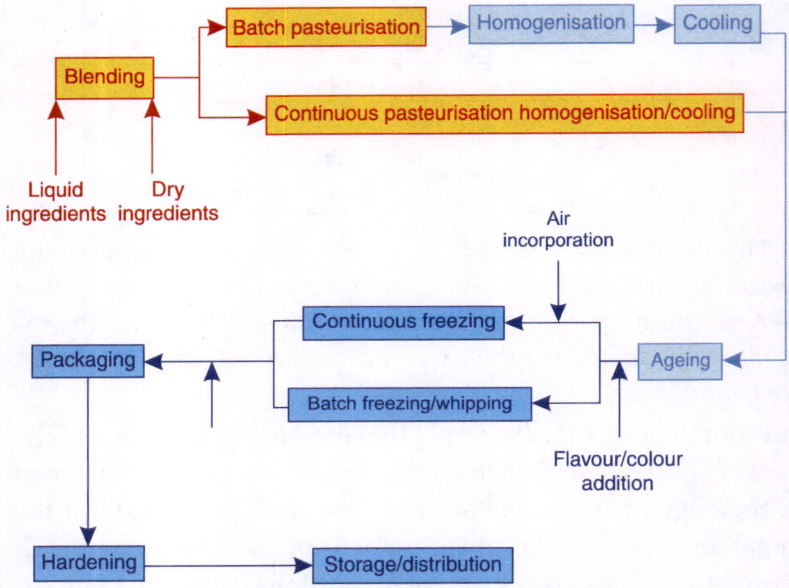

(a) Flow diagram for ice cream manufacture

The red section represents the operations involving raw, unpasteurised mix, the pale blue section represents the operations involving pasteurised mix, and the dark blue section represents the operations involving frozen ice cream.

Blending

First, the ingredients are selected based on the desired formulation and calculation of the recipe, then the ingredients are weighed and blended together to produce what is known as the "ice cream mix". Blending requires rapid agitation to incorporate powders, and often, high speed blenders are used.

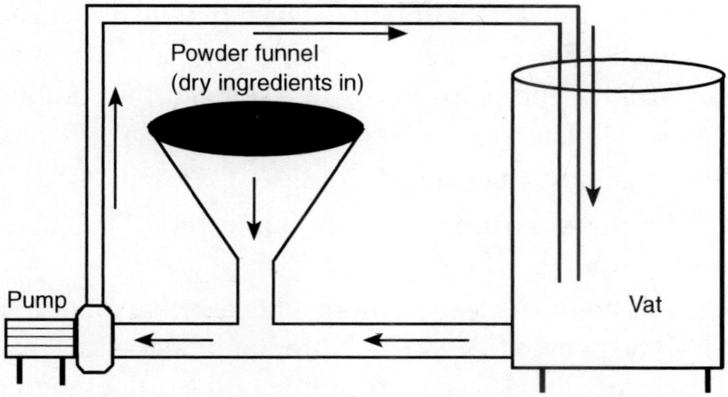

(b) Simple hopper device for incorporating dry ingredients into the recirculating liquids

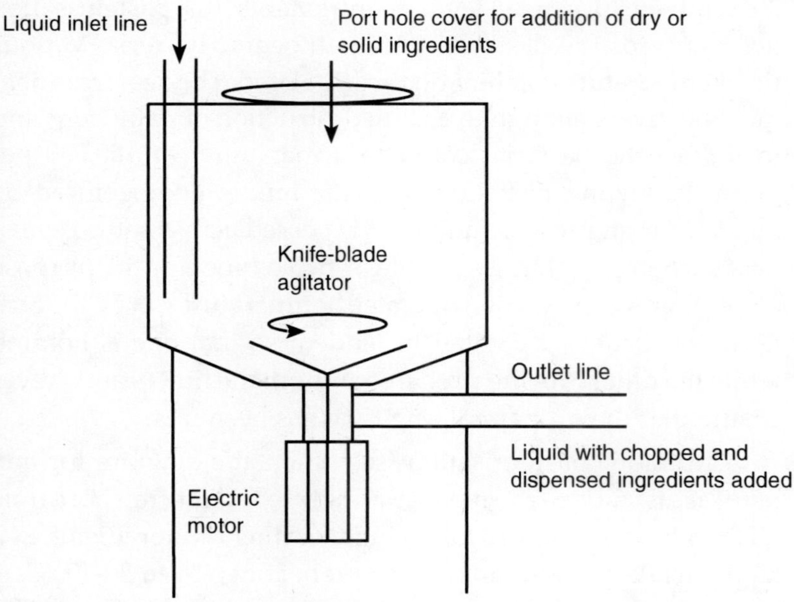

(c) High shear blender for incorporating dry ingredients into ice cream mix.

Pasteurisation

The mix is then pasteurised. Pasteurisation is the biological control point in the system, designed for the destruction of pathogenic bacteria. In addition to this function, pasteurisation also reduces the number of spoilage organisms, such as psychrotrophs, and helps to hydrate some of the components (proteins, stabilizers).

Pasteurisation (Ontario regulations): 69 °C / 30 min. 80 °C / 25 sec.

Both batch pasteurisers and continuous (HTST) methods are used.

Batch pasteurisers lead to more whey protein denaturation, which some people feel gives a better body to the ice cream. In batch pasteurisation system, blending of the proper ingredient amount is done in large jacketed vats equipped with some means of heating, usually steam or hot water. The product is then heated in the vat to at least 69 °C (155 °F) and held for 30 minutes to satisfy legal requirements for pasteurisation necessary for the destruction of pathogenic bacteria. Various time temperature combinations can be used. The heat treatment must be severe enough to ensure destruction of pathogens and to reduce the bacterial count to a maximum of 100,000 per gram. Following pasteurisation, the mix is homogenised by means of high pressure and then is passed across some type of heat exchanger (plate or double or triple tube) for the purpose of cooling the mix to refrigerated temperatures (4 °C). Batch tanks are usually operated in tandem so that one is holding while the other is being prepared. Automatic timers and valves ensure that the proper holding time has been met.

Continuous pasteurisation (see schematic diagram for mix here) is usually performed in a high temperature short time (HTST) heat exchanger following blending of ingredients in a large, insulated feed tank. Some preheating, up to 30-40 °C, is necessary for solubilisation of the components. The HTST system is equipped with a heating section, a cooling section, and a regeneration section. Cooling sections of ice cream mix HTST presses are usually larger than milk HTST presses. Due to the preheating of the mix, regeneration is lost and mix, entering the cooling section, is still quite warm.

Homogenisation

The mix is also homogenised which forms the fat emulsion by breaking down or reducing the size of the fat globules found in milk or cream to less than 1 μm. Two-stage homogenisation is usually preferred for ice cream mix. Clumping or clustering of the fat is reduced thereby producing a thinner, more rapidly whipped mix. Melt-down is also improved. Homogenisation provides the following functions in ice cream manufacture:

- Reduces the size of fat globules
- Increases surface area
- Forms membrane
- Makes possible the use of butter, frozen cream, etc.

By helping to form the fat structure, it also has the following indirect effects:

- Makes a smoother ice cream
- Gives a greater apparent richness and palatability
- Better air stability
- Increases the resistance to melting

Homogenisation of the mix should take place at the pasteurizing temperature. The high temperature produces more efficient breaking up of the fat globules at any given pressure and also reduces fat clumping and the tendency to thick, heavy-bodied mixes. No one pressure can be recommended that will give satisfactory results under all conditions. The higher the fat and total solids in the mix, the lower the pressure should be. If a two-stage homogeniser is used, a pressure of 2000-2500 psi on the first stage and 500-1000 psi on the second stage should be satisfactory under most conditions. Two-stage homogen-isation is usually preferred for ice cream mix. Clumping or clustering of the fat is reduced, thereby, producing a thinner, more rapidly whipped mix. Melt-down is also improved.

Ageing

The mix is then aged for at least four hours and usually overnight. This allows the fat to cool down and crystallize, and for the proteins and polysaccharides to fully hydrate. Aging improves whipping qualities of mix and the body and texture of ice cream, it does so by:

- providing time for fat crystallisation, so the fat can partially coalesce;
- allowing time for full protein and stabilizer hydration and a resulting slight viscosity increase; and
- allowing time for membrane rearrangement and protein/emulsifier interaction, as emulsifiers displace proteins from the fat globule surface, which allows for a reduction in stabilisation of the fat globules and enhanced partial coalescence.

Aging is performed in insulated or refrigerated storage tanks, silos, etc. Mix temperature should be maintained as low as possible without freezing, at or below 5 °C. An aging time of overnight is likely to give best results under average plant conditions. A "green" or unaged mix is usually detected quickly at the freezer.

Freezing

Following mix processing, the mix is drawn into a flavour tank where any liquid flavours, fruit purees, or colours are added. The mix then enters the dynamic freezing process, which both freezes a portion of the water and whips air into the frozen mix. The "barrel" freezer is a scraped-surface, tubular heat exchanger, which is jacketed with a boiling refrigerant such as ammonia or freon. Mix is pumped through this freezer and is drawn off the other end in a matter of 30 seconds (or 10-15 minutes in the case of batch freezers), with about 50 % of its water frozen. There are rotating blades inside the barrel that keep the ice scraped off the surface of the freezer and also dashers inside the machine which help to whip the mix and incorporate air.

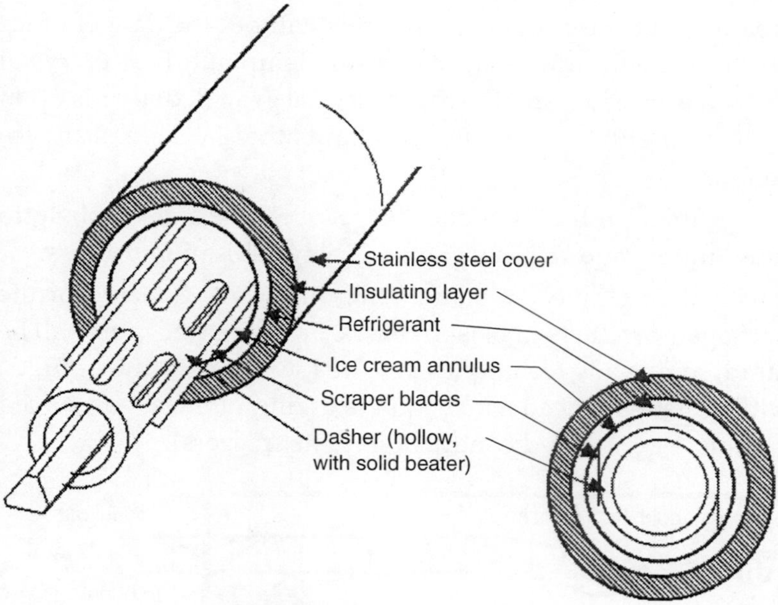

Continuous ice cream (barrel) freezer

Ice cream contains a considerable quantity of air, up to half of its volume. This gives the product its characteristic lightness. Without air, ice cream would be similar to a frozen ice cube. The air content is termed its overrun, which can be calculated mathematically.

As the ice cream is drawn with about half of its water frozen, particulate matter such as fruits, nuts, candy, cookies, or whatever you like, is added to the semi-frozen slurry which has a consistency similar to soft-serve ice cream. In fact, almost the only thing which differentiates hard-frozen ice cream from soft-serve, is the fact that soft serve is drawn into cones at this point in the process rather than into packages for subsequent hardening.

Hardening

After the particulates have been added, the ice cream is packaged and placed into a blast freezer at –30 to 40 °C where most of the remainder water is frozen. Below about –25 °C, ice cream is stable for indefinite periods without the danger of ice crystal growth; however, above this temperature, ice crystal growth is possible and the rate of crystal growth depends upon the temperature of storage. This limits the shelf life of the ice cream.

A primer on the theoretical aspects of freezing will help to fully understand the freezing and recrystallisation process.

Hardening involves static (still, quiescent) freezing of the packaged products in blast freezers. Freezing rate must still be rapid, so freezing techniques involve low temperature (– 40 °C) with either enhanced convection (freezing tunnels with forced air fans) or enhanced conduction (plate freezers).

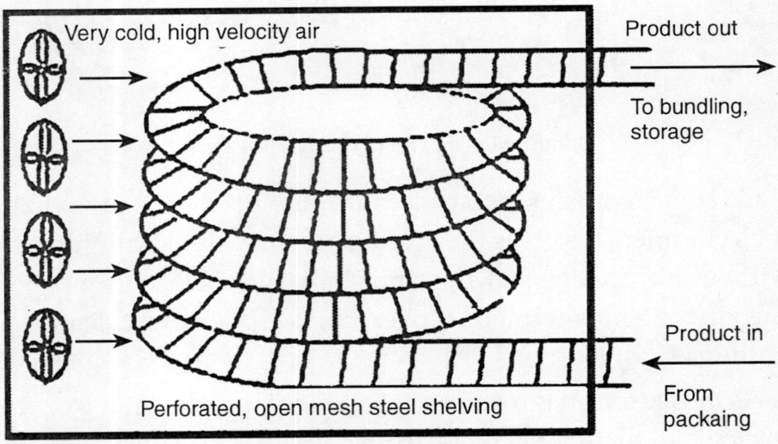

Spiral, wind tunner freezer

The rate of heat transfer in a freezing process is affected by the temperature difference, the surface area exposed and the heat transfer coefficient ($Q = UA\ dT$). Thus, the factors affecting hardening are those affecting this rate of heat transfer:

1. Temperature of the blast freezer, the colder the temperature, the faster the hardening and smoother the product.
2. Rapid circulation of air increases convective heat transfer.
3. Temperatures of ice cream when placed in the hardening freezer, the colder the ice cream at draw, the faster the hardening. Must get through packaging operations fast.
4. Size of container, exposure of maximum surface area to cold air, especially important to consider shrink wrapped bundles. They become a much larger mass to freeze. Bundling should be done after hardening.
5. Composition of ice cream is related to freezing point depression and the temperature required to ensure a significantly high-ice phase volume.
6. Method of stacking containers or bundles to allow air circulation. Circulation should not be impeded, there should be no 'dead air' spaces (e.g., round vs square packages).
7. Care of evaporator, freedom from frost, acts as insulator.
8. Package-type should not impede heat transfer, e.g., styrofoam liner or corrugated cardboard may protect against heat shock after hardening, but reduces heat transfer during freezing, so not feasible.
9. Ice cream from the dynamic freezing process (continuous freezer) can also be transformed into an array of novely / impulse products through a variety of filling and forming machines.

GELATINE-BASED DESSERTS

A pudding not thickened with starch or eggs must be bound or stabilized using another ingredient. Gelatine is often used for this purpose. The most common gelatine-based desserts are:

Panna cotta: It is a moulded chilled dessert, popular throughout Italy. For its preparation, gelatine is softened in a cold liquid, then added to the warm cream mixture. This is poured into moulds and allowed to set.

Bavarois: It is a French mousse made with cream Anglaise base. Gelatine is added before being cooled. Then cream is folded in. The mousse is set in a mould before being de-moulded and served.

Delice: It is same as above but with a layer of sponge in the bottom of the mould. The mousse once set can be finished with a glaze or a fruit jelly.

Charlotte russe: Sponge fingers are layered around the mould, bavarois is made and set, holding the sponge fingers in place.

Jelly: Flavouring, water and sugar are boiled. Gelatine is added and set the mixture in fridge.

EGG-BASED DESSERTS

There are two basic kinds of custards: stirred custard, which is stirred as it cooks and remains pourable when cooked, and baked custard, which is not stirred and sets firm. One basic rule governs the preparation of both types of custard, i.e., do not heat custard higher than an internal temperature of 185 °F (85 °C). This temperature is the point at which egg-liquid mixtures coagulate. If they are heated beyond this, they tend to curdle. An overbaked custard becomes watery because the moisture separates from the toughened protein.

Other major types of custard include:

Crème anglaise: Crème anglaise, or vanilla custard sauce, is a stirred custard. It consists of milk, sugar, and egg yolks, stirred over very low heat until lightly thickened.

Baked custard: Like custard sauce, it consists of milk, sugar, and eggs, usually whole eggs for their thickening power. Unlike the sauce, it is baked rather than stirred over heat, so it sets and becomes firm. Baked custard is used as a pie filling, as a dessert by itself, and as a base for many baked puddings.

Crème caramel, crème brûlée, diplomat pudding and custard tart are some of the famous custard deserts. Egg-based deserts are made from egg custard. The milk/cream, whole eggs or egg yolks and sugar are combined together, poured into a mould and carefully cooked in a bain maire. The eggs are gently cooked, making them the setting agent within these desserts. Once cooked, they are either de-moulded and finished or served in the dish/ ramekin.

CREAM-BASED DESSERTS

Mousse is a sweet dish made with smooth light mass (fruit puree or melted chocolate). The main ingredient in a mousse is whipped cream. Some mousse recipes have whipped egg whites, folded in after the cream has been added, which will lighten the mousse.

RICE DESSERTS

Pear conde: A chilled sweet delight made from rice cooked in toned milk, topped with poached pears, served in silver flat dish and decorated with fresh cherries.

Rice creole: It's a basic rice pudding, served in a hollowed-out baby pineapple.

Empress rice: It's a basic rice pudding, made with the addition of egg yolks. Set in a mould and de-moulded. Topped with stewed fruit and served.

FRUIT-BASED DESSERTS

The fruit is the main element in this dessert. Often, the presentation of the fruit is the key! Examples of fruit-based deserts are fruit terrine, peach melba, fruit salad, poached pear, etc.

ICE CREAM-BASED DESSERTS

Arctic roll: An arctic roll is made of vanilla ice cream wrapped in a thin layer of sponge cake to form a roll, with a layer of raspberry flavoured sauce between the sponge and the ice cream.

Peach melba: It is peaches with raspberry sauce and vanilla ice cream.

Knickerbocker glory: It is a layered ice cream sundae, served in a large tall glass.

Banana split: It is a classic summertime sundae loaded with vanilla, chocolate, and strawberry ice cream, gooey syrups, nuts, whipped cream, and cherries! It is served between the split banana.

Baked alaska: In this, a thin layer of sponge is wrapped around vanilla ice cream. Meringue is then piped over the top of the sponge. It is then baked in the oven and served straightaway.

Sundae: Sundae consists of one or more scoops of ice cream topped with flavoured sauces and whipped cream and some other toppings too.

CHECK YOUR PROGRESS

1. Write a short note on frozen yogurt.
2. Write a detailed note on sorbet.
3. Describe the classification of frozen desserts.
4. Give the example of bakery frozen desserts.
5. Write a short note on freezing and hardening.
6. Write a short note on frozen desserts.
7. Describe the basic steps involved in the manufacturing of ice cream.
8. What is pasteurisation? Explain the different methods of pasteurisation.

Unit 14

Chocolate

Chocolate is widely popular as food and flavouring. People everywhere enjoy chocolate candies, pastries, and drinks. Chocolate was, for many centuries, enjoyed chiefly as a beverage. Its popularity began in America, where the cacao tree grew wild. In the early 1500s when Hernando Cortez conquered Mexico, the Aztec emperor Montezuma served him a drink. Cortez brought the beverage back to Spain. With sugar, vanilla, and cinnamon added to sweeten the bitter drink, it became a favourite with the Spanish aristocracy. In the 1600s, the drink won popularity among the upper classes in France and England. In 1753, the botanist Carolus Linnaeus gave cacao tree a botanical name "Theobroma", meaning "food of the Gods."

In the 1800s, the process for making smooth, tasty chocolate was invented. This increased the popularity of chocolate products further. Today, the chocolate industry in the United States is a big one, absorbing more than one-fourth of the world production of cacao beans. Other important chocolate manufacturing countries are Germany, The Netherlands, Great Britain, and France.

One pound (0.45 kg) of sweet milk chocolate contains nearly 2500 calories, almost twice as many as a pound of beef or a dozen eggs. About half the composition of milk chocolate is carbohydrate and about one-third is fat.

Chocolate contains a small amount of obromine, which is an alkaloid similar to the caffeine found in tea and coffee. The stimulant properties of obromine may account for chocolate's popularity. In some sensitive people,obromine content can produce the same effects as caffeine, i.e., alertness, elevated mood, depression of appetite, and increased mental and physical energy. Too much consumption of chocolate can cause insomnia and tremors.

MANUFACTURING AND PROCESSING OF CHOCOLATE

Chocolate is made from the "seeds" or "beans" of the tropical cacao tree. The beans grow inside leathery pods that are found both on the trunk and on the branches of the tree. Workers cut the pods from the tree trunks with large heavy knives called machetes and from the branches with long-handled knives. The purple or creamy-white beans are shelled from the pod, which is about the size of a small cucumber.

At this stage, the bean has a raw bitter taste. As the first step in the long process of making appetizing chocolates, the beans are piled in bins for several days. Bacterial action causes them to take on a rich-brown colour and the fragrance of chocolate. After several more days, they become dry enough to prevent spoilage, and they are bagged for shipment.

When they arrive at the factory, the beans are roasted in large rotating machines. This improves the flavour and dries the shells of the beans so that they can be easily removed in the next machine, the "cracker and fanner." Here, the beans are cracked and fans blow away the brittle shells, leaving the nibs, or meat. The nibs are the part used for making chocolate products. The shells are saved for use in fertilizer or as feed for cattle.

About 50 % of the nibs are made up of a fatty substance known as cocoa butter. In the next stage, large grinding stones or heavy steel disks crush the nibs, creating frictional heat that melts the butter. The hard parts of the nibs are ground to powder. The result is a smooth, dark-brown liquid known as chocolate liquor. When poured into moulds, the liquid hardens into cakes of unsweetened chocolate, which are used in cooking. To produce cocoa powder, the warm liquor is pumped into a filter press. Pressure exerted by a pump forces much of the cocoa butter, a yellow liquid, through the pores of a strong filter cloth. The filter cloth holds back a light- brown cake of solid particles, which is then ground and sifted to form cocoa powder.

Chocolate for eating is made by adding cocoa butter to chocolate liquor. For sweet or dark chocolate, finely powdered sugar is added. For milk chocolate, a third ingredient, milk, is included. Various flavourings may also be added. These mixtures go through a set of rollers that reduces them to a paste.

Next, more machines with heavy rollers knead the chocolate mass for periods ranging from a few hours to several days. This process, called conching, makes the rather gritty mixture very smooth. Varying the temperature in the machines and the movement of the rollers, produces variations in flavour.

Finally, the chocolate is tempered or heated to a high temperature. This reduces the size of large fat crystals and gives the chocolate a velvety quality. The chocolate is poured into moulds by automatic machinery.

Cocoa butter is sold separately for other purposes. When solid, it is white and pleasant tasting. Baking firms may use it instead of regular butter. It is also an ingredient of soaps and complexion creams.

TYPES OF COCOA AND CHOCOLATE PRODUCTS

Block Cocoa

Unsweetened, finely ground and coached cocoa mass. Cocoa butter content at least 50 %.

Uses: To flavour and colour gianduja, praline mass, marzipan, ganache, butter mixtures and fillings.

Cocoa Butter

It is the fat yielded by pressing of the cocoa mass.

Uses: To thin couverture, in the production of gianduja, praline mass and fillings to have a long shelf life.

Cocoa Powder

This is the finely ground pressed cake which appears as the cocoa butter is pressed out. Minimum fat content is 20 %.

Sweetened cocoa powder is a mixture of cocoa powder and sugar with a maximum sugar content of 68 %.

Uses: To roll pralines or other pastries, for dusting over chocolate specialities, etc.

Chocolate

Chocolate or even block chocolate is a homogenous mixture of cocoa mass and sugar with a minimum cocoa butter content of 18 %.

Uses: For the production of ganaches, fillings and grated for decoration purposes.

Chocolate Powder

It is pulverized chocolate with a minimum of 16 % cocoa butter content.

Uses: For cocoa powder.

Milk Chocolate

Milk chocolate is a chocolate with a minimum of 14 % milk solids, of which atleast 3.5 % is milkfat. Total fat contents at least 25 %, sugar content, maximum 55 %.

Uses: As for chocolate.

Cream Chocolate

Total fat content of at least 25 %, of that atleast 7 % is milkfat, sugar content, maximum 55 %.

Double Cream Chocolate

Same as cream chocolate, but minimum fat content is 10 %.

White Chocolate

White chocolate consists of at least 20 % cocoa butter, 14 % milk solids, of this 3.5 % milkfat and the maximum of 55 % sugar, used solely for confectionery products.

Couverture

This is a chocolate with at least 31 % fat content. The fat content can vary according to the use. For the couverture:

Thick flowing couverture	32-34 %
Couverture for covering goods	36-37 %
Couverture for moulding	38-40 %

Uses: For covering of pralines and chocolate specialities. Also, for the production of gianduja, ganache, praline masses, fillings, decoration and making sprinkling material.

Types of couverture

Apart from the normal couverture, there are several other types in the market, as for example, couverture with a slightly higher content of milk solids and butter, couverture with special ingredients as mocca, caramel, and hazelnuts.

Grated Couverture

Also known as "couverture rapee".

Use: To temper couverture for decoration purposes.

Store couverture in a cool and dry place and particularly away from foreign odour.

Baker's chocolate

It is a mass similar to couverture but with the cocoa butter replaced by another type of fat. This allows for a simpler method of work, as it does not need to be tempered.

Uses: As for couverture, not allowed to be used for truffle fillings or the pouring or covering of chocolate.

Tempering of couverture

The high gloss of couverture is of greatest importance as it gives the end product its appetising appearance. In order to achieve perfect products, it is necessary to work and handle the couverture carefully and the following points must be observed.

Melting the couverture

Melt in a tempering apparatus or in a warm cupboard at a temperature of 45-50 °C. The couverture block should be broken up into small pieces, in this way the warmth can penetrate the pieces better and soften the couverture much quicker. Stir well with a wooden spatula when all is fully melted.

Tempering of the couverture

Tempering is the process needed to handle the couverture so that it will give a lasting gloss, crisp snap break and the best melting properties and a good resistance to warmth.

The confectioner understands the word "tempering", which means the process of melting the couverture, pre-crystallising it and then, rewarming it at a correct temperature.

The necessary work is brought about through the fat phase of the cocoa butter in the couverture. The cocoa butter contains various fat groups with varying melting points from 45 to 16 °C. The various fat groups have the properties of setting when cool into both stable and unstable crystal shapes. In order to achieve the high gloss, with the crisp snap, the couverture needs stable crystals. To make this occur, the couverture must be tempered.

There are various methods of tempering:

- **Tabliering (graining):** Warm the couverture to 45-50 °C and tip about 1/3rd onto a marble slab. Spread it out and rescrape it together with a spatula or palette knife, so that it cools and starts to thicken. This shows that the fat is beginning to crystallise. Just before it sets completely, mix it to the remaining couverture, mix well together and bring back slowly by warming it to 30-32.5 °C, which is then the working temperature.

- **Seeding with grated couverture:** The couverture is seeded with stable fat crystals.

  Melt the couverture with warming to 40-50 °C and stir in about ⅓rd of its weight of grated chocolate and then, rewarm to the working temperature of 30-32.5 °C.

  ***Important*:** The grated couverture used for seeding must only consist of tempered couverture itself, that is, it must be tempered before setting.

- **By direct warming:** Allow the set couverture, which has been tempered before being allowed to set, to melt very slowly in a tempering vessel or a warm cupboard over a period of 24 hours. The working temperature of 30-32.5 °C must not exceed at all during this time.

- **In a tempering machine:** The couverture is warmed between 45 and 50 °C under thermostatic controls. It is then eventually cooled to 26-27 °C to start the re-crystallisation and then, rewarmed to the working temperature.

  The temperature of the working room should be around 20 °C. The temperature of the interiors and filling should coincide with that of the work room, or be slightly higher. Too cold interior works on the couverture in such a way that it sets too quickly from inside to the outside, which hinders the gloss. Such pralines then have too thick a coat and look matt and white-grey.

  If the centres are too warm, then the couverture sets too slowly which creates a false type of crystal as it sets. The pralines are red-grey and show streaks and points. After covering, the product should be left to set at 15 °C, this slight difference in temperature forces the setting a little.

- **Storing the chocolate:** Warmth and moisture are the two enemies of couverture. So, covered products should always be stored in a dry, airy, cool room, protected from sunlight. Stored at temperature of 15-18 °C, with relative humidity, 55-65 %.
- **Pouring of mould:** Remove with chocolate condition of the mould and use only metal and plastic moulds which are in perfect condition. Every scratch, every rusted or unplanted spot will show a disadvantage on the finished product. If any bit of chocolate sticks to the mould, they must not be scrapped with any hard article such as knife tips. Only in this way, the mould remains in good condition.
- **Preparation of the moulds:** To ensure that pouring can be carried out quickly and without trouble, great care must be given to the preparation of the moulds. Wash the moulds in warm soapy water and then rinse with warm water. Rub the moulds dry with a very soft cloth. Metal moulds should then be polished. For this, one can use powdered chalk, rubbed into the mould with cotton until they shine evenly all over. Then it is necessary to rub them out cleanly with cotton wool. Plastic moulds must only be polished with cotton wool. The mould should be at room temperature before pouring.
- **Pouring of the moulds:** In order to avoid the creation of small bubbles on the sides, it is recommended that the moulds are first brushed out with a small brush. The lined moulds are then clipped together, immediately and then filled with couverture. Then lightly tap the edge of the mould to cause any new bubbles to burst. Then turn the mould over and tap, so that the surplus couverture runs out readily. Place on a wire rack to drain. Small moulds must be turned over and knocked out immediately for

filling. Larger moulds can be left for a little while so that the couverture layer is not too thin.

As soon as the couverture starts to set, remove the mould from the wire rack, take off the clips and place the moulds in the fridge to set. They should be removed from the mould only when the couverture is completely set and shrunk away from the mould. Put on a base only after the mould has been taken off. To do this, simply spread couverture onto paper and stand the hollow body on it. Allow it to set in the fridge and then break off any surplus. Before any further decoration, allow the shape to temper itself, i.e., it should be brought back to room temperature.

When the hollow shape is taken from the mould, it often shows a seam which needs to be removed. This can be trimmed off with a fine blade only after 2-3 hours.

- **Colouring of white couverture:** White couverture can readily be coloured as desired, whether it is to be used in moulds, for piping, or for the production of decorative material. It is important to ensure that fat soluble colours are used and not the water soluble ones.

Method

Mix well a small quantity of white tempered couverture with the powder colour and then mix this into larger quantities to be used. Moulds can be poured quite easily with variously coloured couverture.

Spraying with couverture

A spray gun is the best thing to use here. It should have an adjustable nozzle and a compressor with a pressure of about 3-5 atm. The gun itself must be pre-warmed so that the couverture does not set in its container. Any desired type of couverture may be used, but it is important to ensure that there are no lumps in it. So it is advised to sieve it first. The couverture should be thinned with cocoa butter to a piping consistency. The more it is thinned down, the finer and smoother will be the structure of the piping on its background. If the couverture is not thinned much, then it must be tempered with couverture which has been thinned a great deal, then its tempering should mean that the temperature of the mixture should not be too high, at best, not over 35 °C.

The proportion of couverture-cocoa butter for a fairly coarse structure can be two parts tempered couverture and one part cocoa butter (approx. 30 °C). For a fine structure: one part untempered couverture and one part cocoa butter.

If a satin-type of structure is desired, allow the product to cool a little and then spray over, immediately. One pound (0.45 kg) of sweet milk chocolate contains nearly 2500 calories, almost twice as many as a pound of beef or a dozen eggs. About half the composition of milk chocolate is carbohydrate and about one-third is fat.

CANDY

When Hernando Cortez was received in 1519 at the court of the Aztec Emperor Montezuma in Mexico, he was served a drink made from the cacao bean chocolate. This novel substance was soon blended with sugar to make a beverage that became popular throughout Europe. However, it is not more than 300 years that sugar and chocolate were produced in a solid mixture and sold to the public as candy. It is, of course, not the only candy; but it is perhaps the most popular product of a multibillion-dollar business of an industry whose major manufacturers are in Europe and the United States.

There are hundreds of varieties of candy, but they are all classified by manufacturers into three basic types. The classification depends on the ingredients used. Commonly used ingredient is a sugar called sucrose, which is derived from sugarcane or sugar beets. Other sweeteners are honey, molasses, maple sugar, corn sugar, and corn syrup. In recent years, some candies have been made with artificial, non-caloric sweeteners such as saccharin or aspartame.

The more complex candies contain a greater variety of ingredients added to the sweetener. Chocolate, either sweetened or in its bitter-sweet form, is a common ingredient. Other substances are used to affect the consistency, flavour, and colour of a candy. Among these are milk (usually in a powdered or concentrated form), eggs, gelatine, vegetable fats, and invert sugar. Invert sugar is a mixture of glucose and fructose made by heating sucrose and adding an acid, such as cream of tartar or citric acid. Invert sugar affects the sweetness, solubility, and crystallisation of candy. Other common ingredients in more complex candies are fruits, nuts, coconut, jellies, spices, and liquor. Liquor-filled chocolates are popular in Europe.

Candy is a cooked food. The basis for most production is melting or boiling sugar. The process for a specific kind of candy depends on the desired consistency and the number of ingredients.

Types of Candy

Hard candy: Hard candy is also called high-boiled candy and is made from solutions of mixed sugars that are boiled with water until concentrated into an easily shaped mass that can be coloured and flavoured. The material can then be formed into shapes and allowed to harden. Sometimes the material is passed through rollers with grooves or through continuous forming machines. Either process produces a rope of candy. A shiny, satin-like finish can be given to the candy by pulling or stretching. The "rope" can then be cut into candy pieces. High-boiled sugar solutions easily crystallize, changing texture and looks. To stop crystallisation, invert sugar or corn syrup may be added.

Caramel and toffee: Caramel is a fairly chewy candy that is soft at room temperature; toffee is harder and somewhat brittle.

Both are basically a mixture of boiled sugar and butter manufactured in a way similar to that of a hard candy, except that more ingredients are added. Milk in a sweetened, condensed, or evaporated form is normally used. Fats, such as butter or vegetable oil, are mixed with milk or some kind of syrup before being added to the batch of candy. Because caramel is soft enough to be moulded at lower temperatures than hard candy, it can be easily formed into lengths and cut into desired shapes.

Nougats are light, chewy candies similar to caramel in consistency, but they do not usually contain milk. They are aerated by whipping a solution of egg white or gelatin or both into boiled syrup. Vegetable fats are added to give a chewiness, and fruits, nuts, or honey may also be added. Soft, well-aerated nougat has become a very popular filling for some chocolate covered bars.

Fondant or cream candies: Candy corn, seen most during the Halloween season, is a common fondant candy. But fondant is also the basis of most chocolate covered creams. Most of the chocolates made by well-known companies are filled with fondant. The candy is made by cooking syrup at a lower temperature than for hard candy. The cooled mass of white syrup is kneaded like bread dough. Fruits, nuts, flavouring, and colouring are added to make the variety of creams found in boxes of chocolates.

Mechanisation has made it possible for manufacturers to produce as much as 2000 pounds (900 kg) of fondant per hour. After the fondant has been flavoured and coloured, it is shaped by pouring it into trays filled with cornstarch. Shapes have previously been pressed into the cornstarch and withdrawn, leaving cavities that act as moulds. After the fondant is cool, the tray is passed over a sieve, and the cornstarch drops through. The pieces of fondant are dusted and ready to be coated.

The machine that coats candy is called an enrober. Invented in France in about 1900, it can coat 2000 pounds of candy an hour. It has a moving belt that carries the candy centred into the machine. Here, they are transferred to a short belt of wire mesh, through which the soft chocolate is forced from underneath to coat the bottom of each piece. They then move on to another belt and are passed under a suspended tank of warm chocolate. A thin sheet of chocolate flows out to cover the top and sides of the creams, and the surplus chocolate flows through the wire mesh to the pan beneath. The surplus is automatically pumped back into the suspended tank. The chocolates are then cooled and packed.

Very fine grades of chocolate are still coated by hand. The manufacturer's name is often stamped at the bottom of each piece.

Other candies: Chocolate fudge is probably the candy most easily and commonly made at home. It consists of corn syrup, sugar, chocolate, vanilla, milk, and butter cooked together until the desired consistency is reached. It is then cooled and allowed to harden.

Marshmallows are made by whipping air into a mixture of sugar, corn syrup, gelatine, egg whites, and flavourings. The popular form is white and covered with powdered sugar. It can also be purchased in a nearly liquid form for use as ice cream.

ASSORTED PREPARATION OF CHOCOLATE

Following are some preparations and flavours which we use to make it as assorted preparation of chocolates:

- Key lime raw chocolate + sweet cashew cream filling
- Cocoa raw chocolate + raspberry China jam
- Cocoa raw chocolate + raw caramel
- Plain raw chocolate + raspberry jam
- White chocolate

- Almond drops
- Marbel drops
- Chocolate candy

Preparation Method

Dark or white chocolate: Cut small pieces of chocolate compound in a double bowling method or in a microwave safe bowl and microwave it for 30 seconds. Once done, mix the compound using spoon. Again keep it for 20-30 seconds more. Mix the compound well to get a smooth creamy structure. Tap the mould for even distribution of compound. Keep the mould in a freezer for 10-15 minutes, till it sets. Then, unmould the chocolates.

By using different shaped moulds, make different shapes of chocolate.

Marble chocolate: Add white compound first, top with dark compound in the same mould.

For any flavour, fill centre with nuts or flavour the mixture in it after one base filling of chocolate and fill it again and keep it to set. After setting it, unmould the chocolate.

CHECK YOUR PROGRESS

1. Describe the moulding method of chocolate.
2. Define chocolate.
3. How to make flavoured chocolate?
4. Write a short note on chocolate storage.
5. Write a short note on couverture.
6. Describe the chocolate products.
7. Describe the manufacturing and processing of chocolate.

Unit 15

Breads

HISTORY

It is not known who was the first baker, though some of the world's oldest breads can be found in Switzerland and are around thousand years old. Breads from the ruins of Pompeii are found with the makers name still visible.

The discovery of leaven was accidental. Breads were made in the form of unleavened cakes and a batch from the previous day was added to the new dough to avoid wastage. Soon, the baker saw it was leavened and softer in texture.

Bread was leavened only by the addition of sour dough. Books as old as 240 B.C. mention that old dough was used to ferment new doughs. The 1st baker's guild was formed in the reign of Emperor Augustine in Rome in 14 A.D.

The Medieval bakers used barm as a leaven. This was a mixture of malt and hops with water and some of the coarse meal. This was left for some time for air-borne yeast microbes to settle down on the barm and inoculate it. This was then used in the dough. A little dough was left for next day's use. Sour dough is still used in the modern-day bakeries, especially in the making of rye breads.

In the Hebrides, a hazel twig was dipped into this barm or ferment and then, carefully dried in the sun. The next day, all that was required was to swirl the stick in the next ferment and the yeast would begin to get activated. Yeast coming to the surface of home-made wine was collected and dried. This was also used for bread making. At that time, a considerable amount of brewer's yeast was used by bakers.

Up to 1859, it was thought that fermentation just happened, till Louis Pasteur showed that it was the result of microorganisms converting sugar into carbon dioxide (CO_2).

Patent yeasts were soon made, which were used in ferments to multiply and strengthen it further. There were various names given to these barms, used depending upon the area or the time. 'Spon' or 'virgin barm' is one of them and is derived from the word 'spontaneous'. Compound barms were derived from malt, hops, and brewer's yeasts. Some people used bottles of stout beer as starter. Ingredients such as mashed potatoes, brown sugar, ginger, and caraway seeds, were added.

Compressed yeast, which is now available freely, came into existence only in the early days of 19th century.

History of the Bakery Oven

The bakery oven is approximately 7800 years old. Before that, breads were cooked on heated stones after the charcoal fire had died down. In Asia Minor, an oven has been found dating back to 5900 B.C. or 5700 B.C. The Egyptians were the first to have commercial bakeries between 3000 B.C. and 2700 B.C. By 2000 B.C., they had 16 different types of bread. In Bohemia and Bulgaria, bakery ovens dating back to 4800 B.C. have been discovered.

INGREDIENTS USED IN BREAD MAKING

Every ingredient used in the making of bread has a particular role to play. These ingredients, however, perform only when certain conditions are met and are highly dependent on each other to perform that particular function to the desired level, e.g., yeast performs well in the presence of sugar as well moisture. Thus, it becomes essential to understand the nature of each of these ingredients in detail, how they affect the final product and how to manipulate these materials to achieve the desired product.

Flour

The most important ingredient which gives body and structure to the bread. The contents of flour affect the final product to such an extent that it becomes vital to understand its various components and properties.

The most commonly used grain in flour manufacture is the wheat grain.

Structure of the wheat grain: The wheat grain is made up of three main parts:

(a) Bran (12 %)

(b) Germ or embryo (3 %)

(c) Endosperm (85 %)

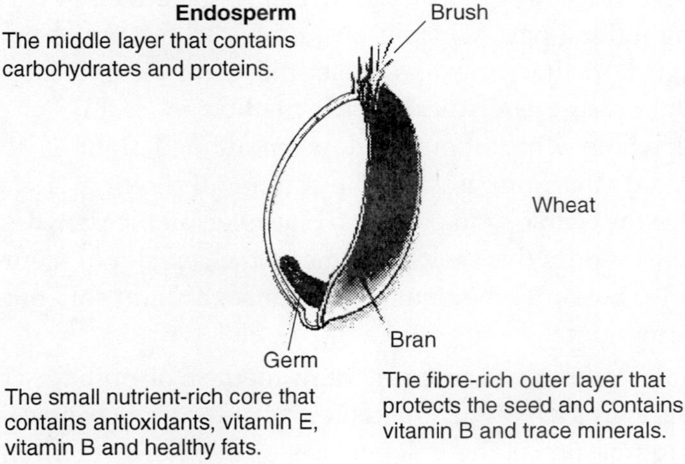

The bran is the outermost layer and is the protective covering of the grain. It has five layers which include epidermis, epicarp, endocarp, epispermortesta and aleurone cells or cerealin.

The endosperm is the portion from where refined flour is milled. It consists of 85 % of the grain and is made up of a number of small compartments of cellulose. These are tightly packed with starch cells, in spaces between them are found other substances like insoluble protein, fats, moisture and sugar.

The germ is the smallest part of the grain and contains most of the oil content and hence, has a tendency to go rancid. It also contains the cellulose and other valuable components which are removed during the milling of refined flour.

Milling

The wheat grain has to be milled in order to extract all the components of the grain and to make it ready for the bread making process. There are two main methods employed to do this job, which are stone milling and roller milling.

Stone milled flour is the more primitive method of milling flour and it consists of 2 heavy stones, on top of each other. The bottom one remains stationary while the top one moves in a circular fashion. There is a small opening on top of the stone through which the grain is passed. Heat is generated by friction during milling part, which is absorbed by the stone. A part of heat goes to the germ and melts the germ oil and mixes it throughout the endosperm. This method is mainly used to make whole wheat flour and when refined flour is to be produced, the flour is sieved through silk bolting cloths to remove the coarse bran particles. However, all the particles are not removed by this method.Some of the cerealin or aleurone cells also pass into the flour which causes a slight softening of the flour / gluten.

Roller milling is a more modern method of milling where there is a gradual reduction in the size of the grain from coarse meal to fine flour. The mill consists of two horizontal rollers, one rotating faster than the other. This rolling has a tearing effect on the grain which is ripped open. Here, the germ is separated from the endosperm before milling and hence the germ oil is not released into the flour. Also, the aleurone cells are released into the flour to a large extent, giving a stronger flour. The only disadvantage that this method has is that the heat generated by the grinding process is transferred to the flour, as there is no stone to absorb it, causing a slight denaturing of certain particles.

Composition of flour	
(approx. values will vary from grain to grain and flour to flour)	
Starch	70 %
Water	13%
Gluten (insoluble protein)	11 %
Soluble protein	2 %
Fat	1 %
Sugar	2.5 %
Mineral matter/ ash content	0.5 %

Important Terms in Bread Making

Terms	Description
Leavening	Such substances as baking powder or yeast, which create bubbles of gas in batter and doughs, causing them to rise.
Raising agents	Same as leavening agents.
Bran	Skin or outer covering of wheat grain.
Caramelised sugar	Dry sugar, heated with constant stirring until melted and dark in colour.
Bake	To cook or roast by dry heat in a closed chamber, such as an oven.
Baking powder	A chemical leavening agent composed of soda, dry acids, and corn starch (to absorb moisture), when heated, carbon dioxide is given off to rise the batter during baking.
Bacteria	Microscopic organisms, various species of which are involved in fermentation and spoilage of food.
Bleeding	Term is applied to dough that has been cut and left unsealed at the cut surface, thus permitting the escape of leavening gas.
Blend	A mixture of several ingredients or grades of any ingredients.
Bread dough	The unbaked mass of ingredients used for making bread.
Bread faults	Deviations from standard of perfection, used to determine wrong factors in the process of production of bread.

(Contd...)

Terms	Description
Buns	Small shapes of bread dough, sometimes slightly sweetened or flavoured.
Carbon dioxide	A colourless, tasteless, edible gas obtained during fermentation or from combination of soda and acid.
Citron	The sweetened rind of fruit.
Clear flour	Lower grade and higher ash content flour remaining after the patent flour has been separated.
Corn meal	A coarse meal made by grounding corn.
Divider	A machine used for cutting doughs into desired size or weight. The dough is cut by volume, not by weight.
Docking	Punching a number of vertical impressions in a dough with smooth, round stick. Docking is done so that dough expands uniformly without bursting during baking.
Dough	The thickened uncooked mass of combined ingredients for bread, rolls and biscuits but usually applied for bread.
Dry yeast	A dehydrated form of active yeast.
Dusting	Distributing a thin film of flour or starch on pans or work bench to prevent dough from sticking.
Fermentation	The chemical changes of an organic compound due to the action of living organism (yeast, bacteria), usually producing a leavening gas.
Fold	To lap yeast dough over itself. With cake batter to lift and lap the batter on to itself to lightly incorporate the ingredients.
Old dough	Yeast dough which has become over-fermented due to long fermentation. This produces finished baked loaf, dark in crumb colour, sour in taste and flavour, low in volume, coarse in grain and open in texture.
Scaling	Apportioning batter or dough according to a unit of weight.
Texture	Describe the measures of silkiness of the interior structure of a baked product as sensed by the touch of the cut surface.
Yeast	A microscopic plant which is reproduced by budding and causes fermentation and gives off carbon dioxide.
Young dough	Yeast dough which is under fermentation. This produces finished yeast goods, which are dark (harsh reddish brown) in crust colour, light in grain and low in volume.

Water

The main functions of water include:

- Hydration of the insoluble protein
- Taking up the soluble protein and other matter
- Dispersing the yeast amongst the entire dough

It is observed that the water content greatly affects the rate of fermentation. Thus, it can be seen that the speed of fermentation is greater in ferment as compared to sponge as compared to a dough, which has an increased level of hydration.

As the fermentation time increases, it becomes essential to reduce the water content to induce higher dough ripening.

The amount of water present also affects the texture of the final product and this is effectively used in various products.

Batter	Hot plate crumpets
Exceptionally soft dough	Hot plate muffins
Very soft dough	Oven muffins, buns
Soft dough, which flows slightly	All doughs baked in pans
Moderately stiff	Crusty bread, malt and rye breads
Very stiff	Fancy breads

Hard water has a higher alkalinity and as yeast works best in an acidic medium, fermentation can be slower in the initial stages. However, as the fermentation proceeds, the acids produced will neutralize this alkalinity and then the fermentation will proceed at a brisk pace. Also, the alkalinity and the mineral salts will tighten the gluten and thus the dough will be firmer. Very hard water also has magnesium sulphate, which has a retarding action on the yeast. Breads can, however, be made with both hard as well as soft water, provided the physical adjustments are made:

- Slacker dough for hard water
- Longer fermentation time to counter alkalinity
- Yeast content increased or salt content decreased

Mineral improver used: This effect, however, is seen only in large manufacturing units.

Ice in Bread Making

Ice is used in large-scale manufacturing of bread doughs to help maintain an optimum dough temperature of 78 °F. Thus, it keeps the fermentation activity of yeast at an ideal rate for gluten ripening. The quantity used will vary depending upon the time of kneading the dough or the friction factor, and the dough temperature required. Ice used must be in the form of flaked ice so that it is evenly distributed in the bread dough and causes an even cooling of the dough. It can be safely said that 10 lb of ice will be equivalent to 1 gallon of water. However, a safer way of determining the requirement will be:

$$\text{Weight of ice} = \frac{\text{Weight of water}}{\text{Tap water temp.} + 112}$$

112 Btu will change the temperature of water by 1 °F. The amount will then have to be removed from the water before adding ice.

Calculation of required water temp.

1. Straight dough method:

   $(3 \times \text{DDT}) - (\text{FT} + \text{RT} + \text{FF})$

   where, DDT = Desired dough temp.

   FT = Flour temp.

   RT = Room temp.

   FF = Friction factor, which is the amount of heat generated in a particular machine for 1 minute.

2. Sponge dough system:

   $(4 \times \text{DDT}) - (\text{FT} + \text{RT} + \text{FF} + \text{SPT})$

   where, SPT = Sponge temp.

Yeast

Yeast is a living microorganism belonging to the fungi family. It obtains its food from carbohydrates. Sugar is essential for panary fermentation and hence, they are called "saccharomyces".

Though there are many strains of yeast, the type used for bread making is "Saccharomyces cerevisae". The primary function of yeast is to change sugar into CO_2 so that the dough is aerated. When dispersed in water with yeast food, the yeast exudes an enzyme which changes sucrose into dextrose, which is then absorbed by the yeast cell. Inside the cell, this is broken down into carbon dioxide and other by-products. Yeast also has enzymes that change protein into simpler compounds, that can pass through the yeast cell membrane.

Invertase⇨ Sucrose➔ Dextrose, levulose

Maltase ⇨ Maltose➔ Dextrose

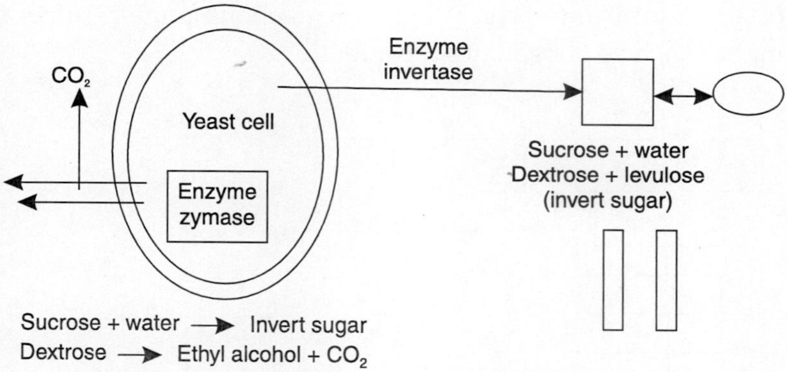

Diagrammatical representation of fermentation of sucrose

Yeast works best within a temperature range of 78-82 °F. Above this, the fermentation becomes rapid but gets weaker successively and is finally killed at 140 °F. At 40 °F, yeast is completely retarded though it is not damaged. Yeast can never dissolve completely in water, though it can disperse well into it. To ensure the distribution well, use a whisk.

Compressed yeast must be cool to touch and must possess a creamy colour breaking with a clean fracture. If it is light in colour, dry, warm and with a pungent odour, it is in a poor condition. If dark brown in colour, with a soft, sticky consistency and an unpleasant odour, it is unsuitable for use.

Commercial Manufacturing of Compressed Yeast

Stage 1: Seed Yeast

It is essential to have a healthy first generation. This is selected to inoculate a prepared plate containing nutrient 'agar' and is incubated. These cells are transferred to small flasks containing yeast food in solution. This is further transferred into progressively larger solution kept in sterile flasks with yeast foods. Thus, in 3 weeks 1 cell can be grown into hundreds of tons.

Stage 2: Preparation of Wort

The yeast food is called a wort. This is mainly a sugar solution of some form into which some nitrogenous matter, mineral matter such as phosphates are added.

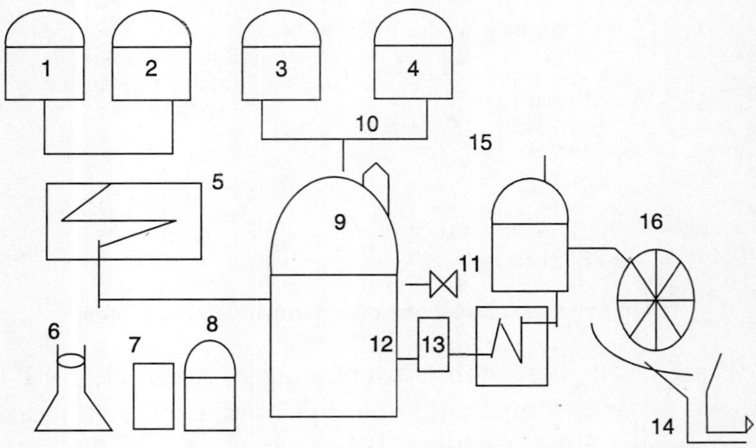

1. Molasses
2. Water
3. Ammonia
4. Phosphate
5. Heat exchanger
6. Pure strain
7. Purely reproduce mother yeast
8. Air
9. Fermentation vat
10. Deaeration
11. Cooling water
12. Centrifuge
13. Cooling
14. Water-water treatment
15. Yeast cream
16. Yeast cream
17. Packing

Diagrammatical representation of commercial manufacture of yeast

Stage 3: Fermentation

Huge tanks are fitted with coils to control the temperature. An aeration system is put into operation, causing the yeast liquid to bubble furiously. The yeast liquid multiplies, rapidly increasing the weight. The alcohol produced lowers the density of the solution and finally, the yeast comes to the surface and the fermentation stops.

Stage 4: Separation, Compressing and Packing

The yeast is passed into centrifugal separators to extract the exhausted yeast liquor. The yeast is then added to water and the liquor is cooled to 38 °F.

The yeast then passes to filter presses where under pressure, water is removed which renders the yeast into a plastic mass.

Salt

Uses of salt:

- Flavour
- Stability to gluten
- Control the rate of fermentation
- Retention of moisture
- Affects the crust colour and crumb, by controlling fermentation rate

The advised usage of salt is 3-4 % solution in water dough making. For smaller doughs, use 5 ounces to a gallon of water.

If salt is less, there is a greater breakdown of sugars into carbon dioxide, which will give:

- Large volume
- Less crust colour
- Weakened crumb due to more action on gluten

When too much salt is added to the dough, there will be a retarded action on the yeast which will cause:

- Dark crust colour, as sugar is not broken down.
- Cheesy crumb structure, as not enough gas is produced.
- Tightening of the gluten.

Sugar

Sugar is the primary food that the yeast feeds on to produce alcohol and CO_2 gas. With the exception of lactose, yeast can break down all the other sugars present in the dough, either naturally in the flour or as an addition of sugar, mainly sucrose or sometimes malt.

Flour naturally contains about 2.5-3 % of sugar in the form of sucrose and maltose. This is enough for the yeast in initial stages of the fermentation. However, in the final proof when maximum of the sugar is required to be broken down for an optimum rise, the natural sugars are exhausted and the addition of sucrose or maltose is required.

Flours with a high diastatic value, however, have a continuous source of supply, as the available starch is broken down into sucrose by diastatic enzymes.

If sugar is added to such flour, the sugar content increases which cause:

- Large volume
- High crust colour
- Weak structure
- Lower yeast activity, as yeast works best in a 10 % solution of sugar

For such dough, it becomes essential to have a longer fermentation time to help break down the sugar by yeast.

Yeast works best in a 10 % solution of sugar. Hence, when a large amount of sugar is to be added, as in a bun dough, a ferment is made to give the initial boost to the fermentation process.

Sugar has a solvent effect on gluten and this greatly affects the quality of the crumb in bread loaves. To counteract this, a mineral improver is used and excess salt is used, as salt has a stabilizing effect on the gluten.

Some sugars have high percentage of monosaccharides and hence, are excellent yeast foods. They are also anti-staling agents due to their moisture-retention capabilities. These include:

Fondant	Golden syrup
Glucose	Honey
Invert sugar	Treacle

These are excellent for short dough process, as they are easily assimilated. Treacle is an excellent moisture retainer used mainly in brown breads.

Functions of sugar

- Primary yeast foods
- Crust colour
- Some are anti-staling agents
- Some are bread improvers
- Glazes for buns
- Moisture retainers
- Imparts flavour, e.g., treacle, honey, barbadoes and demerara sugar

Fats

Fats have a physical effect on breads rather than any chemical reaction. Fat, being a shortening agent, reduces the toughness of the gluten and gives a mellowness to the final product. Fat also has lubricating effect on the fine gluten strands, giving extra volume to the final product. These strands begin to slip over each other and thus, affect the final quality.

As the amount of fat increases, the fermentation rate decreases. This is because the fat will form a thin layer on the yeast cell membrane, hindering the release and the absorption of the materials. Thus, yeast quantity is slightly increased, e.g., the stollen. Also, when a high quantity of fat is used, it is advisable to use milk, as the milk protein has a tightening effect on the gluten and offsets the excessive shortening.

Effects of fat

- Increases the food value
- Reduces elasticity, softens the crust and the crumb
- Moisture retention
- If used in small amounts, increases volume, used extensively, volume is affected
- Butter and lard give flavour to the product
- If used in large amounts, it retards fermentation

Milk

Milk also has a physical effect on bread in the form of the tightening effect of gluten by the action of casein or the milk protein. However, boiling or pasteurisation neutralizes the effect to a great extent.

Lactose or the milk sugar is the only sugar which is not fermentable by yeast and hence, it remains in the dough right till the end, resulting in a good crust colour.

Milk is generally used in powdered and skimmed form and hence, the amount of water taken up in the dough is slightly more, though not considerably.

Points to be considered when using milk in a bread:

- Check if the milk powder is heat-treated.
- Increase the water content.
- More yeast or diastatic enzymes used.
- Reduce fermentation time, as the water and yeast content is increased.
- Lower baking temperature, as the sugar content is higher and the crust gets coloured quickly.

Malt

It is a raw material that is of great importance in bread making, as it is a yeast food and diastatic malt is also a great bread improver. Malt, as an addition, will assist only if there are certain deficiencies in the constituent balance of the basic materials.

Malt is made primarily from barley, which is sprouted. However, wheat can also be sprouted to increase the malt levels before milling into flour.

When the seed is planted, they begin to germinate, the plumule and the radicle break through the germ. Food is used up from the endosperm till the roots are sufficiently developed. To assimilate these starches and proteins, these are first broken down into simple sugars and simplified nitrogenous compounds by active enzymes.

Malting is the process where conditions are controlled to increase the water-soluble substances and the formation and liberation of enzymes, especially of the diastatic group.

Malt is available in three forms:

1. Malt flour
2. Malt extract
3. Dehydrated malt extract

Malt flour is made by passing the malted grain through roller mills. This is reddish-brown in colour, dry and rich in malt sugar.

Malt extract is made by mixing this flour in water and heating it gradually to 130 °F for 1 hour to convert the starch into sugar. This is then transferred to vacuum pans where excess moisture is extracted to give a brown viscous mass.

Dehydrated malt extract is this malt extract further dried and ground to a fine powder.

Malt can be classified into two types:

1. Diastatic malt
2. Non-diastatic malt

This indicates the presence/absence of the diastatic group of enzymes in the final product. Enzymes are natural nitrogenous products which are denatured or killed at high temperatures.

These are killed at temperatures exceeding 170 °F and hence malt, which is heat-treated is said to be non-diastatic or devoid of enzymes. The diastatic quality is lowered by low heat for long hours and hence, the product label should be read to find out the temperatures at which malt is extracted.

Diastatic malt is usually extracted by soaking it in cold water for a long time to facilitate the solubility of malt in the water.

Flour contains a wide range of enzymes which affect the fermentation process. These include:

- Breakdown of starch into sugar.
- Breakdown of soluble protein into simple nitrogenous compounds.
- Mellowing and ripening of the gluten or insoluble protein.

Diastatic enzymes break down starch into sugar. This content can be measured by a maltose test. If a figure below 1.5 is obtained, then the flour will have insufficient gassing in the final stage. A figure in excess of 2.3 will have excessive gassing and hence, require additional fermentation time. This will cause the bread to have a weak structure, dark crumb and a high crust colour.

A high-maltose flour can be used well in the "salt delayed method" of bread making.

A low-maltose flour requires diastatic malt to contribute to the sugar content as well as diastatic value of the flour.

Qualities of malt

1. Increased volume, due to gluten ripening.
2. Better crust, this is due to the conversion of the available starch to sugar.
3. Better bloom, due to better dough fermentation.
4. Brighter and softer crumb, due to better gluten ripening.
5. Increased food value, flavour and keeping qualities.

Diastatic malt

- Adds flavour
- Increases sugar content
- Breaks down starch to provide sugar
- Proteolitic enzymes modify insoluble protein
- Non-diastatic malt
- Adds flavour
- Increases sugar content

BREAD MAKING PROCESS

There are many methods by which bread can be manufactured. These, however can be classified under three broad headings, which are:

1. Straight dough method
2. Ferment or sponge and dough method
3. Continuous dough method

Straight Dough Method

This is one of the most popular methods of manufacturing breads and is simple and straightforward. The fermentation time can vary from 30 minutes to 14 hours. This is varied by altering the quantities of yeast, salt, and water. The type of flour will affect the time of fermentation. A very strong gluten flour will require a long fermentation time to help in the softening and mellowing of the gluten, and so will a high-maltose flour. However, a whole wheat bread or a germ bread will require a shorter fermentation time due to the high-enzyme activity in the germ of the wheat grain, and the higher water content in the dough. The shortest method is the "no time dough method" which call for a high percentage of yeast (2.5 %) and the dough is directly made, scaled and moulded. This is not a very good method of bread making and must be resorted only in dire circumstances. This method is not very efficient as there is not enough time for the gluten to ripen or mellow down and the bread can be said "to be gassed rather than fermented". The finished product is generally not of good quality and the bread stales quickly because of the insufficient gluten ripening. The bread structure will also show uneven expansion as the gas is not evenly distributed in the gluten network. The bread will lack the characteristic aroma of a well-fermented bread as there is not enough time for the various chemical changes to take place.

Germ breads are made with this method or with 30 minutes fermentation dough due to high-enzymic activity that causes the dough to ripen quickly. The dough is made warm preferably to help develop the flavour of the dough quickly.

The most commonly used straight-dough processes are of 1-5 hours of bulk fermentation. This is the time from the dough making to the scaling of the dough. For this, 3-4 hours are most widely used.

The time of fermentation can be controlled by the moisture content, yeast content, and the salt content. Thus, it will be observed that whole wheat breads are made with 1-hour fermentation as the water absorbed by these doughs is more than in white flour.

The temperature of a dough increases with time as the fermentation is an exothermic reaction, i.e., involving release of some heat energy. Thus, it becomes difficult to control the fermentation process in the long processes. The longer processes are used only when the dough or the gluten is too harsh to be made into a bread and the entire gluten can stand long fermentation strains.

As the fermentation time increases, the gluten softens to a larger extent. Thus, the water content is also reduced. Along with this, the salt content is increased and the yeast content is lowered. This will lower the fermentation rate and help conserve maximum gassing power in the final stages. A very long process is not widely practised and is replaced by a shorter sponge or a ferment and dough process as is described below.

Bulk fermentation (in hr)	Quantity of yeast (in lb)	Dough temperature (in °F)	Salt content in (lb)	Water content (in gallon)
0	7	82	4.5	15.5-16
1	6	82	4.5	15.5-16
2	4.5-5	80	5	15-15.5
3	3-3.5	78	5	15-15.5
4	2.25-2.5	78	5	15-15.5
5	1.75-2	76	5	14.5-15.5
6	1.5	76	5	14.5-15
7	1.25	76	5	14.5-15
8	18 oz	76	5	14.5-15
9	16 oz	75	5	14-15
10	15 oz	74	5	14-14.5
11	14 oz	74	5.25	14-14.5

Ferment/Sponge and Dough Method

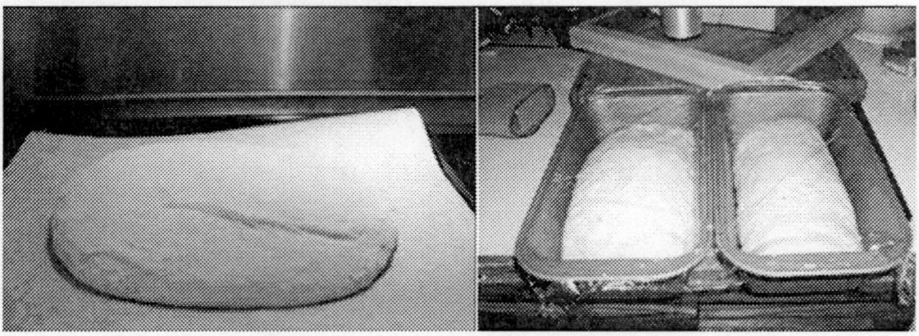

Proofing dough

Breads and buns can be made in two stages to help hasten the fermentation and yet achieve better dough ripening. These are:

(i) **Ferment and dough process:** A ferment is a proportion of water, yeast, yeast food, and flour just enough to make a thin batter. The yeast readily disperses in the water and begins assimilating the food dissolved in water. It begins fermenting immediately and multiplies and is soon active and vigorous. This makes it a first-class condition to undertake the harder work of fermenting the dough. A ferment is made and kept until it shows a sign of collapse. This is when it is considered to be at its optimum for bread fermentation.

This is, however, not necessary as the ferment might be ready in advance. Usually, 30 minutes to 1 hour is sufficient for achieving good results.

A ferment is usually used when the dough to be made is rich and has a high sugar concentration. Usually, the ideal concentration for yeast to work is 10 % sugar. Thus, a ferment made with this concentration will give the bread a boost when the concentration is bound to increase in the final dough, going up to 30 % in buns.

A flying ferment is haphazard guess of water, yeast, sugar and flour which is allowed to stand only till the rest of the ingredients are weighed and the dough is prepared, approximately 10-20 minutes.

(ii) **Sponge and dough process:** A sponge can be said to be a stiffer version of the ferment. The rate of fermentation is hence, lesser and the sponge is kept for a longer time. It is made by mixing a part of the flour, yeast, sugar, and salt (sometimes not), and some or all the water. The speed of the fermentation is controlled by the amount of yeast added, addition of salt, water content and the temperature of both the sponge as well as the holding temperature. When the sponge has dropped down, the remaining materials are added to make a dough which is then given a bulk fermentation.

The size of the sponge in relation to the dough gives the name to the process, or e.g., ¼ sponge, ⅓ sponge, ½ sponge. The sponge quantity will go only uptil 75 % of the dough content.

The main purpose of the sponge is to help develop a mellow flavour which is the result of the long fermentation. This is done without subjecting all the gluten to the harsh fermentation process and thus, staggering the quality of gluten present in the final product. This prevents a weak structure or a collapse of the bread.

In most bakeries, a portion of the previous day's dough is added to achieve this effect. The dough, thus, ripens well at temperature between 5 and 7 °C for a long period of time (16-18 hours minimum) and gives excellent flavour to the bread.

Salt Delayed Bread Making Process

An excellent process used initially for harsh gluten flours but now widely used for all bread making processes as it drastically reduces the fermentation time without giving any change in quality.

This process calls for the omission of salt in the first stage of dough making. As was discussed earlier, salt is helpful in controlling the pace of fermentation by the yeast and hence, when the salt is omitted in the first stages, the action of the yeast will increase. The gluten will ripen or soften well due to the rapid action of the gases released. The chemical changes that take place in the dough will also hasten and the effect of the acids produced will be visible in a short time.

The salt is added later in three ways:

1. By sprinkling the salt over the dough
2. By using some water reserved from the original quantity
3. By using some fat to incorporate the salt

This process is the best method of conditioning a dough without using higher yeast content or an increase in fermentation temperature or time.

The dough is usually given a ⅔rd mixing allowed to rest. This mellows the gluten reasonably. The salt is added at the knock back stage when the rest of the normal mixing time is given to mix the salt evenly in the dough.

Continuous Dough Method

This process was first put to commercial use in U.S.S.R. in 1951 and is very popular there and also in the U.S.A. The process is a speeding up of the old 'barmferment and dough process', though bulk fermentation is eliminated. The fermentation takes place in a brew or a broth, which contains yeast, water, salt, milk solids, malt and yeast foods and is fermented for 6 hours at 100 °F, constantly agitated. The dough ingredients are fed continuously in small amounts into a premixer where under pressure, the dough is developed and conditioned. This is extruded into baking tins. The total mixing time is 90 seconds; 30 seconds in the premixer and 60 seconds in the developer.

Sourdough breads

Also called "mature parent dough", this is the oldest method of leaving a bread dough. This can be attributed to the activity of certain lactic acid bacteria and special yeasts from the atmosphere, the dough begins to ferment and becomes sour. As the yeasts vary from region to region, depending upon the atmospheric conditions and the other external environment, over a period of time, the bread made from these sour doughs gets characteristics of that particular region.

One of the most curious discoveries about the art of bread making is that the yeast present in the sour dough is not *Saccharomyces cerevisae* but is *Saccharomyces exiguous* amongst many others. Exiguous means small or scanty. This implies the condition of the dough as it sours. The acidity of the sour dough exceeds the favourable limits of acidity. Exiguous thrives in an acidic medium and and it cannot metabolize maltose. It is observed that most sour doughs contain lactic acid as the main acid, 75 %, while acetic acid and other acids form the remaining part of the acidic content. The pH of the sour dough lies between 3.8 and 4.5 and hence, has a tightening effect on the gluten. Sour dough is considered to be an excellent rope inhibitor. Sour dough also acts as an anti-staling agent due to the excellent dough conditioning. The lactic acid and acetic acid content is also called the total titrable acid (TTA) content. The pH value is actually a measure of this titrable acid content.

Making a sour dough

The sour dough is developed by leaving the dough to stand for a long time and allowing the wild yeasts to multiply. The acid development can be regulated by controlling the temperature and the moisture content. The lactic acid is developed in a warm and moist dough while the acetic acid is developed in a cool and firm dough. A ripe sour dough has lactic acid and acetic acid in the ratio of 75:25 or 80:20, as high acetic acid has a very strong acidic taste while lactic acid is dull and tasteless.

If microorganisms causing bad taste and bad bread quality are used for a long time, then unwanted yeast will become more conspicuous in the bread at a later date as the sour dough for a long period of time.

It is used in a bread which has a high percentage of wheat flour and is used with a ferment or a sponge in the ratio of 50-100 gm per litre. When storing, it is important not to let it become too sour. This is done by refreshing it every two days, with 1 part of water and 2 parts of flour. This is left at room temperature for 1-2 hours before storing it away.

Finished Dough Temperature

77 °F/25 °C

Dough can be used after 3-4 hours and up to 12 hours at room temperature. The dough can also be refrigerated after 1 hour at room temperature and used up to 36 hours later.

Temperature

It is the temperature of the dough and the room that determines the speed, intensity, and eventually, the time of fermentation. If you can manipulate this variable, you encourage a regulated and nurturing fermentation. Generally, for most of the breads, the ideal temperature during fermentation is 80 °F. In a perfect world, all our elements, air, flour, and water would be at 80 °F, when we stir them together, but this is never the case. In many cases, the temperature of the water is the prime variable. Here is a scientific formula to help you exert control over the temperature of the ingredients by changing the temperature of the water.

Temperature of the flour + temperature of the kitchen + 10 to 14 °F friction factor (this is the amount of heat the dough will gain from being mixed or kneaded). Subtract this total from 240 °F, which would be the ideal total if all ingredients were at 80 °F. The new number indicates what temperature to make the water you combine with the flour. It is important to have all the other ingredients at room temperature (polish, nuts, fruits), so their temperature will be same as the kitchen's and not through another factor into your calculation.

After the dough is kneaded, take its temperature with a long-stemmed thermometer, such as an instant-read thermometer. Be sure the thermometer reads from 0 °F to about 200 °F. The ideal dough temperature is 78 °F. If the final dough temperature is higher than 78 °F, place the dough in a cool place such as the refrigerator.

There are exceptions to these rules, but not the goals and general principles of manipulating the time and temperature of the ingredient at hand.

BREAD IMPROVERS

Flour is of variable quality and hence, it becomes necessary at times to add something to dough to bring the final product to a set standard.

Bread improvers may be divided into three main categories. These include:

1. Those of mineral nature, used by the miller.
2. Those of organic nature, mainly enriching agents.
3. Those of the above categories which are also yeast foods.

Improvers are popular because they increase the yield of the bread by necessitating the use of extra water. Some of the mineral improvers have a slight drying effect on the crumb.

The most commonly used mineral improver is common salt or sodium chloride (NaCl) and it is often a good thing for faults instead of going in for the more expensive improvers.

Mineral Bread Improvers

These include:

1. **Persulphates:** Ammonium or potassium persulphates are used in the ratio of ¼ - ½ oz in 280 lb of flour. These affect the water intake of the flour, which allows for the tightening that takes place as fermentation proceeds.
2. **Potassium bromate:** Bromate has a stabilizing effect on the gluten. This is due to the astringent action on gluten, which necessitates the use of more water. It improves the gas retaining power of the gluten, increasing the loaf volume. It is used in the ratio of 1⁄10 oz per 280 lb of flour and is one of the most effective ingredients and it should be added only if it is not used by the miller.
3. **Sulphates:** Aluminium and copper sulphate were once used extensively in longer fermentation processes, as they delayed the ripening and had a bleaching action on gluten. These, however, are now prohibited by law as they are injurious to health.

   Magnesium sulphates (epsom salts) and sodium sulphate (glauber salts) also have astringent actions. Magnesium sulphate stimulates yeast action, more so in the baking time. It is advised to reduce the salt use when using these sulphates.
4. **Phosphates:** Acid calcium phosphate (ACP) and ammonium phosphate have a tightening action on gluten and in addition to this, phosphates are essential yeast foods. ACP is used 1 lb (pound) per 280 lb of flour, increased to 2 lb to prevent rope of 8 oz ammonium phosphate is used for 280 lb of flour.

Organic Improvers

These include milk and fats. They improve according to ingredients used to make that dough. They improve the texture and quality of the dough.

Yeast Food Improvers

These include malt and sugars, whose roles have also been described earlier.

Three-deck oven with proofing chamber

OVENS

Ovens may be heated by coal, coke, gas, oil, diesel, or electricity. The price of the raw material is not always the only factor which determines the choice of the fuel, as the cheapest fuel may not always be the most economical. This choice depends upon:

1. Availability of material
2. Type of baking
3. Amount of baking & size of oven
4. Usage

Points to be kept in mind while using various types of ovens:

1. Understand the construction and the working of the oven, e.g., the points with higher intensity of heat, methods of controlling the heat, etc.
2. Plan the baking schedule and give enough time for the oven to heat up to the desired temperature before putting in the next product.

Methods of heat transfer

The different methods by which heat is transferred in ovens are:

1. **Conduction:** This is when heat is transferred by the motion of molecules vibrating. Thus, heat is transferred from one part of a metal rod to the other. Thus, in the oven the heat is transferred from the oven floor to the metal trays and then to the food, thus cooking it.
2. **Radiation:** Here, there is no contact between the food particles and the heat source. The cooking comes due to the rays emitted from the heat source. This is the primary method by which surface browning takes place.
3. **Convection:** The actual movement of gasses and liquid molecules to transfer heat from one part to another is called convection. In an oven, the air surrounding the food particles is also heated, which then transfers the heat to the food particles.

Some general points also include:

1. Check temperature with an external thermometer at regular intervals, to keep a check on the thermostat.

2. Load the oven well, only to its maximum capacity with sufficient air space in between them.
3. Plan the baking schedule well to allow for maximum and efficient use of the oven.
4. Close oven doors when not required.
5. Minimum draught of air to minimize heat loss.
6. Regular servicing of the oven.

Types of Ovens

Gas ovens

- Keep a check on the air supply, avoiding excessive air draught.
- Check burners, jets, valves, etc. Clean for maximum efficiency.
- Check burners to maintain the heating efficiency. This will ensure an even distribution of heat in the oven.

Oil / diesel ovens

- Flame should always be checked regularly. Smokeless flame indicates heating effeciency. Smoke shows excess oil in the mixture, while flying sparks show excess air in the flame.
- Keep the burner clean and adjusted.

Electric ovens

- Have internal elements checked for safety and efficiency.
- Pay attention to the top and bottom heat switches and controls for maintaining even heating and economic fuel.

Wood-fired ovens

- These ovens cook food by radiation, conduction and convection and they bring out and enhance the flavours.

- Through these ovens, you get healthy, authentic, refined, inventive and unique dishes.
- Wood-fired cooking is completely natural.
- The wood fired oven is initially very hot and gradually loses its heat until it has cooled.

Steam tube ovens

Invented by Perkins in 1851, stream tube oven is externally heated and is thus, continuous in operation. It is also smoke free as the heat generation is in a different place. The bakery, thus, has a very congenial atmosphere for working.

Principle: The oven works on the principle of induced pressure on water surface, which raises the boiling point of water and the temperature. The oven construction consists of tough cold drawn steel tubes, 15 / 16" diameter. Each tube consists 40 % of the internal volume of distilled water and is heat-sealed.

These are placed in rows on either side of the oven floor. When heat is applied, the water starts boiling at 212 °F. Steam is generated but it cannot escape as the tube is sealed. This increases the boiling point of the water. As the pressure increases, the boiling point increases, eventually water boils at 500 °F. This is then transferred to the oven.

Note: The water pressure at 500 °F is about 700 lb / inch^2 and hence, regular maintenance is necessary.

Advantages

- Continuous baking
- Clean
- No fumes in the bakery
- Can use any kind of fuel

Disadvantages

- High capital outlay
- Danger of bursting of the tubes
- Time needed to raise or lower the temperature

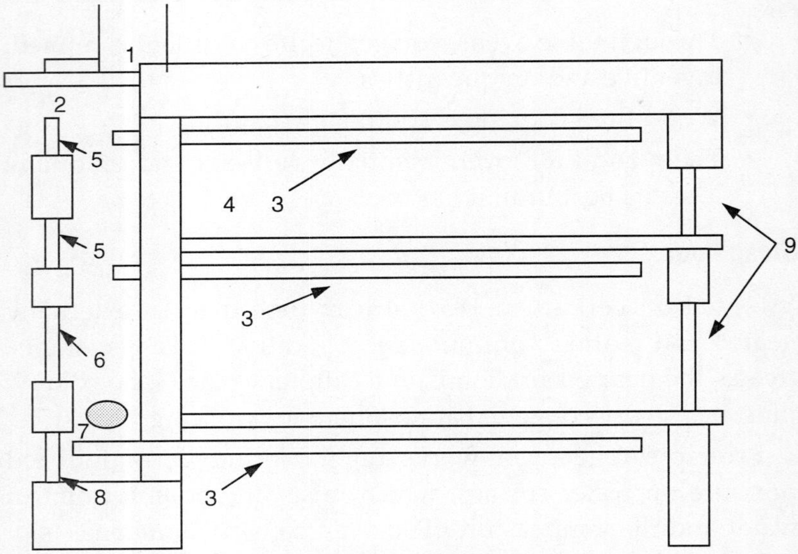

Steam tube ovens

1. Flue
2. Damper
3. Steam tubes
4. Baking chamber
5. Cleaning pots
6. Furnace door
7. Fire
8. Ash pit door
9. Door

Drawplate Ovens

A variation of the traditional ovens which was modified for large scale use. The drawplate oven allows for easy loading and unloading of the goods onto the oven plate. It also allows for a number of people to work simultaneously, thus resulting in speed which was not possible in the traditional ovens.

When the bread is shaped and moulded, it is put on trays of the oven sole and put into proofers. Thus, when it is ready for baking, it is brought to the oven, the oven sole is drawn out and the bread is loaded into the oven.

This is then pushed inside the oven and put for baking. This rests on wheels which allow the bread to be loaded without any jerks. When the bread is baked, the plate is drawn out and the bread is unloaded quickly by a number of people.

Gas ovens

These ovens are a great improvement to the coal-fired or wood-fired ovens as they are much more compact. This is because the burners are placed at the bottom of the oven instead of the sides, as is the case in the earlier ovens. The ovens are also much more heat efficient as the hot air would rise up and the cold air would settle down to be heated again. This gives a convection movement to the air which otherwise is static and baking is not as efficient. The baking atmosphere is also widely improved as smoke-free baking is now possible and this meant not only the bakery but also the surrounding.

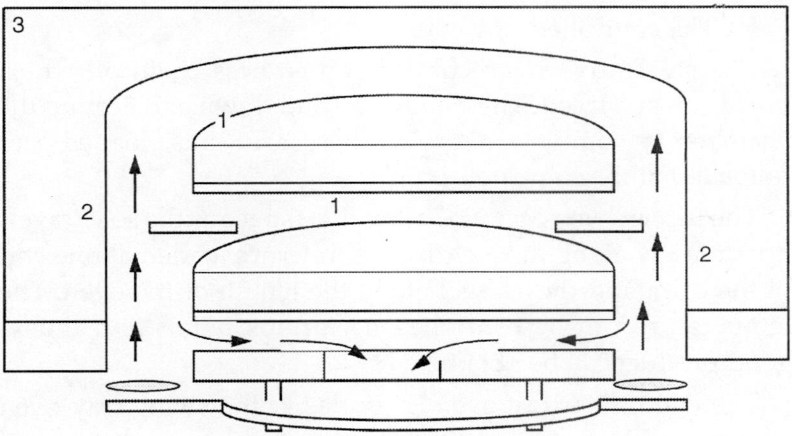

Gas oven

1. Baking chamber 2. Flame with gas pipe 3. Insulated body

Electric ovens

These are more commonly used, though not economical. They are handy, efficient and have excellent baking qualities. They are heated by metal coils on either side of the floor. They can be either peel, drawplate or travelling kind.

Vienna ovens

Very similar to the electric ovens, though small variations have been made to ensure that a steam-saturated atmosphere is maintained for the baking of Vienna breads.

Steam is lighter than air and thus, rises upwards. Thus, the sole of this oven is sloping upwards in two sections; the first one is to facilitate the loading of the oven and is at a very steep angle. The second one is used for baking and is not steep. There is also a steam escape to remove the steam at the end of the baking, to ensure the golden colour and drying out of the crust takes place.

Travelling ovens

This oven is used for uninterrupted baking in the same oven. There are three main types of travelling ovens:

- The swing tray oven
- The tunnel oven
- The controlled tray oven

The swing tray oven contains an endless chain on which bread can be placed. These move up and down and around the chamber to complete a cycle. These are, thus, loaded and unloaded at the same point.

The tunnel oven occupies more floor space as the sole travels horizontally along the length. The trays are loaded at one end of the oven and they travel along the length of the oven. The temperature can be controlled at various points and thus a good product can be obtained.

The controlled tray oven is similar to the swing tray oven with the difference that the trays are held in an horizontal position during their journey through the oven. This is useful in baking goods such as breads, sponges, etc., which would be distorted by the swinging action of the swing tray oven.

Convection ovens

These ovens are based on the principle of turbulent heat. The heat in a conventional oven is static and does not move to a great extent. The bread dough is a bad conductor of heat and it forms a cushion of vapours around it, which insulate it from the surrounding atmosphere. This makes heat penetration difficult, and the bread takes a long time to cook.

In a convection oven, a fan or a blower is used to force the heat onto the bread dough. This turbulence in the heat causes the insulating vapour barrier to break by violent agitation of the hot air. Thus, the heat is constantly in touch with the dough which makes baking a quicker and even process.

The blower ensures even circulation of heat throughout the oven. This facilitates using a greater number of trays at a time as compared to conventional ovens.

This has led to the development of using racks in the oven on which the trays can be loaded, greatly enhancing space efficiency. Some larger ovens even have a trolley on which all the goods are loaded and is transferred to the oven. The oven door is thus kept open for a short time, resulting in saving the energy.

Rotary ovens

A variation of the convection oven was necessitated by the commercialisation of baking techniques. As the quantum of baking increases, the number of trays used in one batch had to be increased. The oven, soon, could not cope with this increased pressure and the baking would not be that even as required.

Thus, very large ovens were fitted with rotating trolleys. These ovens are designed to rotate the trolley around slowly, without any jerks, thus evenly distributing the heat in all the trays at all levels

OTHER EQUIPMENT USED IN BREAD MAKING

1. **Dosed water regulator:** This is an electronic water mixer which provides the desired water at the desired temperature for bread making. This is very useful when water is required at a said temperature in order to maintain the dough temperature at the required level. This can be achieved without the use of ice and makes the process of calculating the amount of ice required.

   Normal range of temperature: 1-60 °C.

2. **Flour siever:** A good bread dough requires loose flour. This is achieved by sieving the flour. This helps make a more homogenous dough and also removes foreign impurities. The machine consists of a bowl into which the flour is emptied. There is a suction motor which sucks in the flour, passes it through a sieve and through a pipe into the machine or storage bins.
3. **Dough mixers:** As the scale of production and increased workload, it made more sense to mechanise things. The dough mixer is an offset of this need. Not only did it speed up the dough making process, it also helped in the even distribution of all the ingredients in the dough and helped in the formation of gluten. It consists of a spiral arm and a kneading bowl. Made from chrome steel or chrome nickel steel, the speed at which the dough hook moves can be controlled for dough making. The bowl is either stationary or rotates in clockwise and anticlockwise directions.

   There are two types of spiral arms. These are spiral kneaders or dough hooks. The dough hook is an older version of commercialisation of dough making. It is not very efficient in kneading the dough, as it moves the dough around in circles rather than knead it through and through. The desired effect is achieved in a longer time. The spiral hook is a newer development and is more human in its kneading techniques. It works the dough in a vertical direction as well as horizontal direction and thus, achieves better gluten formation in less time and more efficiently, i.e., without too much wear and tear of the gluten. This helps in the final crumb texture.

   The rotating bowl is useful in large scale production as the moisture is distributed throughout the dry ingredients and the dough is worked better as the dough is moved from top to bottom and vice versa, regularly.

Most units now have a finger guard through which a grid prevents the hand from accidentally coming into the machine. Most new units also have an inlet for water, so as to remove the cumbersome task of lifting heavy containers of water and avoiding the occasional spill. It could also have the dosed water regulator attached to it.

4. **Proofer:** Yeast and bread's dough require a certain atmosphere while proofing for the final stage. This is usually a temperature of 78-80 °F with a humidity of 80-85%. These are required for two main reasons: the temperature for maintaining an ideal rate of gas production and working of enzymes, while the humidity prevents the bread from forming a skin on top, which will crack on baking. The proofer is an equipment for this.

   However, when the proofer is used, the bread has to be baked when it is proofed. This does not allow the baker to play around with his time and bread cannot be made, shaped and stored for baking as and when required. A retarder / proofer is ideal for this does precisely this. Control the rate of gassing for the bread to be made, and shaped in the evening, while baking can be done at a later stage, i.e., as and when required.

Other Small Equipment

Most traditional professional bakers have more equipment than the home bakers: an electric mixer, a work table, a sharp knife for dividing the dough, a thermometer, a timer, some treasured containers for the dough to rise in, and cabinets, often thermostatically controlled, where the loaves proof. Professionals make bread as a kind of ritual. They place the dough in the same vats for rising in the same corner of the bakery, day-in and day-out. Many home bakers instinctively do the same thing. They possess only a few equipment and use them all the time.

A large clay, wood, or ceramic bowl for mixing the dough and for allowing it to rise. This provides a stable environment that doesn't change temperature quickly. Use this same bowl again and again. If you simply scrape the bowl with a plastic scraper, wipe it clean with a damp cloth, and avoid detergents, it becomes well-seasoned, surviving yeast culture remains in the bowl because you can never kill off all the yeast cells. The old yeast cells enhance the fermentation process and help build flavour in the next dough. If you develop a baking habit, your whole kitchen will be full of yeast cells eager to help your next bread develop.

Weighing scale

A scale is vital. Bakers are incredibly precise about their ingredients. They weigh everything. It is more reliable than measuring cups, and it ensures proper absorption. If you are satisfied with weighing ingredients, you will find that you are less anxious about the quantity and quality. Remember that the exact flour weight varies from brand to brand and also with humidity.

A board or countertop space is essential. Any space as long as it is hard and clean will do. It must also be stable and secure enough to support you and the dough during the kneading process. Wood, marble, formica and stainless-steel surfaces are all fine. Be sure your kneading area is waist high. Sometimes, a couple of inches make all the difference in avoiding kneading fatigue. Shorter bakers could stand on sturdy, shallow boxes in order to reach a comfortable level.

Thermometers are important for the new as well as the experienced baker. You need to know the temperature of everything – the room, the flour, the water, the finished dough, the oven in order to make successful loaves. Buy a good room thermometer, an oven thermometer, and a long-stemmed thermometer that reads from 0 to 200 °F, to stick deep into the flour and the dough. Mercury thermometers are generally more reliable than spring-based models, but the instant read-long thermometers are easy to find and are perfect for taking dough temperature readings. Heavy-duty standing electric mixer like kitchen aid with a dough hook gives you an option to knead by hand, but is not vital. Except for some sweet doughs, which are too sticky to knead with hand, all dough can be successfully kneaded by hand. Use a digital cooking timer that can be set for hours. There are multiple setting timers that allow you to time three items at once perfect when you are preparing a number of dishes and fermenting doughs too.

An assortment of different size bread pans provides variety. Cast iron is really good as it holds heat well, but they are difficult to find. Second best is heavy gauge aluminium rectangular pans in large, medium and small sizes. If you use glass loaves pan, which are a distant third, reduce the oven temperature by 25 °F.

Baskets are a tradition among bakers. You can line them with canvas and raise the dough in them. Soft, moist dough, such as a leavening, needs the support of the basket until the fermentation takes place and the CO_2 gluten partnership holds the bread shape on its own. In European bakeries, there are beautiful willow baskets made especially for certain breads such as German sour dough rise. But you can take any basket or bowl with a diameter of 8 inches and a depth of 3-4 inches and lay inside a clean lightweight linen towel dusted with flour. By letting the dough rise in a cushioned, floured container, you'll get a loaf that will take the shape and markings of the basket and the crust will be thicker and bolder because extra flour is embedded in the dough as it rises. This creates a rustic, earthy-looking crust.

Equipment Used in Bread Making

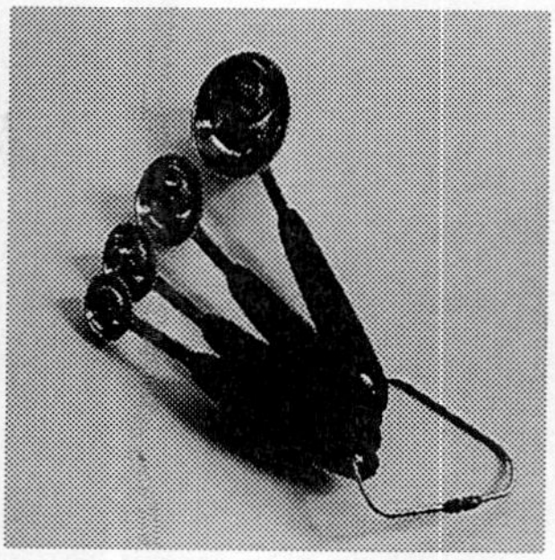

Measuring spoon

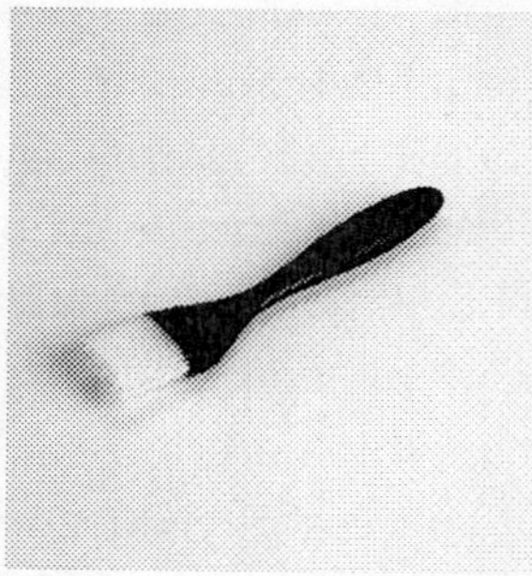

Pastry brush

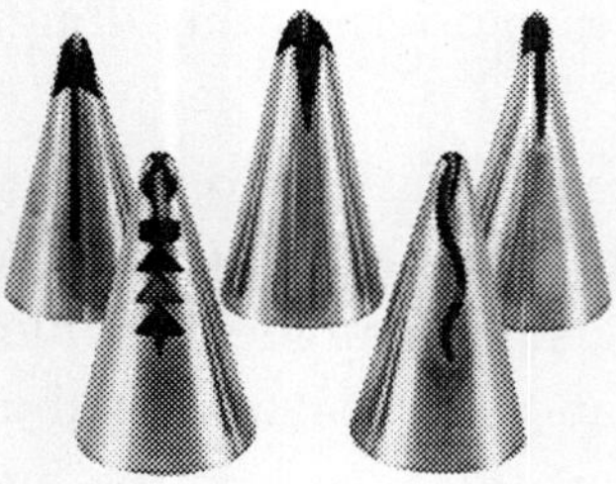

Assorted

Nozzles sieve

Whisk, perforated spoon, perforated flat spoon, ladles

Loaf pan

Rolling pin

Spatula (palate knife)

Tart pan

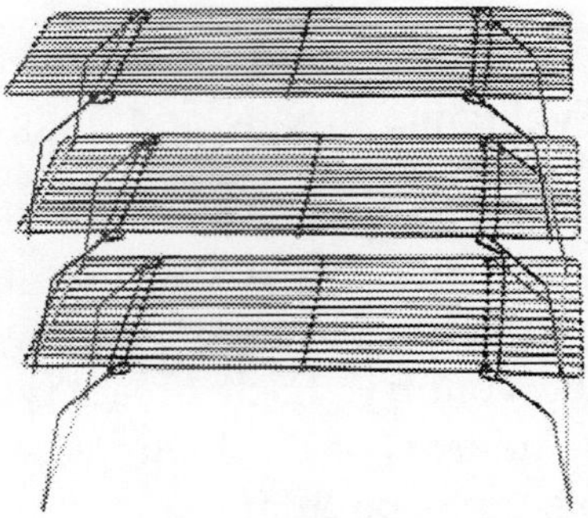

Cooling rack

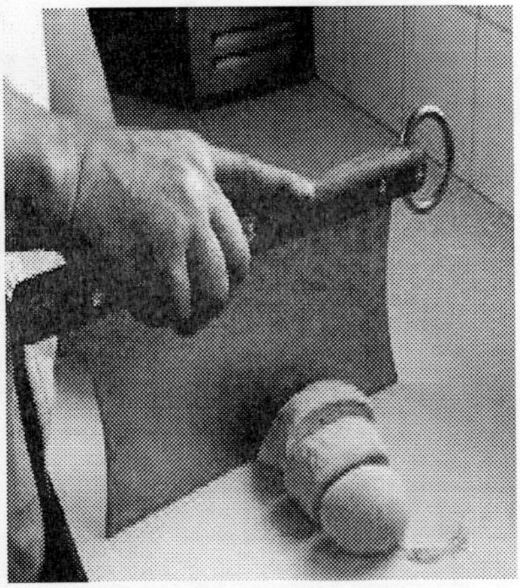

Dough cutter

Dough kneader (three attachments): creamer, whisker & dough kneader

INTERNATIONAL BREAD VARIETIES

No-Time Yeast Raised Doughs

Years ago, bakers made no-time doughs to meet emergency production needs. In countries where quality of wheat and flour were available, bakers found that the weaker flours could produce reasonably good products with the use of chemical additive preparations. The optimum temperature of mixer should be about 78 °F or 26 °C. Proofing of baguettes is usually about 1 hour, depending on conditions.

Evaluating Breads and Rolls

Bakers should be aware that the scoring system for bread and other bakery foods is subject to a great variety of factors that vary from country to country and from area to area and within the country. Each bread type and bakery food has special standards of evaluations; for example, the crusty French baguette, popular in many countries, has variable of crust and volume. Typical or average bread standards must be pre-established, and then point assignments made.

White pan bread

White pan bread is the most popular type of bread made in the United States. It is made of fermented dough that follows the same principles and techniques of fermentation as rolls made up of yeast-raised doughs. The operations involved in making the bread are similar to those of sweet rolls and hard type of rolls.

White pan bread (1 quantity)

Ingredients	Oz	Mixing procedure
Sugar	3	Scale carefully. Dissolve ingredients in water. The temperature of water helps considerably in the rate of fermentation.
Salt	1	
Milk powder	2	
Water	8	

(Contd...)

Yeast	3	Dissolve the yeast and set aside.
Water	8	
Bread flour (pat)	6	Sift, add the flour, stir until absorbed, add the yeast and mix to a dough.
Shortening	2	Add the shortening and develop the dough until smooth.

White mountain bread

White mountain bread is either in round or loaf form. The shape units are given three-four proof and sliced through the top with a sharp knife or blade about half inch deep. The loaf shape is cut through the top centre acid the round shape may be cut across the centre or across the side, after the top is washed with water and lightly dusted with cake flour. It is baked same as white pan bread.

Pullman split-top and round split breads

Pullman bread is similar to the average white pan bread, except it is baked in a pan. It is a square-shaped bread pan with a slightly larger than the average, 1-lb loaf pan. The size varies from 2 to 3-lb loaf. The following recipe may be used for making pullman if a straight dough is not desired.

Ingredients	Oz	Mixing procedures
	Sponge dough	
Sugar	2	Dissolve the yeast in one part of water. Dissolve the sugar and malt in the remaining water. Add the flour and yeast and mix it to a smooth dough. This is the sponge dough. Allow the sponge to rise until it starts to fall back.
Malt	2	
Yeast	6	
Water		
Bread flour	10	
	Final dough	
Sugar	6	Dissolve the sugar, salt, and milk powder in the water. Add to the sponge and mix well to break up the sponge. Add the flour and stir into a dough. Add the shortening and develop the dough.
Milk powder	4	
Salt	2	
Bread flour	10	
Water		
Shortening	4	

French and Italian breads and rolls

French and Italian breads and rolls are bread specialities that have greater sales in many retail bake shops. These breads are generally made by bake shops that specialise in their production. Many bakers purchase these breads and resell them; however, greater sales and prestige accrue to the baker who makes and bakes them on premises.

French bread and oval rolls

Ingredients	Lb	Oz	Mixing procedure
Sugar		2	Blend ingredients together to dissolve.
Salt		2	
Malt		2	
Oil		2	
Water	3		
Yeast		6	Dissolve the yeast and set aside.
Water	1		
Bread flour (high gluten)	7		Sift, add, stir lightly, add the yeast solution, and develop well to a smooth dough.

Baguettes

These are the most popular bread types consumed in most French speaking countries. These are growing popularity of French bread in the U.S. The flour used is carefully aged and not mixed with additives.

Baguettes (10 kg flour)

Ingredients	Lb	Oz	%	Metric	Mixing procedure
Fresh yeast		6-7	2-2.5	200-250 gm	Dissolve the yeast and set aside.
Water	2	4	10	1 l	
Sugar		4	1	85 gm	Mix well to dissolve.
Salt		6	2	575 gm	
Malt		4	1	100 gm	
Water	10-11		50-55	5 l	

(Contd...)

Dough conditioner	50-75 ppm				Add and mix lightly. Add yeast and develop.
Bread flour	22		100		
Shortening		4	1	100 gm	Add in final dough development.

Pistolette rolls

These are oval shaped crisp rolls and are often called petit pain. This is a rich dough used in small amount of sugar.

Ingredients	Lb	Oz	%	Metric	Mixing procedures
Fresh yeast		10	3	350 gm	Dissolve the yeast and set aside.
Water	2	5	5	1 l	
Sugar	10	5	1	175 gm	Stir well to dissolve.
Salt		5	1	175 gm	
Malt syrup		5	1	120 gm	
Water			40	5 l	
Bread flour	20		90	10 kg	
Dough conditioner		¼	0.1	6 gm	Add flour and stir. Add yeast and mix dough. Add shortening and develop.
Shortening		5	1.6	175 gm	

Italian bread, rolls and bread-sticks

Italian bread is similar in many respects to French bread. The similarity exists in the nature of the dough, handling of the dough and the appearance of the baked product.

Ingredients	Mixing procedure
Salt	3 gm
Malt	3 gm
Water	125 mL
Yeast	Dissolve the yeast and set aside.
Water to dissolve yeast	3 mL
Bread flour (high gluten)	Add, stir slightly, add the yeast solution and develop well.

Italian bread (international version) (10 kg)

Ingredients	Lb	Oz	%	Metric	Mixing procedure
Fresh yeast		7	2	190 gm	Dissolve yeast and set aside.
Water	2	5	10	1 l	
Salt		5	1.5-2	150-185 gm	Stir to dissolve.
Malt		4	1	100 gm	
Water	11		50-55	5 l	
Bread flour	20		100	10 kg	Add flour and stir. Add yeast and develop dough.
Dough conditioner		3/4	0.2	20 gm	
Shortening		4	1	100 gm	

Vienna bread

In many respects, it is similar to French and Italian bread. The difference lies in the richness of the dough and the slight variation in the shape of the loaf. Its dough is also similar to that used for hard rolls such as Kaiser rolls. The crust is crisp but not as thick as that of Italian bread.

Bolillos

Bolillos are oval shaped rolls. These are popular bread type in Mexico. They have the appearance of Vienna loaves and are of standard weight. The dough is relaxed for about 20 minutes and then scaled and divided. They may be placed on canvas clothes as for baguettes or placed on lightly greased pan.

Egg bread and rolls

Egg bread is a bread variety of great popularity among people of all faiths. Egg bread is made from a dough that has a high percentage of eggs. Egg provides added richness, increases volume, better-keeping quality and protein. The mixing time is shorter because the dough develops quickly.

Ingredients	Oz	Mixing procedure
Sugar	6	Stir well to dissolve dry ingredients.
Salt	11/4	
Oil	4	
Egg yolk	12	
Water	8	
Yeast	3	Dissolve yeast and set aside.
Water	8	
Bread flour	8	Sift, add and stir lightly. Add yeast and develop well.

Common problems with hard roll

- Rolls lack volume.
- Rolls have too light or too dark a crust colour.
- Rolls have closed grain and very moist texture.
- Rolls firm up soon after baking and have poor shelf life.

Pumpernickel Bread and Rolls

This bread has a darker colour due to pumpernickel flour sugar colour added in it. A sour dough must be used as it is for sour rye bread.

Ingredients	Lb	Oz	Mixing procedure
Salt		10	Break up the sour dough in the water and dissolve salt. Add sugar colour and mix until blended.
Fermented sour dough	8		
Sugar colour			
Water	6		
Water	2		Dissolve the yeast and set aside.
Yeast		9	
Pumpernickel flour	2		Sift and add the flour, stir lightly, add the yeast solution, and develop the dough.
Clear or common flour	15		

Whole wheat bread

Whole wheat bread varies to the percentage of whole wheat flour it contains. It contains bran flakes, which gives the bread coarse grains with a more nut-like flavoured texture.

Ingredients	Oz	Mixing procedure
Sugar	8	Scale carefully and mix ingredients well to dissolve.
Salt	2	
Milk powder	4	
Molasses	3	
Water		
Yeast	6	Dissolve yeast and set aside.
Water (warm)		
Whole wheat flour	3	Sift the flour. Do not remove bran flakes. Add to the above and stir slightly. Add yeast solution and mix until flour is absorbed and dough is formed. Add the shortening and develop to a smooth dough.
Bread flour	4	
Shortening	4	

Peta bread

Peta bread is also known as pocket bread. This bread is packaged soon after baking. It is served with hummus.

Armenian cracker bread-biscocho

This dry, cracker-type bread is quite popular in many restaurants. It has the characteristics of a cracker with its oval shaped interior grain. The process is similar to that of a cracker production, since the dough is very firm can be sheeted readily when relaxed.

BREAD VARIETIES WITH RECIPES

Grissini (Italian Bread Sticks)

These iconic Italian bread sticks are easy to make using this Italian bread stick recipe and taste far better than anything you will get in a restaurant.

S. No.	Ingredients	Quantity
1.	Strong white flour	225 gm (8 oz)
2.	Lukewarm water	135 mL
3.	Extra virgin olive oil	2 tbsp
4.	Salt	1½ tsp
5.	Dried yeast	1½ tsp
6.	Grated parmesan cheese (optional)	1-2 tbsp
7.	Olive oil for brushing	

Method

1. Mix the yeast with water and leave it for 10 minutes to allow the yeast to activate.
2. Sift the flour and salt into a bowl. Make a well in the centre and add yeast in water and olive oil. Mix to a soft, slightly sticky dough.
3. Knead the dough on a floured surface for about 10 minutes until smooth and elastic. (Add parmesan into the dough and knead.)
4. Roll the dough out to about 15 cm × 20 cm (6″ × 8″) on a floured surface. Brush with olive oil, cover and leave to double in bulk (for about 1 hour).
5. Cut the dough in half across the shorter length, then cut each half into 10 strips.
6. Stretch and roll each piece of dough to about 30 cm (12″) long and place on a lightly oiled baking sheet.
7. When the baking sheet is full, brush each piece of dough with olive oil. Leave the baking sheet in a warm place uncovered for about 15 minutes for the dough to rise a little again.
8. Bake the grissini at 200 °C (392 °F) 5-10 minutes, until it is slightly brown. Place on a wire rack to cool.

White Bread

S. No.	Ingredients	Quantity
1.	Refined flour	450 gm
2.	Salt	10 gm
3.	Milk powder	20 gm
4.	Fresh yeast	20 gm
5.	Grain sugar	20 gm
6.	Oil	20 mL
7.	Water	200 mL

Baking temperature = 180 °C

Baking time = 20-25 minutes

Method

1. Sieve the flour and milk powder.
2. Dissolve yeast in lukewarm water and salt-sugar solution in another mug.
3. Pour yeast solution in the flour and mix it well.
4. Add gradually the salt-sugar solution and knead it to a smooth, soft dough.
5. Cream the fat and mix it with the dough.
6. Keep this dough into a greased bowl and put in a wet proofing chamber under a wet cloth for about 30-40 minutes.
7. Remove the dough and knock back and keep it again for proofing for about 30 minutes.
8. Remove the dough from proofing chamber, make dough round in a ball shape and cover it with wet cloth for intermediate proofing for about 10 minutes.
9. Give the shape of bread to the dough and place it in a greased bread mould.
10. Keep the mould in a proofing chamber for final proofing for about 45 minutes.

11. Bake at 180 °C for about 20-25 minutes. Take it out, apply melted fat wash and cool it on a cooling rack for 12-16 hours and cut them into slices and pack.

Brown Bread

S. No.	Ingredients	Quantity
1.	Refined flour	200 gm
2.	Whole wheat flour	200 gm
3.	Salt	5 gm
4.	Cumin seeds	2.5 gm
5.	Fresh yeast	10 gm
6.	Grain sugar	15 gm
7.	Oil	25 mL
8.	Water	200 mL
9.	Caramel colour	25 gm

Baking temperature = 180 °C

Baking time = 20-25 minutes

Method

1. Sieve the flour on a working top.
2. Add and mix cumin seeds and caramel colour in the flour.
3. Dissolve the salt and sugar with lukewarm water and yeast in another mug.
4. Make smooth, soft dough, using yeast, sugar, and creamed fat /oil in the end when dough is ready.
5. Keep in wet proofing chamber for 15 minutes. Knock back it and keep it in proofing chamber again for 10 minutes.
6. When double the size put it into the greased bread mould with the required weight.
7. Keep it for final proofing for about 25-30 minutes.
8. Bake at 180 °C for about 15-20 minutes.
9. Keep it for cooling on a wire rack.

French Bread

S. No.	Ingredients	Quantity
1.	Refined flour	500 gm
2.	Salt	10 gm
3.	Fresh yeast	12 gm
4.	Grain sugar	10 gm
5.	Oil	50 mL
6.	Water	250 mL

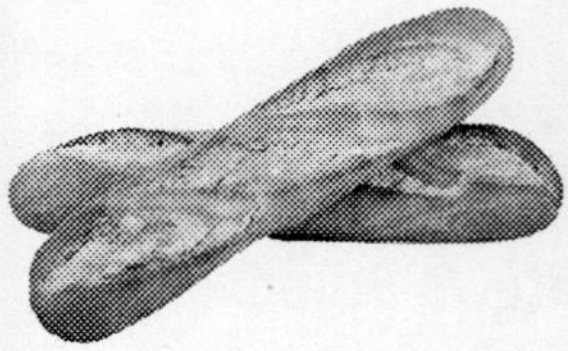

Baking temperature = 180 °C

Baking time = 15-20 minutes

Method

1. Sieve the flour and salt together.
2. Take the yeast and sugar and soak in lukewarm water.
3. Make dough of flour with the help of soaked yeast.
4. Mix oil in the dough and keep it for fermentation in a greased bowl under wet cloth in wet proofing chamber for half an hour.
5. Knock back the dough to original size and again keep it in a wet-proofing chamber for 15-20 minutes.
6. Divide it and keep it for intermediate proofing for 10 minutes.
7. Make required shape of the dough and keep it in a greased-baking tray, egg wash them, give some cuts on top and keep it for final fermentation.
8. Bake it at 180 °C for about 10 minutes.
9. Apply melted fat with brush and cool it. When completely cooled, cut into slices and serve.

Broiche

S. No.	Ingredients	Quantity
1.	Refined flour	200 gm
2.	Salt	5 gm
3.	Fresh yeast	15 gm
4.	Grain sugar	15 gm
5.	Butter / fat	150 gm
6.	Milk	100 mL
7.	Egg	1

Baking temperature = 180 °C

Baking time = 10-15 minutes

Method

1. Sieve the flour on the marble top.
2. Dissolve salt and sugar in half of the lukewarm milk and in the other half, dilute the yeast.
3. Beat the egg in salt and sugar mixture.
4. Pour the salt and sugar mixture into the flour and mix it.
5. Add yeast solution into the flour and knead a soft and smooth dough.
6. Add butter and fold it nicely into the dough.
7. Allow it to ferment for 1 hour. Grease some moulds, remove the dough and punch it.
8. Divide it into 50 gm size, shape them into a BROICHE.
9. Brush them with egg wash and keep it in proofing chamber for 10-15 minutes.
10. Bake at 180 °C for 10-15 minutes. Remove and polish with melted fat.
11. Serve with jam or butter.

Bread Rolls

S. No.	Ingredients	Quantity
1.	Refined flour	225 gm
2.	Salt	5 gm
3.	Milk powder	10 gm
4.	Fresh yeast	10 gm
5.	Grain sugar	10 gm
6.	Oil	10 mL
7.	Water	100 mL
8.	Egg for wash	Half
9.	Poppy seeds	5 gm

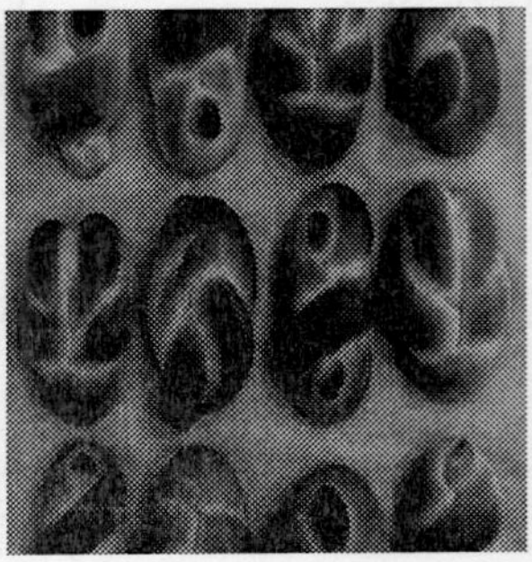

Baking temperature =180 °C

Baking time = 15-20 minutes

Method

1. Sieve the flour along with milk powder on the working top.
2. Dissolve the salt and sugar in lukewarm water and yeast in another mug.
3. Pour yeast solution in the flour and mix it well.
4. Add gradually the salt and sugar solution in the flour mixture and knead it well to a soft dough.
5. Cream fat and mix it with the dough.
6. Keep this dough in wet-proofing chamber for about 15-20 minutes. Take it out and knock back.
7. Again keep it in wet-proofing chamber for about 15-20 minutes and take it out, then divide it in eight portions.
8. Make round smooth balls and keep it under wet cloth in proofing for 10 minutes.
9. Convert them into cylindrical shape and give them required shape.

10. Place on a greased baking tray, give egg wash and sprinkle poppy seeds and keep it for proofing in a wet-proofing chamber for about 15-20 minutes.
11. Bake at 180 °C for about 15-20 minutes or till they obtain nice golden-brown colour.
12. Remove from the oven, apply melted butter or oil for wash and use as required.

BREAD FAULTS

Before discussing the various faults in bread, it is vital to look at the various points on which the bread can be judged:

1. Volume
2. Bloom of crust
3. General shapeliness
4. Colour of the crumb
5. Evenness of texture
6. Sheen of the crumb
7. Moistness
8. Flavour

They may not be necessarily in order of importance, as each one has a vital role to play in guest satisfaction and each person's preference is different.

Skinny Doughs

If a fermented dough is left uncovered in an atmosphere which is not saturated with moisture (80-85 %), water evaporates from the surface of the dough, leaving a skin of the dried ingredients. This skin, once formed, is difficult to eliminate and when a skinny dough is scaled off and moulded, the dry skin breaks off and some which remains on the exterior will get folded into the interior and show as whitish coloured patches, which are hard and knotty.

When moulded dough pieces become skinned, it will give an unsatisfactory bloom to the crust. Also, there will be a number of bursts or 'flying tops'.

Breads From Under Fermented Dough

1. 'Flying tops' and unshapely doughs
2. Lack of volume
3. Uneven texture, showing large irregular holes
4. Lack of sheen or sparkle on the crumb
5. Unsatisfactory crumb colour
6. Lack of flavour and aroma
7. Dry eating, and rapid staling qualities

Most of these faults can be said to be a direct effect of the insufficient gluten ripening. It has already been discussed in detail how fermentation affects the gluten structure and the final flavour of the bread.

When the dough is not fermented long enough, the gluten does not reach its maximum extensibility. As the gluten is not fully extended, the loaf will be smaller in volume. Also, some of the smaller gluten strands will break down under the expansion pressure of the gas creating irregular large holes in the baked product. The sheen of the crumb depends upon there being in any cut surface a sufficient number of fine glossy cell surface to reflect the light. Greater the web-like structure of the gluten, greater will be the reflection of the light.

Bread From Over-Fermented Dough

1. Lack of volume
2. Lack of crust colour or bloom
3. Crumb lacking in sheen
4. Large unsightly holes
5. Crumbliness
6. Acidic flavour in the bread

Longer fermentation time increases the acid production, giving a very sour taste. This coupled with excessive proteolytic activity will weaken the gluten for lack of volume and large holes. It will also give a bad structure to the baked bread which will begin to crumble easily.

Faults from Incorrect Proofing

Even if the dough has been handled with extreme care, it is not completely impossible to waste all these efforts. This is most easily done by incorrect proofing. High proofing temperatures, low humidity, under-proofing, over-proofing, etc., are all common faults, which can happen and spoil the final appearance of the bread.

Under-Proofed Bread

Unless the dough is given a sufficient time to proof, there will be a lack of volume, unless the oven is very cool which again will cause problems like excessive drying out, leathery crusts, etc. An under-proofed bread will lack volume, and have a harsh crumb, ugly bursts which will spoil the shape or some flying tops. If the bread is under-proofed, there will be expansion even though the outer crust has set causing the bread to break from the top or the side,whichever is weaker. The inner unbaked dough will come out giving an ugly appearance. However, a bread baked in a steam-saturated chamber will delay the formation of the crust, thus resulting in very few breads having that fault. This is used in the commercial travelling ovens, which thus give a uniform product.

Over-Proofed Bread

It is difficult to describe the ideal moment when the bread should be loaded into the oven. Generally, this is decided by looking at the product or by pressing it lightly with the fingers. If allowed to prove too much, the bread will be too large in volume, its texture will be open and holey and the crumb will fall away, when the butter is spread. There may be collapsing under the crust, caused by the breaking of over-stretched gluten. The top crust will not fall because the oven heat sets the crust quickly, but the uncooked dough beneath it can thus cause seams and cores in the crumbs.

Bread Baked in a Very Hot Oven

If the oven is too hot and the bread dough is properly proofed, the effect will be the same as in under-proofing. This is because the crust will set too quickly, causing the bread to burst under the internal pressure caused by the gas, water vapour pressure and alcohol pressure. The only difference will be that this will be accompanied by a high crust colour or even a burnt crust with a doughy interior. This again can be prevented by the use of steam in the oven.

Bread Baked in a Cool Oven

Most of the faults that occur due to over-proofing of the bread can also be brought about by baking in a cool oven. Under these conditions, the dough pieces continue to proof in the oven before the yeast is killed and a strong crust is formed, thus, giving all the signs of over-proofing, accompanied by pale crusts, crumbliness, excessive dryness and loss in weight.

Rope

Rope is one of the main diseases that affect the bread. The spores of *Bacillus Mesentericus vulgatus*, the microorganism, are responsible for the development of rope. It is usually present in the flour itself. This is not apparent until the bread is some hours old. This develops in the form of patchiness and the crumb becomes sticky. At the same time, a peculiar odour similar to that of a pineapple develops. This will occur only when the spore is given suitable conditions for it to develop, increase, grow, and so produce an attack of the disease. These conditions include warmth, moistness, and a deficiency of acid in the medium. Spores cannot develop in an acidic medium. Also, as the spores require warm weather rather than cold, it becomes even more important to cool the bread quickly and completely.

Note: The heat of the oven does not destroy all the spores of the microbe.

This can be prevented by using a sour dough in the making of bread. Thus, the bread made from the sour dough, will have a sufficient acid content to prevent the formation of rope. This is called the 'mature parent dough' method.

CHECK YOUR PROGRESS

1. What is blind baking?
2. Write a detailed note on fermentation of bread.
3. Give the recipe for brioche.
4. List the examples of international breads.
5. Write the role of yeast in bread making.
6. Draw the structure of a wheat grain.
7. Describe the equipment used in bread making.
8. Describe the role of ingredients used in bread making.

Unit 16

Meringues

It is light as air and is made by whipping egg whites and is used in a variety of desserts, such as pavlova, macaroons and baked Alaska.

Three basic techniques are used for meringue and each one originates from a different European tradition. French, Swiss and Italian meringues.

FRENCH MERINGUE

Egg whites are beaten until they coagulate and form soft peaks, at which point sugar is slowly incorporated until the mixture attains full volume; and stands at attention when the whip is lifted. French meringue is customarily spooned or piped into different forms, including dessert shells (such as vacherins) and cake layers, and baked, later to be topped with fruit, mousse, or whipped cream. It is also often folded into batters (for lady finger, sponge, cakes, soufflés and the like) and baked.

SWISS MERINGUE

Prepared by gently beating egg whites and sugar in a pan that sits above the boiling water, without touching it. When the mixture reaches 120-130 °F and the sugar is completely dissolved, the mixture is pulled off the heat and beaten vigorously to increase and attain full volume and then at a lower speed until cool and very stiff. Swiss meringue is smoother, silkier, and somewhat denser than French meringue and is often used as a base for buttercream frostings.

ITALIAN MERINGUE

Italian meringue is made by beating egg whites to firm peaks, then slowly whisking in hot sugar syrup to produce a dense meringue with a satiny texture. Whipping continues until the meringues are fully voluminous, satiny, stiff, and cool. Italian meringues are often used to frost cake (alone or as a base for buttercream frostings), to top filled pies or to lighten ice cream, sorbets, and mousses.

PART 3

RECIPES

Pastry Recipes

RECIPE 1

Sweet Paste

S. No.	Ingredients	Quantity
1.	Sugar	200 gm
2.	Shortening	400 gm
3.	Flour	600 gm
4.	Eggs	2
5.	Baking powder	7 gm
6.	Vanilla essence	Few drops

Preparation

1. Cream butter at room temperature.
2. Add equal quantity of sugar & continue creaming.
3. Add refined flour with ¾ tsp salt in it, till the texture is fine for baking & add egg.
4. The sweet paste can be used to make varieties of cookies.

RECIPE 2

Flaky Pastry/Puff Pastry

S. No.	Ingredients	Quantity
1.	Flour	200 gm
2.	Oil / fat	10 gm
3.	Salt	1 gm
4.	Water	100 mL
5.	Rolling fat (pastry margarine)	100 gm
6.	Lime juice	1 drop

Preparation

1. Make dough with the help of flour, water, salt and oil and lime juice. Keep the dough at rest for 15-20 minutes.
2. Roll out dough into a rectangular shape with 1 cm thickness and spread one-third of fat on it and fold like a book. Rest the dough for 15 minutes.
3. Again, roll it and spread the part of fat and again fold it like the book. Repeat the process thrice.
4. Finally, roll it and make the desired product.

Cream Roll

Roll out the dough and cut into thick strips. Roll the strips individually on the moulds and bake. Meanwhile, prepare the filling of cream, by whisking 100 gm of powdered sugar in 1 kg of cream. Pipe the cream into the baked rolls.

Apple Turnovers

Allow 50 gm pastry for each turnover.

1. Roll out the pastry and cut out circles of 12-13 cm in diameter.
2. Place a spoonful of apple, prepared as for apple flan in the centre and lightly brush the edges with egg wash.
3. Fold the pastry in half and seal the edges with the back of a cutter.
4. Place on a baking sheet and brush evenly with egg wash.
5. Bake in an oven at 220 °C.
6. When cooked, dust with icing sugar.
7. Serve hot with custard or vanilla sauce.
8. *Note*: Pears, apricots, cherries and rhubarb can be used in this recipe.

RECIPE 3

Danish Pastry

S. No.	Ingredients	Quantity
1.	Flour	1 kg
2.	Yeast	25 gm
3.	Eggs	2 (egg wash)
4.	Salt	15 gm
5.	Sugar	60 gm
6.	Fat	60 gm
7.	Water	600 mL
8.	Rolling fat	500 gm
For felling		
9.	Milk	500 mL
10.	Custard powder	50 gm
11.	Sugar	100 gm
12.	Cake crumbs	150 gm
13.	Raisins	50 gm
14	Apple jam	100 gm

Preparation

1. Make a dough with the help of flour, yeast, sugar, salt, water and after three-fourths kneading, add liquid fat and make a dough.
2. Roll out the dough after 15-20 minutes and apply a thin layer of rolling fat on it.
3. Fold it like a puff pastry and keep into refrigeration, till the fat is set.
4. Roll out with the help of rolling pin and apply for folding method twice to thrice, according to the strength of flour.
5. Make milk custard with the help of milk, sugar, and custard powder. Cool and keep aside.
6. Add cake crumbs and raisins into it.

7. Now roll out Danish paste into rectangular shape with one-fourth of thickness and cut into square pieces of equal size. Put custard along with crumbs and raisins in the centre. Take all corners and fold them in the centre; and make a square shape.
8. Arrange on a baking tray, keep in proving chamber for 40-45 minutes or till it is done. Apply egg wash on it.
9. Bake at 200 °C for about 20-25 minutes. Take out from oven and apply jam on it. Serve hot as a breakfast roll.

RECIPE 4

Choux Paste

S. No.	Ingredients	Quantity
1.	Refined flour	117 gm
2.	Butter	100 gm
3.	Moisture	180 mL
4.	Egg	3
5.	Vanilla essence	½ tsp

Preparation

1. Place the butter and water in a saucepan. Bring the water to boil and stir until the butter has melted. Remove from the stove.
2. Stir in the sifted flour. Add the flour all at once. Beat until smooth.
3. Return to the heat, and stir vigorously until the mixture leaves the sides of the saucepan and forms a smooth ball.
4. Allow the mixture to cool slightly.
5. Whisk the eggs well and then add them to the choux ball. Beat the eggs into the mixture.
6. Use a piping bag to pipe 7-10 cm lengths for éclairs, or place in spoonful on greased cookie trays for cream puffs or profiteroles.
7. Bake in a hot oven, −220 °C, for 10 minutes. Reduce the heat to 200 °C and continue to cook for 15-20 minutes, or until golden and crisp.

8. Turn the oven off.
9. Remove from the oven and immediately make a small slit in the side of each puff to allow the steam to escape. Return to the oven for a few minutes to help dry them out. The oven has already been turned off.
10. After that, fill the fillings and serve with attractive icings.

RECIPE 5

Profit Rolls

S. No.	Ingredients	Quantity
1.	Basic choux paste	1 part
2.	Whipped cream	200 mL
3.	Any flavouring agent	2-3 drops
4.	Chocolate	1 no.
5.	Milk	1 cup

Preparation

1. Pipe out small bulbs of mixture onto a lightly greased tray, using a savoury bowl and a 10-12 mm plain tube.
2. Space regularly and evenly to ensure even cooking.
3. Bake at 215 °C for 18 minutes.
4. Do not open the oven during cooking as the steamy atmosphere will be lost.
5. Ensure that the filling is fine enough to pass through the pipe.
6. Fill the puffs with whipped cream while seasoning, dip each puff in chocolate or other sauce.
7. Pour over the sauce to coat the pile.

Cream Puffs (Choux a la cream)

Cream puffs are piped and baked in the same way as profiteroles, but the bulbs of choux pastry are made a little larger. Fill with vanilla-flavoured whipped cream, and ice with fondant that is flavoured and coloured with different toppings.

Eclairs

Pipe these with a 10-12 mm plain tube about 10 cm long, and mark lightly with the back of a fork. Bake as for profiteroles. When cold, split one side and fill with whipped cream or flavoured pastry cream. Ice with a good coating of chocolate or coffee fondant.

RECIPE 6

Palmiers

S. No.	Ingredients	Quantity
1.	Flour	1 kg
2.	Shortening	0.5 kg
3.	Refined oil	50 mL
4.	Salt	10 gm
5.	Breakfast sugar	250 gm

Preparation

1. Roll out the puff pastry with one-fourth of thickness.
2. Sprinkle breakfast sugar on it and roll with the rolling pin.
3. Fold it from both sides and keep the folded piece into refrigeration, till it sets.
4. Cut into pieces and arrange on baking sheet.
5. Bake at 190 °C for about 25-30 minutes.

RECIPE 7

Genoise Sponge

S. No.	Ingredients	Quantity
1.	Flour	85 gm
2.	Sugar	85 gm
3.	Eggs	3
4.	Vanilla essence	½ tsp
5.	Melted butter / fat	30 mL

Preparation

1. Before starting this génoise sponge recipe, make sure you have organised all the necessary ingredients.

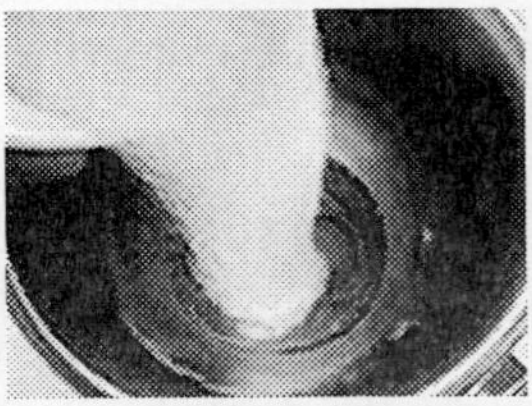

2. Combine the eggs and sugar in a mixing bowl or in the stand mixer recipient.

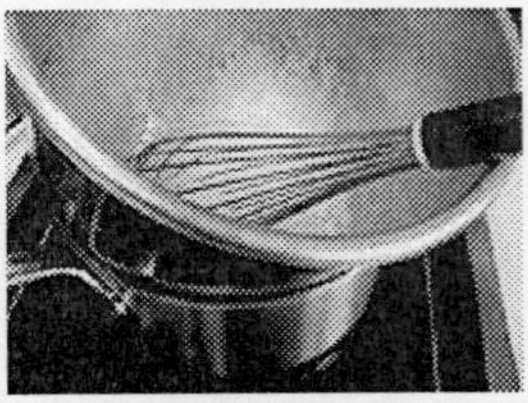

3. Using a hand whisk, beat the preparation over a bain-marie.

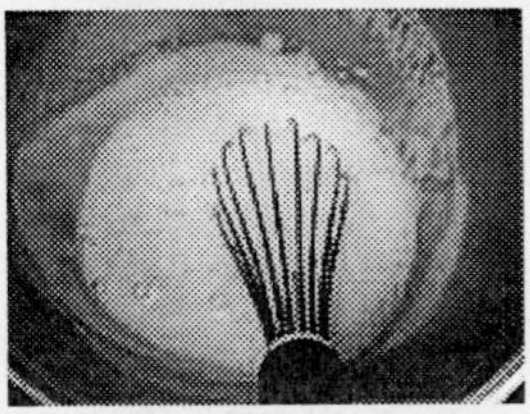

4. The temperature should be roughly 40 °C.

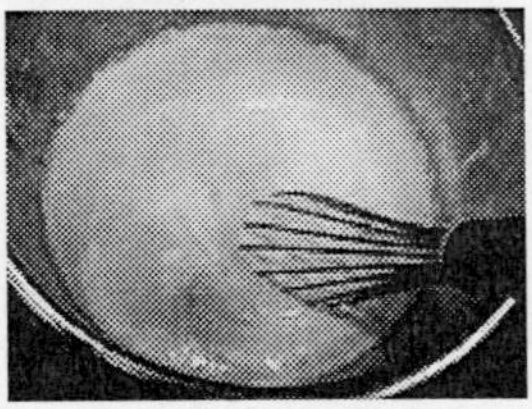

5. Finish beating with an electric whisk, until cooled down completely. If you do not have an electric whisk, you can finish beating manually. The preparation is ready when doubled in volume.

6. Add the sifted flour.

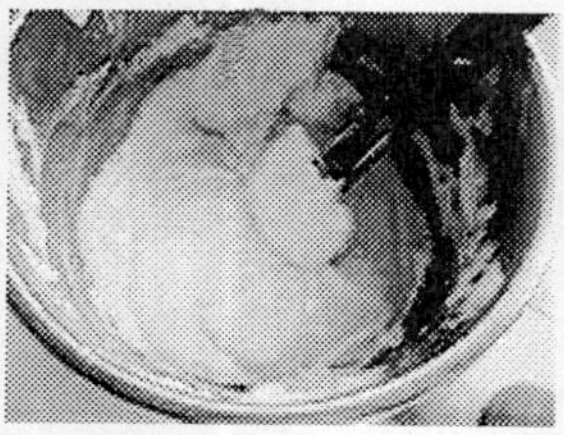

7. Stir gently with a rubber spatula or a skimmer, in rotating motion.

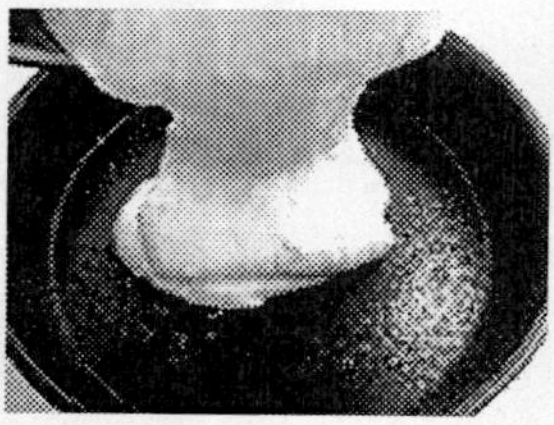

8. Butter and flour a round cake tin. Pour the mixture.

9. Bake at 180 °C.

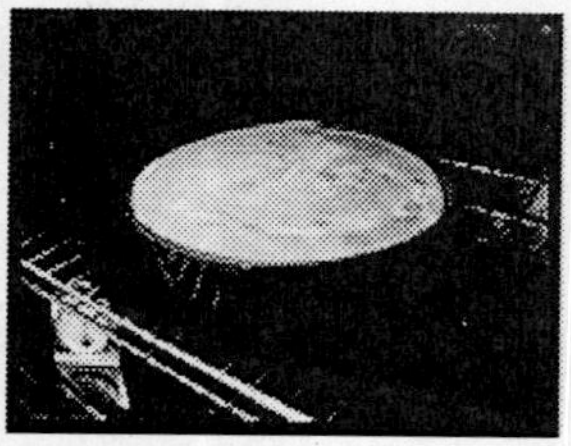

10. The génoise sponge is ready when golden. To check whether the génoise is cooked, insert a knife in the cake. If nothing sticks to the knife, you can remove the dish from the oven.

11. Remove from the mould. Leave to cool on a rack.

RECIPE 8

Butterscotch Sponge

S. No.	Ingredients	Quantity
1.	Flour	85 gm
2.	Golden castor sugar	85 gm
3.	Eggs	3
4.	Yellow colour	Few drops
5.	Melted butter / fat	30 mL
6.	Milk	1 tbsp
7.	Cream cheese	40 gm
8.	Butterscotch essence	Few drops

Preparation

1. Before starting this génoise sponge recipe, make sure you have organised all the necessary ingredients.
2. Combine the eggs and sugar in a mixing bowl or in the stand mixer recipient.
3. Using a hand whisk, beat the preparation over a bain-marie.
4. The temperature should reach roughly 40 °C.
5. Finish beating with an electric whisk until cooled completely. If you do not have an electrical whisk, you can finish manually. The preparation is ready when doubles in volume.
6. Add the sifted flour.
7. Stir gently with a rubber spatula or a skimmer, in rotating motions.
8. Add all ingredients and then, it is ready to mould.
9. Butter and flour a round cake tin. Pour the mixture.
10. Bake at 180 °C.
11. The génoise sponge is ready when golden. To check whether the génoise is cooked, insert a knife in the cake. If nothing sticks to the knife, you can remove the dish from the oven.
12. Remove from the mould. Leave to cool on a rack.

RECIPE 9

Lemon Sponge

S. No.	Ingredients	Quantity
1.	Flour	85 gm
2.	Golden castor sugar	85 gm
3.	Eggs	3
4.	Lemon colour	Few drops
5.	Melted butter / fat	30 mL
6.	Lemon zest 1	1
7.	Milk	1 tbsp
8.	Lemon juice	2 tsp

Preparation

1. Before starting this génoise sponge recipe, make sure you have organised all the necessary ingredients.
2. Combine the eggs and sugar in a mixing bowl or in the stand mixer recipient.
3. Using a hand whisk, beat the preparation over a bain-marie.
4. The temperature should reach roughly 40 °C.
5. Finish beating with an electrical whisk until cooled completely. If you do not have an electrical whisk, you can finish manually. The preparation is ready when doubles in volume.
6. Add the sifted flour.
7. Stir gently with a rubber spatula or a skimmer, in rotating motions.
8. Add all ingredients and pour it into the mould.
9. Butter and flour a round cake tin. Pour the mixture.
10. Bake at 180 °C.
11. The génoise sponge is ready when golden. To check whether the génoise is cooked, insert a knife in the cake. If nothing sticks to the knife, you can remove the dish from the oven.
12. Remove from the mould. Leave to cool on a rack.

RECIPE 10

Fatless Sponge

S. No.	Ingredients	Quantity
1.	Flour	60 gm
2.	Castor sugar	170 gm
3.	Eggs	4
4.	Vanilla essence	Few drops
5.	Cornflour	35 gm
6.	Baking powder	1 tsp

Preparation

1. Separate eggs. Whisk egg whites in sugar.
2. Whisk yolks. Whisk all together.
3. Fold in flour, cornflour and baking powder.
4. Divide between two 20 cm (8″) tins.
5. Bake at 180-190 °C.

RECIPE 11

Swiss Roll

S. No.	Ingredients	Quantity
1.	Butter	For greasing
2.	Castor sugar	125 gm
3.	Eggs	3
4.	Refined flour	125 gm
5.	Warm water	1 tbsp
6.	Jam	200 gm
7.	Icing sugar	For dusting

Preparation

1. Heat the oven to 200 °C/180 °C.
2. Cut a piece of grease-proof paper to fit the base of a Swiss roll tin approx 30 × 25 cm. If you do not have a Swiss roll tin, a roasting tin will do just fine. Grease the

bottom of the tin, then put in the paper and grease that too, dust with castor sugar and a little flour.

3. Beat the eggs and castor sugar in a large bowl with an electric whisk for about 10 minutes. The mixture will almost triple in volume and become pale in colour, it will be thick enough so that when you lift the whisk out of the mixture, it will leave a visible trail on the surface (you will notice this more prominently if you leave the mixture to stand for a minute or so). Sift in the flour in three parts, gently folding it in until the flour is blended in completely. It is important to go slowly and not to be too vigorous or you will lose some of the air in the sponge. Fold in a tablespoon of warm water.
4. Pour the mixture into the prepared tin and smooth it out evenly to the edges. Bake in the middle of the oven for 10-12 minutes, until lightly golden and just firm to the touch. Put the jam in a bowl and stir it so it is spreadable; heat it up a little in the microwave, if necessary.
5. Lay out a clean damp cloth or a couple of sheets of damp kitchen paper on your work surface, this is to stop the paper slipping when you roll the cake. Place a large piece of grease-proof paper that is at least 5 cm bigger than the Swiss roll on top of the cloth. Dust it with castor sugar.
6. Loosen the sponge with a knife and turn it out quickly onto the dusted paper (topside down). You may need to support the sponge with your hand as you turn it. Peel the paper off the sponge. Trim the edges so you have a tidy rectangle.
7. Using a spoon, spread the jam evenly onto the sponge, leaving about 2 cm, clear the edges as the jam will spread when rolling.
8. Make a little incision at the edge of the sponge (not all the way through), about 1 cm from the end of the sponge, and another cut opposite this on the other side. This just helps with the rolling. Roll the shorter side inwards.

9. Now you're ready to roll! The cuts at the edges are to help you start rolling. Use the paper to keep the roll tight. It is best to the take the paper between your index finger and thumb, and use the rest of your fingers to push the roll over. Leave the roll with the seam side down to cool.
10. Dust with a little castor or icing sugar and serve.

RECIPE 12

Rich-Butter Cake

S. No.	Ingredients	Quantity
1.	Butter	250 gm
2.	Breakfast sugar	200 gm
3.	Eggs	3
4.	Refined flour	313 gm
5.	Milk	160 mL
6.	Essence	Few drops
7.	Icing sugar mixture	To serve

Preparation

1. Heat oven to 180 °C / 160 °C, fan-forced. Grease and line an 8 cm deep, 19 cm (base) square cake pan with baking paper.
2. Using an electric mixer, cream butter, castor sugar and vanilla in a medium bowl on medium-high speed until light and fluffy.
3. Add eggs, one at a time, beating to combine. Add half the flour, stir to combine. Add half the milk, stir to combine. Repeat with remaining flour and milk to mix it well.
4. Spread the mixture into a prepared pan. Bake for 1 hour or until a skewer inserted into the centre comes out clean. Stand in pan for 10 minutes. Turn out onto a wire rack to cool. Dust with icing sugar. Serve.

RECIPE 13

Fruit Cake

S. No.	Ingredients	Quantity
1.	Butter	250 gm
2.	Breakfast sugar	250 gm
3.	Eggs	6
4.	Refined flour	250 gm
5.	Mix dry fruits	75 gm
6.	Vanilla essence	Few drops

Preparation

1. Prepare a sponge cake mixture in usual manner.
2. Adjust the consistency with caramel colour and water.
3. Add milk-meshed fruits into the mixture.
4. Pour the mixture into the prepared cake mould.
5. Bake at 180 °C for about 15-20 minutes.
6. Remove and cool on cooling racks. Brush with some sugar wash and cut it into pieces and serve.

RECIPE 14

Dundee Cake

S. No.	Ingredients	Quantity
1.	Butter	175 gm
2.	Brown sugar	175 gm
3.	Eggs	3
4.	Refined flour	225 gm
5.	Dry fruits	400 gm
6.	Orange marmalade	3 tbsp

Preparation

1. Heat the oven to 150 °C and grease and double line 20 cm in loose base cake tin with grease proof paper.
2. Beat the butter and sugar in a bond until very light and fluffy.

3. Add a marmalade and mix for a minute.
4. Slowly add the eggs, one at a time, beating well after each addition.
5. Add the flavour, almonds to the batter, mix slowly until well combined.
6. Stir the mixture, dried fruits and cherries with a large metal spoon. Add milk until well combined.
7. Spoon the mixture into the cake tin, smooth the surface and carefully arrange the blanched almonds in circle on top.
8. Bake for 1½-2 hours, until well risen, firm and golden brown. Test the cake by inserting a skewer into it, if it comes out clean, cake is done.
9. Leave the cake to cool for 10 minutes, then remove from the tin peel of the lining paper.
10. Set aside to cool on a wire rack.

RECIPE 15

Madeira Cake

S. No.	Ingredients	Quantity
1.	Flour	170 gm
2.	Sugar	115 gm
3.	Fat	115 gm
4.	Eggs	3
5.	Baking powder	4 gm
6.	Vanilla essence	3 drops
7.	Yellow colour	Few drops
8.	Lemon essence	Few drops
9.	Orange peel	25 gm

Preparation

1. Take flour along with fat, rub them together to a very grainy texture.
2. Whisk eggs along with sugar, till it is of frothy consistency.

3. Mix rubbed flour into this stiff egg and sugar mixture.
4. Add vanilla essence, yellow colour and lemon essence.
5. Pour the mixture into the lined cake tin mould and arrange a slice of orange peel on top.
6. Bake at 180 °C for about 40 minutes.

RECIPE 16

Honeycomb Mould

S. No.	Ingredients	Quantity
1.	Gelatine	3 tsp
2.	Breakfast sugar	½ cup
3.	Eggs	3 large
4.	Whipping cream	1/3 cup
5.	Milk	1 ½ cup
6.	Lemon	2 zest, juice

Preparation

1. In a 2-quart heavy saucepan, whisk together the egg yolks, lemon zest, gelatin, sugar and cream.
2. Place the saucepan over medium-low heat and warm gently. Meanwhile, warm the milk in the microwave or in another saucepan, until it is hot but not boiling. Whisk into the egg yolk mixture.
3. Cook the egg yolk and milk mixture for 5-10 minutes over medium-low heat, whisking frequently.
4. Heat the custard until it reaches a temperature between 170 and 180 °F. Do not let it boil or go over 185 °F. The custard should coat the back of a spoon.
5. When it reaches this point, set it aside for 5 minutes to cool. Stir in the lemon juice.
6. Using a stand mixer or hand beater, beat the egg whites until they hold stiff peaks. When they make stiff peaks that stand straight up, slowly pour the hot custard into the bowl and fold everything together with a large spatula.

7. Let the mixture sit for a few minutes.
8. Divide the mixture among 8 small glasses or wine glasses or pour it into a medium-sized bowl (spray it lightly first with cooking spray). Cover the dishes and refrigerate for at least 2 hours for small glasses, and overnight for a full bowl.
9. Top with a touch of whipped cream.
10. To demould the large mould, run a thin knife around the edge, dip the mould quickly into hot water and invert it onto a plate.
11. Serve with attractive platting.

RECIPE 17

Chocolate Mousse

S. No.	Ingredients	Quantity
1.	Milk	300 mL
2.	Sugar	100 gm
3.	Gelatine	20 gm
4.	Cocoa powder	30 gm
5.	Glazed cherry	1
6.	Cream	400 mL
7.	Egg yolk	3
8.	Egg white	5

Preparation

1. Place sugar in a bowl and add milk and mixture with a wooden spoon.
2. Take hot milk gradually and go on stirring, put this mixture in room temperature.
3. Beat the chilled cream till it just thickens.
4. Make a mixture of cocoa powder and milk. Mix it well with all.
5. Add diluted gelatine and mix it well. Finally, pour this mixture into greased jelly mould.
6. Allow it to set for 2-3 hours. Demould it in a service dish and garnish it with cherries.

RECIPE 18

Mousse au Chocolate

S. No.	Ingredients	Quantity
1.	Milk	1 L
2.	Sugar	200 gm
3.	Cornflour	40 gm
4.	Cocoa powder	100 gm
5.	Gelatine	50 gm
6.	Chocolate	200 gm
7.	Whipped cream	1 kg

Preparation

1. Add sugar in milk and heat it.
2. When it begins to heat, add cocoa powder and cornflour.
3. When it is at boiling stage, add gelatine (dissolve in lukewarm water).
4. Now put the mixture in a bowl and put the bowl on an ice bowl.
5. Stir till the consistency is similar to the whipped cream.
6. Mix the cream and mixture together.

RECIPE 19

Coffee Mousse

S. No.	Ingredients	Quantity
1.	Milk	300 mL
2.	Breakfast sugar	100 gm
3.	Gelatine	20 gm
4.	Coffee powder	20 gm
5.	Glazed cherry	1
6.	Whipped cream	400 mL
7.	Egg yolk	3
8.	Egg white	5

Preparation

1. Place sugar in a bowl and cream with a wooden spoon.

2. Add hot milk gradually and go on stirring. Put this mixture at room temperature. Take small amount of water for double boiling.
3. Remove it and soak gelatine in it.
4. Beat the chilled cream till it just thickens.
5. Mix dissolved coffee powder in a greased jelly mould.
6. Allow it to set the freezer for 2-3 hours.
7. After it gets set, demould it in a serving dish and decorate the top with sweetened cream and cherry.
8. Serve cold.

RECIPE 20

Lemon Soufflé

S. No.	Ingredients	Quantity
	White vanilla sauce	
1.	Milk	300 mL
2.	Sugar	30 gm
3.	Vanilla essence	Few drops
4.	Flour	40 gm
5.	Butter	40 gm
6.	Egg yolks	40 mL (2)
	Meringue	
7.	Egg whites	2
8.	Castor sugar	20 gm

Preparation

1. Prepare the soufflé dishes by greasing well with butter and dredging with sugar.
2. Making white vanilla sauce:
   (a) Heat the milk and vanilla bean in a saucepan. Add the sugar and dissolve it. Infuse the vanilla bean.
   (b) Make a white roux using the butter and flour.

(c) Remove the vanilla bean, and add the milk to make a smooth sauce.

(d) Cook gently for 5 minutes, stirring occasionally to prevent burning and to prevent skin from forming.

(e) Cool the mixture, but while still warm, add the egg yolks one at a time. Keep warm in a bain-marie. (If using essence, add the vanilla now.)

3. Make a meringue. Whisk the egg whites to froth. Add the sugar and whisk to a firm peak.
4. Fold the egg whites into the sauce with a metal spatula.
5. Pour the mixture into the prepared moulds so that each is three-quarters full.
6. Bake in an oven at 175-180 °C for about 25 minutes.

RECIPE 21

Pineapple Soufflé

S. No.	Ingredients	Quantity
1.	Milk	1 L
2.	Grain sugar	200 gm
3.	Eggs	10
4.	Vanilla essence	10 mL
5.	Fresh cream	1 kg
6.	Sugar powder	100 gm
7.	Pineapple slice	250 gm
8.	Yellow colour	As required
9.	Gelatine	50 gm
10.	Cherries	200 gm
11.	Water	150 mL

Preparation

1. Prepare the egg custard, taking milk, sugar, eggs and vanilla essence.
2. Dissolve gelatine into water, till it is transparent and grain free.

3. Mix into hot egg custard.
4. Whip fresh cream, along with powdered sugar to a thick consistency.
5. Take custard on the ice bed and cool it, stirring it continuously like whipped cream.
6. Mix whipped cream into the cool custard and mix uniformly.
7. Add yellow colour, pineapple essence and slices.
8. Pour the mixture in the serving dish or moulds and put in refrigeration for about 2 hours.
9. Remove it from the fridge and demould, if required.
10. Decorate with whipped cream, pineapple slices, cherries and serve cold.

RECIPE 22

Vanilla Souffle

S. No.	Ingredients	Quantity
	White vanilla sauce	
1.	Milk	300 mL
2.	Sugar	30 gm
3.	Vanilla bean or essence	1
4.	Flour	40 gm
5.	Butter	40 gm
6.	Egg yolk	40 mL
	Meringue	
1.	Egg white	50-60 gm
2.	Castor sugar	20 gm

Preparation

1. Prepare the soufflé dishes by greasing well with butter and dredging with sugar.
2. Making white vanilla sauce:
   (a) Heat the milk and vanilla bean in a sauce pan. Add the sugar and dissolve it. Infuse the vanilla bean.
   (b) Make a white roux using the butter and flour. Allow to cool

(c) Remove the vanilla bean, and add the milk to make a smooth sauce.

(d) Cook gently for 5 minutes, stirring occasionally to prevent burning and to prevent a skin layer from forming.

(e) Cool the mixture, but while still warm, add the egg yolk one at a time. Keep warm in a bain-marie. (If using essence, add the vanilla now.)

3. Make a meringue. Whisk the egg white to froth. Add the sugar and whisk to a firm peak.
4. Fold the egg whites into the sauce with a metal spatula.
5. Pour the mixture into prepared moulds so that each is three-quarters full.
6. Bake in an oven at 175-180 °C for about 25 minutes.

RECIPE 23

Bread and Butter Pudding

S. No.	Ingredients	Quantity
1.	Bread	3
2.	Milk	3 L
3.	Sugar	200 gm
4.	Egg	24
5.	Butter	200 gm
6.	Dry fruits – Kaju – Kishmish	150 gm (each)
7.	Vanilla essence	7 mL

Preparation

1. Cut bread into slices and put them in a baking tray.
2. Mix milk, sugar, vanilla essence, eggs and pour it over the bread pieces.
3. Press slices of bread, so that it completely submerges in the mixture.
4. Bake at about 150 °C, for about 20-25 minutes.

RECIPE 24

Caramel Custard

S. No.	Ingredients	Quantity
1.	Milk	1 L
2.	Sugar	200 gm
3.	Eggs	9
4.	Vanilla essence	Few drops
5.	Sugar for caramel	300 gm

Preparation

1. Take 300 gm grain sugar in a non-stick pan and keep it on fire. Stir it continuously till the sugar gets melted and is light brown in colour.
2. Pour sugar caramel into a clean mould.
3. Take milk, sugar and eggs, mix them nicely. Pass the mixture through the muslin cloth or strainer.
4. Fill the caramel mould with the mixture and keep the mould into the baking tray.
5. Pour water into the tray and keep it in the oven.
6. Steam at 170 °C (moderate).

RECIPE 25

Albert Pudding

S. No.	Ingredients	Quantity
1.	Refined flour	170 gm
2.	Baking powder	½ tsp
3.	Eggs	2
4.	Sugar	115 gm
5.	Margarine	115 gm
6.	Glazed cherries	15 gm
7.	Milk	1 tsp

Preparation

1. Cream margarine and sugar. Beat eggs and add gradually. Beat mixture well, with each addition of egg.
2. Shift flour and baking powder together and fold it gradually.
3. Grease a pudding mould and decorate with glazed cherries.
4. Pour over the mixture to fill three-fourths of the basin / baking mould.
5. Cover with greased proof paper and steam for 1 ½ hour.
6. Serve hot with Melba sauce.

RECIPE 26

Christmas Pudding

S. No.	Ingredients	Quantity
1.	Sultanas	50 gm
2.	Cherry	30 gm
3.	Raisins	30 gm
4.	Tooty fruity	50 gm
5.	Lemon zest	½
6.	Lemon juice	1 tsp
7.	Rum (old monk)	500 mL
8.	Brandy	500 mL
9.	Whiskey	500 mL
10.	Refined flour	100 gm
11.	Sugar	100 gm
12.	Butter	100 gm
13.	Spices	To taste
14.	Cinnamon	2 sticks
15.	Black paper	4
16.	Orange (for rind)	½
17.	Orange (juice)	½

Preparation

1. Heat oven to 150 °C. Grease a deep 22 cm round cake pan with melted butter, line the base and sides with three layers of non-stick baking pan. Line up paper.
2. Combine the dried fruits with useful cuts, orange rind and orange juice in a large saucepan over medium low heat. Remove from heat and set aside for 30 min to cool. Once the fruit softens, add brandy in it. Mix it well. Soak it for some time.
3. Add butter and sugar to fruit mixture and add the flour with mixed spices.
4. Add eggs, mix well to make a smooth batter. After that, put this mixture into a pan. Add almonds on top.
5. Bake this into a preheated oven.
6. After 20-30 minutes when it's done, serve it.

RECIPE 27

Plum Pudding

S. No.	Ingredients	Quantity
1.	Raisins	370 gm
2.	Currants	250 gm
3.	Sultanas	140 gm
4.	Craisins (dried cranberries)	150 gm
5.	Rum	250 mL
6.	Melted butter	To grease
7.	Butter	240 gm
8.	Brown sugar	180 gm
9.	Eggs	4
10.	Sponge crumbs	150 gm
11.	Refined flour	140 gm
12.	Mixed spices	1 tsp
13.	Ground cinnamon	1 tsp

Preparation

1. Combine raisins, currants, sultanas, craisins and rum in a bowl. Set aside for 6 hours to macerate.
2. Brush a pudding basin with melted butter to grease. Line the base with baking paper.
3. Use an electric beater to beat the butter and sugar in a bowl, until mixed well and creamy. Add egg one by one. Stir in sponge crumbs, combined flour, mixed spices and cinnamon. Add raisins and mix well.
4. Place an upturned heat-proof saucer in the base of the saucepan. Fill one-third of the saucepan with boiling water and bring it to a simmer over low heat.
5. Repeat it twice after the whole procedure. Check if it is done or not, once it's done, serve hot at room temperature with some toppings.

RECIPE 28

Cabinet Pudding

S. No.	Ingredients	Quantity
1.	Bread	225 gm
2.	Eggs	2
3.	Salted butter	30 gm
4.	Milk	300 mL
5.	Sugar	100 gm
6.	Sultanas	55 gm
7.	Cashew nuts	30 gm
8.	Lemon juice	Few drops
9.	Lime rind	½ slice

Preparation

1. Grease the pudding mould and decorate bottom and sides with nuts and sultanas.

2. Butter the slices of bread, cut off the crust and cut bread into cubes.
3. Arrange a layer of bread into the mould and sprinkle with sultanas and sugar. Continue in layers, till mould is half full.
4. Beat eggs in a bowl, boil milk and pour; pour beaten eggs and stir well. Add the flavouring and some sugar.
5. Pour over bread and let it stand for 90 minutes, soak bread thoroughly. Cover the mould with butter paper & steam for an hour.
6. Turnover and serve hot with jam sauce (Melba sauce) or custard sauce.

RECIPE 29

Queen of Pudding

S. No.	Ingredients	Quantity
1.	Milk	250 mL
2.	Butter	30 gm
3.	Fresh bread	115 gm
4.	Jam	30 gm
5.	Lime rinds	A little
6.	Eggs	2
7.	Sugar	55 gm

Preparation

1. Heat milk and butter together and pour over the bread.
2. Add half the sugar, egg yolk and grated lime rind.
3. Mix well and allow to stand for half an hour. Pour into the greased pie dish and bake till quite firm.
4. Heat jam and spread over the pudding. Beat egg white stiffy, fold in sugar and pile on the pudding.
5. Bake in the oven for about 15 minutes, till the meringue is set and is pale brown.

RECIPE 30

Bavaroie

S. No.	Ingredients	Quantity
1.	Egg	2
2.	Breakfast sugar	50 gm
3.	Milk	180 mL
4.	Vanilla pod	1
5.	Gelatine	4 leaves
6.	Double cream	240 mL
7.	Strawberries	4

Preparation

1. Separate the egg, putting the yolks into a clean bowl and saving the whites for another use.
2. Add the sugar to the bowl.
3. Pour the milk into a saucepan.
4. Split the vanilla pod into half lengthways, scrape out the seeds and add to the milk. Also add the pod itself to the milk. Allow it to stand for a while to help infuse the vanilla flavour into the milk.
5. Soak the gelatin in a bowl of cold water. You will find that it soon goes limp.
6. Place the milk onto the hob over a low heat and bring almost to the boil.
7. Meanwhile, using a small electric whisk, whisk the egg yolks and sugar until they become thick and creamy and pale.
8. When the milk is almost boiling, remove it from the hob and carefully pour over the egg mixture, stirring constantly with a wooden spoon. Now, pour the mixture back into the saucepan and return to the hob over a low heat. Keep stirring with the spoon until the mixture begins to thicken slightly, until it coats the back of your spoon. Do not allow the mixture to boil.

9. Remove from the heat.
10. Take the leaf gelatin between your fingers and squeeze out all the excess water and place it in the mixture. They will dissolve in a few seconds.
11. Pass the mixture through a fine strainer into a clean bowl. Allow it to cool. Keep stirring from time to time.
12. When the mixture is cool enough, place the vanilla bavarois in the fridge.
13. Lightly whisk the double cream into soft peaks.
14. When the mixture in the fridge is almost about to set, remove the vanilla bavarois cake from the fridge and gently fold into the whisked cream. Mix well. Ladle into the moulds and return to the fridge to finish setting for about 2 hours.
15. When ready to serve, garnish it with whipped cream and fresh fruits.

RECIPE 31

Baba au Rhum

S. No.	Ingredients	Quantity
1.	Savarin paste	1 mixing
2.	Refined flour	225 gm
3.	Yeast	30 gm
4.	Sugar	50 gm
5.	Egg	4-5
6.	Salt	½ tsp
7.	Milk	50 mL
8.	Butter	150 gm
9.	Currants	50 gm
10.	Sweet cream	100 gm
11.	Apricot jam	100 gm
12.	Glazed cherry	30 gm
13.	Rum	30 mL

Preparation

1. Mix 50 gm of washed, picked currant into a savarin dough.
2. Fill two-thirds well greased baba moulds with the mixture; proving is done until double in size.
3. Bake at 420 °F for 10-15 minutes, and then reduce the temperature to 160 °C and bake for another 15 minutes until dry.
4. Soak it in hot savarin syrup, pineapple with rum, brushed with hot apricot jam in order to serve.
5. Place on a slices flat disk; chill and decorate the top with sweet cream, garnish with half cherry on top.
6. Serve as desired.

RECIPE 32

Chocolate Parfait

S. No.	Ingredients	Quantity
1.	Egg yolk	1
2.	Egg white	3
3.	Salt	1 pinch
4.	Dark chocolate	100 gm
5.	Cookies	1 packet
6.	Butter	1 tbsp
7.	Cinnamon powder	For flavour
8.	Nuts	For garnish

Preparation

1. Chop the dark chocolate and melt in double boiler.
2. Melt sugar with water, i.e., 50 mL and boil them.
3. Whip the cream.
4. Mix the cream and the syrup.
5. Whisk yolk and mix with chocolate.
6. Mix syrup with chocolate and whisk the remaining cream.

7. Pour in glass or a parfait glass cover along with film and keep it in freezer, till chilled.

RECIPE 33

Tart Tartin

S. No.	Ingredients	Quantity
	For short crust pastry	
1.	Refined flour	300 gm
2.	Butter	142 gm
3.	Icing sugar	75 gm
4.	Salt	½ tsp
5.	Almonds	1/3 cup
6.	Egg	1
	For the apples	
7.	Apples	4
8.	Sugar	60 gm
9.	Butter	100 gm
10.	Lemon juice	1 tbsp
11.	Salt	1 pinch
12.	Vanilla	Few drops

Preparation

Short crust pastry

1. In the bowl of a stand mixer, mix the butter and icing sugar at medium speed for a few minutes until reaching a sandy texture.
2. Add salt and almonds and mix for one minute.
3. Add the egg and continue mixing for one minute.
4. Add the flour and mix very quickly until reaching a homogeneous dough.
5. Spread the dough between two sheets of parchment paper to a thickness of about ¼ inch, trying to give it the shape of the mould that will be used for baking.
6. Place the dough in the refrigerator for 4 hours or even overnight.

Apples

1. Heat the oven to 400 °F.
2. Melt the butter in a saucepan over low heat. Add the sugar and stir for 2-3 minutes.
3. Split the vanilla bean in half and extract the seeds. Add lemon juice and vanilla seeds to the saucepan, and stir.
4. Pour the whole mixture in a spring-formed pan and bake for 15 minutes.
5. Remove the pan from the oven and let it cool.
6. Place apples on top of the caramel, with the curved part facing the mould. Sprinkle lightly with fleur de sel.

Pie assembly and baking

1. Remove the dough from the refrigerator and place it on the apples, making sure to fold the edges inside around the mould.
2. Make two light cross-shaped incisions in the middle of the dough using a knife.
3. Bake for about 15-20 minutes or until golden.
4. Remove from the oven and wait at least 10 minutes before unmoulding.

RECIPE 34

Crepe Suzette

S. No.	Ingredients	Quantity
1.	Refined flour	11/2 cup
2.	Salt	A pinch
3.	Egg	3
4.	Breakfast sugar	½ cup
5.	Milk	2 cups
6.	Orange liqueur	1 tbsp
7.	Vanilla essence	1 tsp
8.	Orange zest	1 tbsp
9.	Butter clarified	½ cup

Preparation

1. Whisk together the refined flour and salt in a medium bowl.
2. Whisk together the egg and sugar in a large bowl, until whisked in a 1½ cup of the milk, orange liqueur, vanilla essence, orange zest and flavour, and combine.
3. If the mixture is too thick, add the remaining milk until a thin consistency is achieved.
4. Cover and refrigerator the batter for 30 minutes.
5. Heat on 8-inch syrup suzette pan or skillet over a medium for about 1 minute.
6. Cover the surface of the pan with clarified butter until it gets sizzling hot.
7. Ladle some butter onto the middle of the suzette pan and immediately start swirling the pan to distribute the butter over the surface.
8. Cook for 45-60 seconds or until lightly golden brown.
9. Flip over and cook the other side for 20 seconds.
10. Remove to a plate and repeat with the remaining batter.

RECIPE 35

Crepe Suette Sauce

S. No.	Ingredients	Quantity
1.	Orange, peeled	3 no.
2.	Orange juice	11/2 cup
3.	Sugar	2 tbsp
4.	Orange zest	2 tbsp
5.	Orange liqueur	2 tbsp
6.	Vanilla ice cream	As per serving

Preparation

1. In a large skillet over high heat, bring the orange juice to boil.

2. Add the sugar and orange zest, reduce the heat to a simmer and cook until the sugar is melted and the mixture is slightly reduced for about 5 minutes.
3. Remove from the heat and add the orange liqueur.
4. Orange slice sections are set aside.
5. Working in batches, gently place syrup into the pan holding the orange juice and orange sections, leave for 1 minute to absorb some juice using a narrow spatula, remove the syrup to a warm serving plate.
6. Repeat with remaining syrup.
7. Roll the syrup into a cylinder spoon on some of the orange sections.
8. Serve two syrups per person.
9. Garnish with vanilla ice cream scoop and serve immediately.

RECIPE 36

Chocolate Cream Puff

S. No.	Ingredients	Quantity
1.	Puff paste	1 mixing
2.	Chocolate glaze	1 mixing
3.	Sugar	450 gm
4.	Cream	300 gm
5.	Water	300 mL
6.	Cocoa powder	150 gm
7.	Gelatine	20 gm
8.	Water	60 mL for soaking gelatine

Preparation

1. Prepare puff pastry in usual manner
2. Finally, roll out the pastry approve 1/8″ thickness and cut into stripes and approve 1-½″ width.
3. Clean the cream cones and wrap the strips of puff, i.e., cream roll.

4. Egg wash the rolls and bake at 190 °C for about 15-20 minutes.
5. Place the cones on cooking rack and remove the cones from the shelf.
6. Fill the shelfs with chocolate glaze and serve.

RECIPE 37

Coffee Crème Brulee

S. No.	Ingredients	Quantity
1.	Yolk of eggs	12
2.	Coffee soaked	12 gm
3.	Breakfast sugar	100 gm
4.	Cream	500 gm

Preparation

1. Mix dough, sugar, cream and soaked coffee.
2. Keep it in a small bowl till three-fourths and bake in oven at 140 °C for 25 minutes, till it sets.
3. Sprinkle some brown sugar on top of custard and bake again for another 2 minutes on high temperature so that sugar caramelizes.
4. Serve hot or cold as desert.

RECIPE 38

Soufflé Milanaise

S. No.	Ingredients	Quantity
1.	Eggs	3
2.	Breakfast sugar	85 gm
3.	Water	25 mL
4.	Lemon	1
5.	Cream	500 mL
6.	Lemon essence	Few drops
7.	Yellow lemon	Few drops
8.	Gelatine	15 gm

Preparation

1. Soak gelatine in water.
2. Separate egg yolks and egg white.
3. Add sugar in it and dissolve it.
4. Put this in a double boiler.
5. Remove the mixture from the double boiler.
6. Add cream in it.
7. Then put soaked gelatine, mix it well.
8. Set this into a soufflé mould in refrigerator.
9. Serve cold with some attractive toppings and platting.

RECIPE 39

Pate Des Pommes

S. No.	Ingredients	Quantity
1.	Potatoes	4-5
2.	Puff pastry	2 rounds
3.	Onion	1
4.	Shallots	2
5.	Parsley	A bunch
6.	Crème fraiche	To taste
7.	Egg yolk	1

Preparation

1. Peel and slice in thin rounds for dish.
2. Chop finely– an onion or two shallots.
3. Chop finely– a bunch of fresh parsley.
4. Line your dish with one sheet of pastry (keep paper under it, as it makes it easier to lift out of the dish).
5. Layer the potatoes in your dish (usually about four layers) and sprinkle each layer with onions and parsley, then season each layer with salt and pepper.
6. Cover with the second sheet of pastry (no paper obviously).

7. Seal the edges and brush with egg yolk for a nice golden glaze.
8. Cut a small round hole on the top of a pastry to let out the steam whilst cooking.
9. Prick several times with a fork.

RECIPE 40

Savarin Des Fruit

S. No.	Ingredients	Quantity
	Savarin pastry	
1.	Refined flour	500 gm
2.	Breakfast sugar	50 gm
3.	Eggs	5
4.	Yeast fresh	20 gm
5.	Salt	10 gm
6.	Milk	240 mL
7.	Melted butter	240 gm
8.	Lemon rind	Half lemon
	Syrup 900 mL	
9.	Water	500 mL
10.	Sugar	375 gm
11.	Orange, zest and juice	1
12.	Lemon, zest and juice	1
13.	Cinnamon stick	1
14.	Clove	2
15.	Rum	50 mL

Preparation

1. Mix savarin dough well. Add butter at last.
2. Cover with a cloth and let it stand for 30 minutes in a warm place.
3. Fill the pastry into a piping bag and pipe evenly to half prepared moulds.
4. Allow to rise in a warm place until moulds are full.

5. Bake at 224 °C.
6. Make the savarins in ring-shaped savarin mould as directed above.
7. Soak the savarin in warm syrup for one minute, making sure it penetrates evenly. Drain on a cooling rack.
8. Brush with apricot glaze.
9. Dress on a serving dish and fill the centre with the fruit chosen.
10. Pipe a rosette of fresh cream for each portion.

RECIPE 41

Charlotte Royal

S. No.	Ingredients	Quantity
	For the charlotte	
1.	Raspberry jelly	1 pack
2.	Raspberries	400 gm
3.	Icing sugar	2 gm
4.	Milk	150 mL
5.	Castor sugar	100 gm
6.	Egg yolks	3
7.	Gelatine	6 sheets leaf
8.	Double cream	300 gm
	For the Swiss roll	
9.	Egg	8
10.	Castor sugar	150 gm
11.	Vanilla bean paste	1 ½ tsp
12.	Refined flour	150 gm
13.	Raspberry jam	150 gm
	To serve	
14.	Strawberries	According to flavour

Preparation

1. For the charlotte, prepare the raspberry jelly. Leave to set in a small round bowl in the fridge for one hour.

2. Blend the raspberries and icing sugar to a purée in a food processor, and then strain the purée through a fine sieve into a bowl, discarding the seeds.
3. Heat the milk and half of the sugar in a saucepan until just simmering. Meanwhile, whisk the remaining castor sugar and all of the egg yolks in a bowl until pale and thick.
4. Pour the warm milk over the egg yolk mixture, whisking all the time, until combined well.
5. Return the custard mixture to the saucepan and cook, whisking well, until it thickens just enough to coat the back of a spoon. Make sure that it doesn't boil. Add the drained, squeezed gelatine to the custard and stir until dissolved.
6. Whisk the hot custard with the raspberry purée until smooth and combined well. Set aside to cool, then chill in the fridge for at least 30 minutes.
7. Meanwhile, for the Swiss roll, heat the oven to 190 °C / 170 °C fan/gas 5. Line 2 × 25 × 38 cm/10 × 15 in Swiss roll tins with baking parchment.
8. Whisk the eggs, sugar and vanilla bean paste in a large bowl until very light, fluffy and thickened. Fold the flour into the mixture using your hand, carefully lifting and mixing until it has all been incorporated.
9. Divide the Swiss roll mixture between the prepared tins and smooth the top until evenly spread out. Bake for 10-12 minutes, or until springy and just firm to the touch.
10. Wet two large clean tea towels and wring them out. Place them on a work surface and dust with castor sugar. Turn the sponges out onto the tea towels, then peel away the parchment.
11. Spread the raspberry jam all over the sponges, leaving a 2 cm / 1 inch border at one of the narrow ends. Tightly roll up the sponges, starting with the end with a border and using the tea towel to help you.
12. Grease a large pudding or trifle bowl withlittle vegetable oil and line it with 3 sheets of cling film.

13. Slice the Swiss rolls into 1 cm / ½ inch-thick slices and use them to line the sides and base of the pudding bowl, starting at the bottom, and working your way up to cover all inside the bowl, making sure there are no holes.
14. Add the set jelly to the pudding bowl, breaking it up if necessary.
15. Whisk the double cream until soft peaks form when the whisk is removed. Fold the cream into the chilled raspberry custard, then spoon the mixture on top of the jelly. Chill in the fridge for at least 4 hours.
16. To serve, upturn the pudding bowl onto a serving platter. Remove the cling film and decorate with the strawberries and mint. Serve in slices.

RECIPE 42

Assorted Doughnuts

S. No.	Ingredients	Quantity
1.	Flour	1 kg
2.	Sugar	50 gm
3.	Salt	7.5 gm
4.	Fresh yeast	15 gm
5.	Milk	500 mL
6.	Egg	6
7.	Yellow colour	Few drops
8.	Refined oil	50 mL
9.	Fats / butter	400 gm
10.	Breakfast sugar	500 gm
11.	Frying fat	100 gm

Preparation

1. Roll out the chilled dough into rectangular shape of 1 cm/1/2″ thickness and cut into by the doughnut cutter.
2. Arrange on a dusted tray and keep into the proving chamber for final proving and fry the doughnut on medium heat.

3. Roll out on the breakfast sugar.
4. Serve as breakfast roll.

Doughnut Variations

1. Strawberry-frosted doughnut
2. Cinnamon-sugar doughnut
3. Jelly doughnuts
4. Marble-frosted doughnut
5. Apple-crumb doughnut
6. Blueberry doughnut
7. Chocolate-kreme-filled doughnut
8. Bavarian kreme-filled doughnut
9. Vanilla-frosted doughnut
10. Boston kreme pie doughnut
11. Coconut doughnut
12. Chocolate-frosted doughnut
13. Old-fashion doughnut
14. Powdered sugar doughnut
15. Sour cream doughnut
16. Cruller
17. Glazed doughnut
18. Chocolate-glazed cake doughnut

RECIPE 43

Gateau de Fruit

S. No.	Ingredients	Quantity
1.	Genoise	1 mixing
2.	Sweetened cream	300 mL
3.	Mix fruits	300 gm
4.	Roasted cashew nut	100 gm

Preparation

1. Prepare genoise in usual manner.
2. Cool it on a cooling rack.

3. Split the cake into two.
4. Sprinkle sugar syrup on both parts.
5. Spread sweetened cream over one part and spread chopped mix fruits. Sandwich both the parts.
6. Cover the cake with rest of the sweetened cream.
7. Cover the sides of cake with roasted chopped cashew nuts.
8. Decorate the top with nuts.
9. Serve cold.

RECIPE 44

Chocolate Brownie

S. No.	Ingredients	Quantity
1.	Cocoa powder	75 gm
2.	Refined flour	150 gm
3.	Castor sugar	225 gm
4.	Butter	225 gm
5.	Baking powder	7 gm
6.	Salt	2 pinches
7.	Chocolate essence	5 mL
8.	Caramel colour	15 mL
9.	Rum	5 mL
10.	Dark melted chocolate	50 gm
11.	Walnuts	100 gm
12.	Egg	7-8

Preparation

1. Heat the oven to 180 °C / fan 160 °C.
2. Line a 22 cm square brownie tin with baking parchment. Melt the butter and chocolate together in a microwave or in a bowl set over a pan of simmering water.
3. Cool to room temperature.

4. Whisk the eggs and sugar together until the mixture is light and fluffy.
5. Fold the chocolate mixture into the egg mixture and sift on the flour, baking powder and cocoa.
6. Fold this to give a fudgy batter. Add 100 gm chopped dark chocolate chunks.
7. Add flavour with walnuts. Put the mixture into a lined mould.
8. Bake for 25-30 minutes or until the top is cracked but the middle just set. Cool completely, then lift out of the tin and cut.

RECIPE 45

Tiramisu

S. No.	Ingredients	Quantity
	Ladyfingers cookies	
1.	Egg	3-4
2.	Breakfast sugar	85 gm
3.	Refined flour	125 gm
4.	Baking powder	½ tsp
5.	Vanilla essence	1 tsp
6.	Salt	A pinch
7.	Sugar powder for dusting	4 tbsp
	Preparing Tiramisu	
8.	Egg yolk	6
9.	White sugar	¾ cup
10.	Milk	⅔ cup
11.	Heavy cream	1-¼ cup
12.	Vanilla extract	½ tsp
13.	Mascarpone cheese	1 pound
14.	Brewed coffee	¼ cup
15.	Rum	2 tsp
16.	Ladyfinger cookies	2-3
17.	Cocoa powder	1 tsp

Preparation

1. Prepare a 9 × 13 baking dish. If you want to remove the Tiramisu from the pan, so that you can see the layers, I suggest lining the pan with parchment paper that sticks up over the sides, then putting a cardboard cake rectangle in the bottom of the pan. The Tiramisu will be supported by the cardboard when you remove it using the parchment paper.
2. Combine egg yolks and sugar at the top of a double boiler, over the boiling water. If you don't have a double boiler, you can use a metal mixing bowl set over a pot.
3. Cook for about 10 minutes, with heat on low, stirring constantly.
4. When done, whip yolks with mixer until they thicken and yellow a bit.
5. Add mascarpone to whipped yolks and mix until combined.
6. If you have a second metal mixing bowl, use it for your whipped cream. If not, put mascarpone mixture into another bowl and get your metal mixer bowl clean.
7. Place metal bowl and whisk into freezer for about 15-20 minutes.
8. Remove bowl and whisk from freezer, add whipping cream to bowl and whip with mixer. Whip until soft peak forms, about 5-7 minutes.
9. Fold whipped cream into mascarpone mixture.
10. Dissolve espresso into warm water, and then combine it.
11. One at a time, dip the ladyfingers into the mixture for about 4-6 seconds. The longer you dip the ladyfingers, the stronger the flavour will be. As you dip the ladyfingers, lay them into the bottom of the 9 × 13 pan. You should be able to get two rows in a layer.
12. Spoon half of the mascarpone mixture over the ladyfingers.

13. Repeat ladyfinger layer, then top with remaining mascarpone mixture.
14. Dust the top with cocoa powder.
15. Refrigerate for several hours or overnight, remove from pan (if desired) and serve.

RECIPE 46

Apple Strudel

S. No.	Ingredients	Quantity
	Puff pastry dough	
1.	Flour	200 gm
2.	Oil/fat	10 gm
3.	Salt	1 gm
4.	Chilled water	100 mL
5.	Rolling fat (pastry margarine)	100 gm
6.	Lime juice	1 drop
	Filling for strudel	
7.	Brown sugar	¼ cup
8.	Raisins	¼ cup
9.	Egg	½
10.	Apple	3
11.	Cinnamon powder	2 gm
12.	Butter	50 gm

Preparation

1. Make dough with the help of flour, water, salt and oil and lime juice. Keep the dough at rest for 15-20 minutes.
2. Roll out dough into a rectangular shape with 1 cm thickness and spread one-third of fat on it and fold like a book. Rest the dough for 15 minutes.
3. Again, roll it and spread the part of fat and again fold it like the book. Repeat the process thrice.
4. Finally, roll it and make the desired product.

5. Next step is making filling. Place apple in a large bowl. Stir in brown sugar and raisins, set aside.
6. Place full pastry on baking sheet. Roll lightly with a rolling pin.
7. Arrange apple filling down the middle of the pastry lengthwise around the mixture.
8. Fold pastry lengthwise around the mixture.
9. Seal edges of pastry by using a bit of water on your fingers, and rubbing the pastry edges together.
10. Make egg wash brush onto the top of pastry.
11. Bake in oven for 35-40 minutes, until golden brown.

RECIPE 47

Yorkchire Curd Tart

S. No.	Ingredients	Quantity
	For short crust pastry	
1.	Plain flour	170 gm
2.	Salt	To taste
3.	Margarine	25 gm
4.	Cold water	As required
	For filling	
5.	Curd	225 gm
6.	Breakfast sugar	55 gm
7.	Sultanas	55 gm
8.	Egg	1
9.	Margarine	40 gm
10.	Cinnamon	A pinch
11.	Nutmeg	A pinch

Preparation

1. Sieve the flour and salt into a large mixing bowl.
2. Add the margarine and rub into the flour until the mixture resembles bread crumbs.

3. Sprinkle with cold water, a table spoon at a time and mix it using a knife.
4. Add more water only if the dough does not clump together.
5. With hands gather together into a firm but pliable dough, handling as little as possible.
6. Line a flax or tart with the rolled-out pastry.
7. Mix all filling ingredients together and do proving into the pastry case.
8. Bake at about 180 °C for about 25 minutes or until the mixture is set.

RECIPE 48

Baklava

S. No.	Ingredients	Quantity
	Phyllo pastry dough	
1.	Refined flour	200 gm
2.	Salt	½ tbsp
3.	Water	105 mL
4.	Refined oil	2 tbsp
5.	Vinegar / lemon	½ tbsp
6.	Butter	150 gm
	For syrup	
7.	Water	200 mL
8.	Sugar	200 gm
9.	Honey	100 mL
10.	Lemon juice	2 tbsp
11.	Cinnamon spice	1
	For filling	
12.	Chopped nuts	200 gm
13.	Butter	50 gm
14.	White sugar	50 gm
15.	Ground cinnamon	1 tbsp
16.	Phyllo dough	400 gm

Preparation

1. Heat oven to 350 °F (175 °C).
2. Butter the bottom and sides of 9 × 13 inch pan.
3. Chop nuts and toss with cinnamon.
4. Set aside. Unroll phyllo dough. Cut whole stack in half to fit pan. Cover phyllo with a damped cloth to keep from drying out.
5. Place two sheets of dough, butter, nuts layering as you go.
6. The top layer should be about 6-8 sheets deep.
7. Using a sharp knife, cut into diamond or square shapes all the way to the bottom of the pan.
8. You may cut into four long rows to make diagonal cuts.
9. Bake for 50 minutes until baklava is golden and crisp.
10. Make sauce while baklava is making.
11. Boil sugar and water until sugar is melted.
12. Add vanilla and honey.
13. Simmer for about 20 minutes.
14. Remove baklava from oven and immediately spoon sauce over it.
15. Let it cool.
16. Serve in cupcake papers.
17. This freezes well. Leave it uncovered as it gets soggy if it is wrapped up.

RECIPE 49

Crepe Normandy

S. No.	Ingredients	Quantity
1.	Butter	50 gm
2.	Apple	5

(Contd...)

S. No.	Ingredients	Quantity
3.	Brown sugar	50 gm
4.	Cinnamon	¼ tsp
5.	Brandy	1 tbsp
6.	Orange juice	50 mL
7.	Orange zest	1/2 tsp
8.	Crepes	10
9.	Melted butter	2 tsp
10.	Whipped cream	As required
	Crepe	
11.	Refined flour	150 gm
12.	Salt	A pinch
13.	Eggs	2
14.	Milk	200 mL
15.	Sugar	20 gm

Preparation

1. Heat the butter and add apples and sauté.
2. Add the brown sugar and cinnamon and cook till the sugar is dissolved.
3. Remove from the heat and add the brandy, orange juice and zest.
4. Spoon about 2 tbsp of the apple mixture into the centre of the crepe.
5. Fold over. Place in a shallow pan.
6. Brush with melted butter and place in 350 °C oven for 10-15 minutes.
7. Serve with cream of choice.

RECIPE 50

Crossiants

S. No.	Ingredients	Quantity
1.	Refined flour	250 gm
2.	Yeast	12 gm
3.	Salt	¼ tsp
4.	Sugar	30 gm
5.	Milk	60 mL
6.	Egg	1
7.	Fat	150 gm

Preparation

1. Sieve the flour and salt, keep it aside.
2. Dissolve sugar and yeast in lukewarm milk and then dissolve and add egg and mix well.
3. Mix the fat into the flour till flaky bread crumbs texture appears.
4. Using the milk and yeast solution, make a soft dough.
5. Keep it for fermentation, till it doubles in volume.
6. Once the temperature of fermentation is complete, knock back and keep the dough into the fridge for 30-60 minutes.
7. Take out the dough and roll it into a rectangular shape.
8. Apply the rest of 150 gm of creamed butter on the two-thirds of the dough, fold it like flaky paste and repeat the procedure thrice.
9. Roll out the dough into ¼ inch thick.
10. Roll to make croissants shape.
11. Bake at 200 °C for 25 minutes.

RECIPE 51

Black Forest Cake

S. No.	Ingredients	Quantity
1.	Flour	2 ⅛ cups
2.	White sugar	2 cups
3.	Cocoa powder	¾ cups
4.	Baking powder	1 ½ cups
5.	Salt	¾ tsp
6.	Baking soda	¾ tsp
7.	Eggs	3
8.	Vegetable oil	½ cup
9.	Vanilla extract	1 tsp
10.	Cherries	2 cans
11.	Sugar	1 cup
12.	Cornstarch	¼ cup
13.	Whipping cream	3 cups

Preparation

1. Heat oven to 350 °F (175 °C).
2. Grease and flour two 9 inches round cake pans, cover bottom with waxed paper.
3. In a large bowl, combine flour, two cups of sugar, cocoa powder, baking powder, and baking soda.
4. Add egg, milk, oil and 1 teaspoon vanilla, beat until well-blended. Pour the batter into prepared pans.
5. Bake for 35 minutes or until wooden toothpick inserted in centre comes out clean.
6. Cool layer in pan on a wire rack 20 minutes.
7. Loosen edges and remove from racks to cool completely.
8. Drink cherries reserving half cup juice. Combine reserved juice, cherries, one cup sugar and cornstarch in a two-quart sauce pan, cook over heat until thickened, stirring constantly.

9. Stir in one teaspoon vanilla, cool before using.
10. Combine whipping cream and confectioner's sugar in a chilled medium bowl.
11. Beat with an electrical mixer at high speed until stiff peaks form.
12. With a long separated knife, split each layer horizontally in half.
13. Tear one split layer into crumbs, set aside.
14. Reserve one and a half cup.
15. Frosting for decorating cakes, set aside.
16. Gently brush loose crumbs off top and side of each cake layer with pastry brush or hand.
17. To assemble, place one cake layer on cake plate.
18. Spread with one cup frosting, top with ¾ cup cherry topping.
19. Top with the third cake layer.
20. Frost side of cake.
21. Pat reserved crumbs on to frosting on side of cakes.
22. Spoon reserved frosting into pastry bag fitted with star decorator tip
23. Pipe around top and bottom edges of cake.
24. Spoon remaining cherry topping onto top of cake.

RECIPE 52

Lavash

S. No.	Ingredients	Quantity
1.	Butter	5 tsp
2.	Sugar	1 tsp
3.	Eggs	1
4.	All-purpose flour	2 ½ cup
5.	Salt	1 tsp
6.	Water	2/3 cup
7.	Sesame seeds	2 tbsp

Preparation

1. Place the flour, salt and sugar into a medium size bowl and whisk to combine.
2. In a small bowl, whisk together the water, egg and 2 tbsp of the butter.
3. Add egg mixture to the dry ingredients and stir until the dough comes together, adding additional water if the dough is dry.
4. Knead the dough in the bowl 5-6 times.
5. Turn the dough out onto the counter, divide into the third, cover with tea towel and allow to rest for 30 minutes.
6. Lightly butter the back of a half sheet pan using some of the remaining butter.
7. Place the sheet pan upside down on a surface that will prevent sliding.
8. Place the dough bowl into the back-sheet pan and roll out to an even one-eighth inch thickness. Gently stretch the edges, brush with butter and bake at 375 °F until golden brown.
9. Break each sheet into shape and sizes as desired.

Bread Recipes

RECIPE 1

Bread Rolls

S. No.	Ingredients	Quantity
1.	Refined flour	225 gm
2.	Milk powder	10 gm
3.	Yeast	12 gm
4.	Sugar	12 gm
5.	Salt	5 gm
6.	Fat / oil	5 gm
7.	Egg for wash	½

Preparation

1. Prepare dough as per bread roll dough and keep it for fermentation in a proving chamber for about 25 minutes.
2. Take it out, punch it and keep it again in proving chamber for about 20 minutes.
3. Take it out and divide the dough in eight equal sized balls. Make round smooth balls and place them in a greased baking tray.
4. Apply egg wash and keep it for final proving.
5. Bake at 400 °F or till they obtain a nice golden brown colour.
6. Take it out and brush them with melted fat and use as required.

RECIPE 2

French Bread

S. No.	Ingredients	Quantity
1.	Refined flour	1 kg
2.	Water	500 mL
3.	Fermented yeast	25 gm
4.	Sugar	20 gm
5.	Salt	20 gm
6.	Oil	50 mL

Preparation

1. Sieve the flour and salt together.
2. Take the yeast and sugar and soak in lukewarm water.
3. Make dough of flour with the help of soaked yeast.
4. Mix oil in the dough and keep it for fermentation in a greased bowl under wet cloth in proving chamber for half an hour.
5. Knock back the dough to original size and again keep it in a proving chamber for 15-20 minutes.
6. Divide it and keep it for intermediate proofing for 10 minutes.
7. Make required shape of the dough and keep it in a greased baking tray, egg wash them, give some cuts on top and keep it for final fermentation.
8. Bake it at 210 °C for about 10 minutes first and then, at 140 °C for the next 10 minutes.
9. Apply melted fat with brush and cool it.
10. When completely cooled, cut into slices and serve.

RECIPE 3

Clover Leaf Rolls

S. No	Ingredients	Quantity
1.	Refined flour	225 gm
2.	Milk powder	10 gm
3.	Yeast	12 gm
4.	Sugar	15 gm
5.	Salt	5 gm
6.	Fat / oil	5 gm
7.	Egg for wash	½
8.	Water	180 mL

Preparation

1. Sieve the flour along with milk powder on the table.
2. Put sugar and salt in it.
3. Dissolve the fresh yeast with some warm water in a mug.
4. Pour the yeast into a making dough gradually.
5. Kneed into smooth dough.
6. Keep this dough into a neat proving chamber.
7. Take a garlic with fat and mix it with the dough and again keep this dough for proving about 15-20 minutes.
8. Take it out and punch it, reduce the original volume so that excess CO_2 escapes.
9. Again, keep it in the neat proving chamber for 10-15 minutes.
10. Till it rises up, take it out and divide the dough into even size and portion.
11. Make round-like smooth balls and place them on a baking tray. Give them some rest. Again place them into the proving chamber for 15 minutes till it doubles in volume.

12. Take them out, bake at 200-250 °C for about 15-20 minutes till they obtain nice golden-brown colour. Take out of the oven and brush it with fat or oil.
13. Serve it with hot soup.

RECIPE 4

Whole Wheat Bread

S. No	Ingredients	Quantity
1.	Refined flour	600 gm
2.	Wheat flour	400 gm
3.	Water	600 mL
4.	Butter	100 gm
5.	Milk powder	60 gm
6.	Yeast	40 gm
7.	Sugar	30 gm
8.	Salt	20 gm
9.	Egg	1

Preparation

1. Sieve flour, dissolve salt and sugar.
2. Add caramel colour to it.
3. Dissolve yeast separately.
4. Make a ball and prepare a soft dough, using salt, sugar solution and yeast solution.
5. Break the lumps of fat and add to the dough.
6. Keep for fermentation, let it double, knock back and keep for intermediate proving on the tabletop for 5 minutes.
7. Place the roll dough on baking tray and bake at 375 °F for 15-20 minutes.
8. Remove and let it cool on a cooling rack.

RECIPE 5

Pizza Base

S. No.	Ingredients	Quantity
1.	Flour	200 gm
2.	Yeast	6 gm
3.	Sugar	8 gm
4.	Salt	4 gm
5.	Water	180 mL
6.	Oil	10 mL

Preparation

1. Make a dough with flour, sugar, salt, yeast and water.
2. Keep the dough in a proving chamber for 20-25 minutes.
3. Remove it from bowl. Divide the dough in 100 gm pieces and make a ball of each. Relax it for 10 minutes.
4. Cut each piece into round shapes, according to the size.
5. Place on a baking tray and put them into proving chamber for final proving.
6. Prick them with fork before baking.
7. Bake at 200 °C for 10-12 minutes.
8. Apply topping and serve after baking.

RECIPE 6

Cheese Straws

S. No.	Ingredients	Quantity
1.	Flour	1 kg
2.	Shortening	1/2 kg
3.	Refined oil	50 mL
4.	Salt	10 gm
5.	Amul cheese	250 gm
6.	Red chilli powder	10 gm

Preparation

1. Roll out the puff pastry with one-third (1 cm) inch of thickness.

2. Apply egg wash / water / milk.
3. Sprinkle grated processed cheese on top of the sheet.
4. Cut into 3″ × 1″ pieces and twist it like a bow.
5. Arrange on the baking tray.
6. Bake at 200 °C for about 25 minutes.

RECIPE 7

Kulcha

S. No.	Ingredients	Quantity
1.	Refined flour	250 gm
2.	Water	125 mL
3.	Sugar	10 gm
4.	Oil	10 mL
5.	Salt	5 gm
6.	Yeast	7-8 gm

Preparation

1. Make a dough with the help of given ingredients and keep it in the proving chamber.
2. Now take out the fermented dough and divide it into pieces and make balls. Keep again in the proving chamber.
3. Bake it.

RECIPE 8

Masala Bread

S. No.	Ingredients	Quantity
1.	White bread dough	1 part mix
2.	Herbs	30 gm
3.	Salt	To taste
4.	Black pepper	To taste
5.	Egg	For wash

Preparation

1. Take all the dry ingredients and mix.
2. Add all ingredients into the white bread dough at the knock and brick stage and keep it for fermentation.
3. Make a French loaf and keep it up for fermentation again.
4. Remove it from the proving chamber, give it an egg wash and bake it at 200-220 °C for about 20-25 minutes.
5. Remove it from the oven and give oil wash for shine.

RECIPE 9

Brown Bread

S. No.	Ingredients	Quantity
1.	Refined flour	200 gm
2.	Whole wheat flour	200 gm
3.	Sugar	15 gm
4.	Poppy seeds	2.5 gm
5.	Yeast	10 gm
6.	Salt	5 gm
7.	Oil	25 gm
8.	Water	220 gm
9.	Caramel colour	25 gm

Preparation

1. Mix the flour very well.
2. Soak yeast with water and sugar.
3. Mix poppy seeds, salt, oil, sugar and caramel colour in the flour.
4. Make the dough out of the mixture with water and yeast and add oil at the end when the dough is ready.
5. Ready the dough and put it into the proving chamber for 30 minutes.

6. After 30 minutes, remove it from proving chamber and bake it at 200-220 °C for about 20-25 minutes.
7. Remove it from the oven and brush oil on top of it for the shine.

RECIPE 10

Brioche

S. No.	Ingredients	Quantity
1.	Refined flour	200 gm
2.	Yeast	15 gm
3.	Sugar	15 gm
4.	Salt	5 gm
5.	Egg	1
6.	Milk	100 mL
7.	Butter / fat	150 gm

Preparation

1. Sieve flour on the marble top.
2. Dissolve salt, sugar in half of the lukewarm milk and in the other half, dissolve yeast.
3. Beat the egg in salt-sugar mixture.
4. Pour the salt and sugar mixture into the refined flour and mix it.
5. Add yeast solution into the flour and kneed a soft dough.
6. Add butter and fold it nicely into the dough.
7. Allow to ferment for 1 hour. Grease some patty tins, remove the dough and punch it.
8. Divide it into 50 gm size, shape them in a brioche.
9. Brush them with egg wash, keep it in proving chamber for 10-15 minutes.

10. Bake at 400 °F for 10-15 minutes. Remove and polish with melted fat.
11. Serve with jam or butter.

RECIPE 11

Garlic Bread

S. No.	Ingredients	Quantity
1.	Refined flour	225 gm
2.	Salt	5 gm
3.	Sugar	10 gm
4.	Yeast	10 gm
5.	Butter	10 gm
6.	Refined oil	5 mL
7.	Garlic	35 gm

Preparation

1. Sieve the flour.
2. Take the yeast and soak it with little sugar.
3. Make a dough of the flour with the help of soaked yeast and water.
4. Mix the garlic.
5. Garnish with oil.
6. Wrap it with wet cloth and keep it for half an hour.
7. After half an hour, knock back to the dough and keep it for 10-20 minutes after the dough is ready to bake.
8. Make the required design of the dough.
9. Grease the tray.
10. Put that dough in the tray and place it in the oven.
11. Bake them at 200 °C for 10 minutes first, then bake it at 140 °C for 10 minutes.

RECIPE 12

Bread Sticks

S. No.	Ingredients	Quantity
1.	Flour	500 gm
2.	Refined oil	100 mL
3.	Yeast	10 gm
4.	Salt	10 gm
5.	Sugar	30 gm
6.	Water	150 mL
7.	Poppy seeds	For sprinkling, 5-6 gm

Preparation

1. Make a light dough with the help of given ingredients and rest it for 15-20 minutes.
2. Make thin strips out of the dough.
3. Keep on the baking tray.
4. Keep for proofing until done.
5. Apply egg wash and sprinkle poppy seeds on top.
6. Bake at 200 °C for about 20 minutes.

RECIPE 13

Herbsand Potatoes

S. No.	Ingredients	Quantity
1.	Refined flour	300 gm
2.	Fermented yeast	10 gm
3.	Salt	6 gm
4.	Potatoes	250 gm
5.	Herbs	½ tsp
6.	Egg yolk	For wash
7.	Grounded pepper	To taste
8.	Sugar	40 gm

Preparation

1. Boil the potatoes and grate them.
2. Mix herbs, salt, grounded pepper in the grated potatoes.
3. Dissolve yeast and salt separately in water.
4. Make dough using salt, sugar and yeast solution.
5. Use extra water if required.
6. Knead the dough properly and keep in a greased bowl for first fermentation or till double in volume.
7. Knock back and keep for second fermentation.
8. After mixing the potato filling in the dough, divide the dough as per the shape.
9. Roll and shape likea French bread, like a loaf or square size.
10. Use egg yolk for washing and bake at 200 °C for 30-35 minutes.
11. Remove and brush with melted butter or olive oil.

RECIPE 14

Milk Bread

S. No.	Ingredients	Quantity
1	Refined flour	450 gm
2	Fresh yeast	20 gm
3	Sugar	20 gm
4	Salt	10 gm
5	Milk	2 tsp
6	Fat	20 gm
7	Milk powder	2 tbsp

Preparation

1. Sieve the flour and milk powder.
2. Dissolve yeast in lukewarm and salt-sugar solution in another mug.

3. Pours the yeast solution in the flour and mix it well.
4. Add gradually, salt-sugar solution and kneed it to a smooth, soft dough.
5. Cream the fat and mix with dough. Keep the dough into a greased bowl and put in a proving chamber under a wet cloth for about 30 minutes.
6. Remove the dough and knock back and keep it again for proving for about 30 minutes.
7. Remove the dough from proving for about 10 minutes.
8. Give the shape of bread to the dough and place it in a greased mould.
9. Keep the mould in a proving chamber for final proving for about 45 minutes.
10. Bake at 210 °C for about 20-25 minutes. Take it out, apply melted butter, wash and cool on a cooling rack for 12-16 hours and cut them into slices and serve.

RECIPE 15

Grissini

S. No.	Ingredients	Quantity
1.	Refined flour	200 gm
2.	Fresh yeast	6 gm
3.	Semolina	20 gm
4.	Salt	2.5 gm
5.	Water	85 mL
6.	Barley malt	1 tsp
7.	Olive oil	4 tbsp

Preparation

1. Make light dough with the help of given ingredients and rest it for 15-20 minutes.
2. Make thin strips out of the dough.
3. Keep it on the baking tray.

4. Keep for proofing until done.
5. Apply egg wash.
6. Bake at 200 °C for about 20 minutes.

RECIPE 16

Clove Leaf Rolls

S. No.	Ingredients	Quantity
1.	Refined flour	450 gm
2.	Fresh yeast	20 gm
3.	Sugar	20 gm
4.	Salt	10 gm
5.	Clove powder	2 tsp
6.	Fat	20 gm
7.	Milk powder	2 tbsp

Preparation

1. Sieve the flour and milk powder.
2. Dissolve yeast in lukewarm water and salt, sugar, crushed clove, solution in another mug.
3. Pour the yeast solution in the flour and mix it well.
4. Add gradually salt-sugar solution and kneed it to smooth, soft dough.
5. Cream the fat and mix with dough. Keep the dough into a greased bowl and put in a proving chamber under a wet cloth for about 30 minutes.
6. Remove the dough and knock back and keep it again for proving for about 30 minutes.
7. Remove the dough from proving for about 10 minutes.
8. Give the shape of bread to the dough and place it in a greased mould.
9. Keep the mould in a proving chamber for final proving for about 45 minutes.

10. Bake at 210 °C for about 20-25 minutes. Take it out, apply melted butter wash and cool on a cooling rack for 12-16 hours and cut them into slices and serve.

RECIPE 17

Whole Wheat Bread

S. No.	Ingredients	Quantity
1.	Whole wheat flour	450 gm
2.	Fresh yeast	20 gm
3.	Sugar	20 gm
4.	Salt	10 gm
5.	Fat	20 gm
6.	Milk powder	2 tbsp

Preparation

1. Sieve the flour and milk powder.
2. Dissolve yeast in lukewarm water and salt-sugar solution in another mug.
3. Pour the yeast solution in the flour and mix it well.
4. Add gradually salt-sugar solution and kneed it to a smooth, soft dough.
5. Cream the fat and mix with dough. Keep the dough into a greased bowl and put it in a proving chamber under a wet cloth for about 30 minutes.
6. Remove the dough and knock back and keep it again for proving for about 30 minutes.
7. Remove the dough from proving for about 10 minutes.
8. Give the shape of bread to the dough and place it in a greased mould.
9. Keep the mould in a proving chamber for final proving for about 45 minutes.

10. Bake at 210 °C for about 20-25 minutes. Take it out, apply melted butter wash and cool on a cooling rack for 12-16 hours and cut them into slices and serve.

RECIPE 18

Baugette Bread

S. No.	Ingredients	Quantity
1.	Water	100 mL
2.	Refined flour	250 gm
3.	White sugar	10 gm
4.	Salt	75 gm
5.	Yeast	12 gm
6.	Egg yolk	½

Preparation

1. Place the cup of water, bread flour, sugar, salt and yeast into a bread machine pan, in the order recommended.
2. When the dough cycle is completed, place dough in a greased bowl, turning to coat all sides.
3. Cover and let it rise in a warm place for about 30 minutes or until doubles in bulk.
4. Dough is ready if indentation remains when torched.
5. Punch down dough. On a lightly flavoured surface, roll into 16 × 12-inch rectangle.
6. Cut dough in half, creating two 8 × 12-inch rectangle.
7. Roll up each half of dough lightly, beginning at 12-inch side, pounding out any air bubbles as you go.
8. Roll back gently and forth to taper end.
9. Place 3 inches apart on a greased cookie sheet.
10. Make deep diagonal slashed across leaves, every 2 inches, or make any lengthwise slash on each loaf, cover and let rise in a warm place for 30-40 minutes, or until doubles in bulk.

11. Heat oven to 190 °C.
12. Milk, egg yolk, with tablespoon water; brush over tops of layers.
13. Bake it.

RECIPE 19

Pizza Base

S. No.	Ingredients	Quantity
1.	Refined flour	225 gm
2.	Water	115 mL
3.	Yeast	5 gm
4.	Sugar	10 gm
5.	Salt	2 tsp
6.	Refined oil	15 gm

Preparation

1. Sieve the flour.
2. Dissolve yeast in lukewarm water and salt-sugar solution in another mug.
3. Pour the yeast solution in the flour and mix it well.
4. Add gradually salt-sugar solution and kneed it to smooth, soft dough.
5. Cream the fat and mix with dough. Keep the dough in a greased bowl and put in a proving chamber under a wet cloth for about 30 minutes.
6. Remove the dough and knock back and keep it again for proving for about 30 minutes.
7. Remove the dough from proving for about 10 minutes.
8. Give the shape of bread to the dough and place it in a greased mould.
9. Keep the mould in a proving chamber for final proving for about 45 minutes.
10. Bake at 210 °C for about 20-25 minutes. Take it out, apply melted butter, wash and cool on a cooling rack for 12-16 hours and cut them into slices and serve.

RECIPE 20

Pumpernickle Bread

S. No.	Ingredients	Quantity
1.	Cornmeal	120 gm
2.	Molasses	20 gm
3.	Butter	20 gm
4.	Salt	½ tsp
5.	Sugar	15 gm
6.	Caraway seeds	5 gm
7.	Cocoa	5 gm
8.	Yeast	25 gm
9.	Refined flour	300 gm
10.	Whole wheat flour	300 gm
11.	Mashed potatoes	50 gm

Preparation

1. Mix cornmeal in a saucepan, cooked over into a thick texture.
2. Remove the pan from heat; add molasses, butter, salt, sugar.
3. Add caraway seeds and cocoa powder.
4. Stir, combine and set aside to cool.
5. Add yeast in bowl.
6. Add molasses mixture and mashed potatoes.
7. Stir in the pumpernickel and whole wheat flour mix.
8. Knead the dough at medium speed for 10 minutes.
9. Transfer the dough to a greased bowl. Sprinkle the top with flour, cover the bowl and let it rise, until the dough is not quite double, for about 1 hour.
10. When the dough rises, it will expand and you will see cracks in the flour you sprinkled.
11. Shape the dough into a loaf and place it in a greased 8 ½ × 4 ½ inch loaf pan.

12. Sprinkle the top with nose flour or brush with the mixture of 1 egg, beaten with a tablespoon of water.

RECIPE 21

Ginger Bread

S. No.	Ingredients	Quantity
1.	Refined flour	450 gm
2.	Fresh yeast	20 gm
3.	Sugar	20 gm
4.	Salt	10 gm
5.	Ginger	15 gm
6.	Fat	20 gm
7.	Milk powder	2 tbsp

Preparation

1. Sieve the flour and milk powder.
2. Dissolve yeast in lukewarm water and salt-sugar solution in another mug.
3. Pour the yeast solution in the flour and mix it well.
4. Add gradually, salt-sugar solution and kneed it to smooth, soft dough.
5. Cream the fat and mix with dough. Keep the dough into a greased bowl and put in a proving chamber under a wet cloth for about 30 minutes.
6. Remove the dough and knock back and mix chopped ginger, keep it again for proving for about 30 minutes.
7. Remove the dough from proving for about 10 minutes.
8. Give the shape of bread to the dough and place it in a greased mould.
9. Keep the mould in a proving chamber for final proving for about 45 minutes.
10. Bake at 210 °C for about 20-25 minutes. Take it out, apply melted butter wash and cool on a cooling rack for 12-16 hours and cut them into slices and serve.

RECIPE 22

Cinnamon and Raisins Rolls

S. No.	Ingredients	Quantity
1.	Refined flour	450 gm
2.	Fresh yeast	20 gm
3.	Sugar	20 gm
4.	Salt	10 gm
5.	Cinnamon powder	2 tsp
6.	Raisins	15 gm
7.	Fat	20 gm
8.	Milk powder	2 tbsp

Preparation

1. Sieve the flour and milk powder.
2. Dissolve yeast in lukewarm and salt, sugar, cinnamon powder, solution in another mug.
3. Pour the yeast solution in the flour and mix it well.
4. Add gradually salt-sugar solution and kneed it to smooth, soft dough.
5. Cream the fat and mix with dough. Keep the dough in a greased bowl and put in a proving chamber under a wet cloth for about 30 minutes.
6. Remove the dough and knock back and mix raisins, keep it again for proving for about 30 minutes.
7. Remove the dough from proving for about 10 minutes.
8. Give the shape of bread to the dough and place it in a greased mould.
9. Keep the mould in a proving chamber for final proving for about 45 minutes.
10. Bake at 210 °C for about 20-25 minutes. Take it out and apply melted butter wash. Cool on cooling rack for 12-16 hours and cut them into slices and serve.

RECIPE 23

Ciabatta Bread

S. No.	Ingredients	Quantity
1.	Refined flour	128 gm
2.	Fresh yeast	5 gm
3.	Warm milk	2 tbsp
4.	Water-room temperature	2/3 cup
5.	Olive oil	1 tbsp
6.	Salt	1 ½ tsp

Preparation

1. Make dough; stir together, warm water and yeast.
2. Let it stand for 5 minutes, until creamy.
3. Transfer yeast mixture to another bowl and add room-temp water and flour.
4. Stir for 4 minutes.
5. Cover bowl with plastic wrap.
6. Let it stand at room temperature for at least 12 hours or up to 1 day.
7. Make bread: stir together yeast and milk in a small bowl and let it stand for 5 minutes, until creamy.
8. In a bowl of standing electric mixer with dough hook, blend together milk mixture, sponge, water, oil and flour at low speed, until flour is moistened.
9. Beat on a medium for 3 minutes.
10. Add salt and beat for 4 more minutes.
11. Scrape the dough into oiled bowl and cover with plastic wrap, until doubles, about 1 ½ hours.

    Note: dough will be very sticky and full of bubbles.
12. Cut two pieces of parchment paper, approx. 12 inches by 6 inches.
13. Place on a baking sheet and flour well.
14. Turn dough onto a well-floured.

RECIPE 24

Harlyqueen Bread

S. No.	Ingredients	Quantity
	For white dough	
1.	Refined flour	250 gm
2.	Fresh yeast	10 gm
3.	Sugar	10 gm
4.	Butter	2/3 cup
5.	Salt	To taste
6.	Egg	1 ½ tsp
	For brown dough	
7.	Refined flour	125 gm
8.	Flour	125 gm
9.	Yeast	10 gm
10.	Sugar	10 gm
11.	Fat	10 gm
12.	Salt	To taste
13.	Caramel	5 mL
14.	Poppy seeds	5 gm
15.	Fat	5 gm

Preparation

1. Make white and brown dough with water and keep it covered in a moist cloth till the dough proves or doubles in size. The dough should be soft.
2. After proofing, knock back the dough and roll it into a rectangle.
3. Put the brown dough over the white dough and roll them together. Seal the seam (edges) with a little water.
4. Put it in a greased tray and proof for another 20 minutes.
5. Gash cut on the bread with a blade and sprinkle poppy seeds.
6. Bake at 200 °C for 30-35 minutes.
7. Remove from oven and brush it with a little fat.

Cookies Recipes

RECIPE 1

Nan Khatai

S. No.	Ingredients	Quantity
1.	Flour	1 kg
2.	Shortening	650 gm
3.	Powder sugar	650 gm
4.	Curd	30 mL
5.	Sodium bicarbonate	5 gm
6.	Ammonium bicarbonate	5 gm
7.	Small cardamom	10 gm

Preparation

1. Cream fat and sugar, till it has a very light and fluffy consistency.
2. Dissolve ammonium bicarbonate and sodium bicarbonate to the curd and add mixture to the creamed shortening.
3. Fold flour and make soft and smooth dough.
4. Divide dough into small balls and arrange it on a baking tray.
5. Keep aside for 1 hour (60 minutes) for rest.
6. Bake at 150 °C for about 25-30 minutes.

RECIPE 2

Golden Goodies

S. No.	Ingredients	Quantity
1.	Flour	200 gm
2.	Sugar	120 gm
3.	Shortening	125 gm
4.	Egg	1
5.	Vanilla essence	2 mL
6.	Coconut powder	75 gm
7.	Baking powder	9 gm
8.	Glazed cherries	50 gm
9.	Salt	1 gm

Preparation

1. Cream fat and sugar, till it has a light and fluffy consistency.
2. Add egg and cream, along with vanilla essence.
3. Mix half of the coconut powder and salt.
4. Fold flour mixture into the creamed mixture and make a smooth paste.
5. Divide it into small balls and roll into cylindrical shape.
6. Roll into coconut powder and place glazed cherries at the centre.
7. Bake at 160 °C for about 25-30 minutes or till it is done.

RECIPE 3

Melting Moments

S. No.	Ingredients	Quantity
1.	Flour	200 gm
2.	Bakery shortening	130 gm
3.	Sugar	130 gm

(Contd...)

4.	Egg	1 no.
5.	Vanilla essence	5 mL
6.	Baking powder	3 gm
7.	Corn flakes	50 gm

Preparation

1. Cream fat and sugar, till it has a very light and fluffy consistency.
2. Add egg, little by little, into the creamed mixture.
3. Fold sieved flour along with baking powder and make soft smooth dough.
4. Divide the dough into small units and make balls out of it and roll it on cornflakes.
5. Arrange it on a baking tray and bake at 150 °C for about 25 minutes.

RECIPE 4

Tricolour Biscuits

S. No.	Ingredients	Quantity
1.	Flour	200 gm
2.	Sugar	120 gm
3.	Fat	120 gm
4.	Baking powder	3 gm
5.	Salt	2 gm
6.	Vanilla essence	Few drops
7.	Yellow colour	One drop
8.	Lemon essence	One drop
9.	Cocoa powder	10 gm
10.	Egg	1

Preparation

1. Make the biscuit dough, with the help of creaming method and divide it into three parts.

2. In one of the parts, add vanilla essence. In the second, add vanilla essence and yellow colour and in the third part, add cocoa powder.
3. Roll out each part with 1 cm thickness and cut into thin strips.
4. Arrange these strips of different colours, one over the other.
5. Make a square bar and keep into refrigeration.
6. Take out from the fridge when the bar is set & cut it into the required slice size (1 cm).
7. Arrange on the baking tray and bake at 150 °C for about 20-25 minutes.

RECIPE 5

Chocolate Chip Cookie

S. No.	Ingredients	Quantity
1.	Flour	1 kg
2.	Fat	650 gm
3.	Sugar	650 gm
4.	Eggs	5
5.	Cocoa powder	100 gm
6.	Sodium bicarbonate	7 gm
7.	Baking powder	7 gm
8.	Chocolate chip	250 gm

Preparation

1. Cream fat and sugar.
2. Take flour along with cocoa powder, sodium bicarbonate and baking powder.
3. Add creamed sugar in it. Then add eggs one after another and cream it continuously, till dough is formed.
4. Roll out the dough to a ½″ thickness. Sprinkle chocolate chips on top, apply egg wash. Bake at 150 °C for about 20-25 minutes.

RECIPE 6

Bachelor Buttons

S. No.	Ingredients	Quantity
1.	Flour	140 gm
2.	Butter	55 gm
3.	Sugar	55 gm
4.	Sugar for coating	15 gm
5.	Egg	1
6.	Vanilla essence	Few drops
7.	Baking powder	3 gm

Preparation

1. Cream fat and sugar, till it becomes light & fluffy in consistency.
2. Add egg, little by little, into the creamed mixture, add essence into it.
3. Add flour along with baking powder and make soft and smooth dough.
4. Divide it into small units and make round balls like nan khatai and roll it on sugar.
5. Arrange on a baking tray and bake at 150 °C.

RECIPE 7

Coconut Biscuits

S. No.	Ingredients	Quantity
1.	Flour	1 kg
2.	Shortening	½ kg
3.	Castor sugar	½ kg
4.	Eggs	6
5.	Baking powder	10 gm
6.	Vanilla essence	10 mL
7.	Coconut powder	200 gm

Preparation

1. Cream sugar and fat.
2. Add eggs, little by little.
3. Now add the vanilla essence and flour to it. Mix it till it has a light consistency.
4. Add coconut powder into the dough and make a soft dough.
5. Keep the dough in refrigeration, till the dough gets the rolling consistency.
6. Take out the dough, roll out with the help of sheeting machine or rolling pin to ¼ inch of thickness.
7. Apply egg wash on top of the roll sheet and sprinkle coconut powder.
8. Cut with small biscuit cutter.
9. Arrange the pieces on a baking tray.
10. Bake at 160 °C for about 25 minutes.

RECIPE 8

Khara Biscuits

S. No.	Ingredients	Quantity
1.	Flour	1 kg
2.	Shortening	½ kg
3.	Refined oil	50 mL
4.	Salt	10 gm
5.	Kalaunji/jeera/ajwain	20-25 gm

Preparation

1. Roll out the puff pastry into a rectangular shape with ¼ th of thickness.
2. Apply egg wash and sprinkle ajwain / jeera / kalaunji over it.
3. Cut it into rounds with a round biscuit cutter.
4. Prick it in the centre with the help of a fork.
5. Arrange on a baking tray and bake at 200 °C for about 25 minutes.

RECIPE 9

Whole Wheat and Oats Cookies

S. No.	Ingredients	Quantity
1.	Whole wheat flour	100 gm
2.	Oats	100 gm
3.	Egg	½
4.	Brown sugar	70 gm
5.	Butter	130 gm
6.	Baking powder	½ tsp

Preparation

1. Cream fat and sugar till it has a very light and fluffy consistency.
2. Add egg, little by little, into the creamed mixture.
3. Fold sieved whole wheat flour along with baking powder and make soft, smooth dough.
4. Divide dough into small units and make balls out of it and roll it on oats.
5. Arrange it on a baking tray and bake at 150 °C for about 25 minutes.

RECIPE 10

Almond Cookies

S. No.	Ingredients	Quantity
1.	Refined flour	200 gm
2.	Almond powder	25 gm
3.	Egg	½
4.	Breakfast sugar	70 gm
5.	Butter	130 gm
6.	Baking powder	½ tsp
7.	Almond slivers	10 gm
8.	Almond essence	Few drops

Preparation

1. Cream fat and sugar till it has a very light and fluffy consistency.
2. Add egg, little by little, into the creamed mixture.
3. Fold sieved refined flour along with baking powder and make soft, smooth dough.
4. Add almond powder and essence.
5. Divide dough into small units and make balls out of it and add almonds on top.
6. Arrange it on a baking tray and bake at 150 °C for about 25 minutes.

RECIPE 11

Multigrain Cookies

S. No.	Ingredients	Quantity
1.	Butter	250 gm
2.	Breakfast sugar	200 gm
3.	Baking powder	7 gm
4.	Milk powder	25 gm
5.	Multigrain flour	300 gm
6.	Water	50 gm

Preparation

1. Cream fat and sugar, till it has a very light and fluffy consistency.
2. Add egg, little by little, into the creamed mixture.
3. Fold sieved multigrain flour along with baking powder and milk powder and make a, soft, smooth dough.
4. Divide dough into small units and make balls out of it and roll multigrain in it.
5. Arrange it on a baking tray and bake at 150 °C for about 25 minutes.

List of Culinary (Common and Basic Terms)

Aeration	The incorporation of air and/or gas in bakery products by mixing, beating or whisking. Gas is introduced by baking powder and yeast.
Ala	According to the style or a standard in vogue, such as a la francaise or according to the French way.
Allumette	French word for 'matchstick'. Various puff pastry items are made in thin sticks or strips.
Almond Paste	A mixture of finely ground almond and sugar.
Angel Food Cake	A type of cake made with meringue (egg white and sugar) and flour.
Angel Food Method	A cake mixing method involving folding a mixture of flour and sugar onto a meringue.
Au Four	Baked in the oven.
Baba	A yeast-raised cake. A famous variety is flavoured and soaked in rum before serving. Fruit whipped cream is added. Banaau rum is cooked in rum, a type of yeast cake that is soaked in syrup.
Baking	Usually the food is put in the oven and cooked by dry heat.
Babka	A type of sweet yeast bread or coffee cake.
Barquette	A boat-shaped pastry tartlet with a filling.
Baked Alaska	A dessert consisting of ice cream on a sponge base, covered with meringue, browned in the oven.
Baking Ammonia	Leavening agent that releases ammonia gas and carbon dioxide.
Baklava	A Greek or Middle Eastern dessert, made of nuts and phyllo dough and soaked in syrup.

Bavarian Cream	A light, cold dessert made of gelatine, whipped cream, and custard sauce or fruit.
Beignet Soufflé	A type of fritter made with éclair paste, which puffs up greatly when fried.
Bechamel	A basic sauce, white in colour, prepared with flour, butter and milk.
Beurre Fondue	Melted butter.
Beurre Noisette	Butter heated to nut brown colour.
Beurre Noir	Butter heated to a very dark brown colour.
Black Forest Torte	A chocolate sponge layer cake filled with whipped cream and cherries.
Blanc Mange	(1) An English pudding made with milk, sugar and cornstarch. (2) A French dessert made of milk, cream, almonds and gelatine.
Bloom	A whitish coating on chocolate, caused by separated cocoa butter.
Blown Sugar	Pulled sugar that is made into thin walled, hollow shapes by being blown up like a balloon.
Bombe	Type of frozen dessert made in a dome-shaped moil.
Boston Cream Pie	A sponge cake or other yellow cake filled with pastry cream and topped with chocolate fondant or confectioner's sugar.
Bran	The hard outer covering of kernels of wheat and other grain.
Bran Flour	Flour to which bran flakes has been added.
Bread Flour	Strong flour, such as patent flour, is used for breads.
Brioche	Rich-yeast dough containing large amounts of eggs and butter, or a product made from this dough.
Brown Sugar	Regular granulated sucrose containing various impurities that give it a distinctive flavour.
Buttercream	An icing made of butter and / or shortening blended with confectioner's sugar or sugar syrup and sometimes other ingredients.

Blend	Mixing of two or more ingredients.
Batch	The content of the oven. One mixing of bread or cakes.
Batter	A soft completed cake mixture.
Bay	A well, made in heap flour.
Beat	The aeration of fat, sugar, eggs and other materials.
Body	Firmness and response of the crumb or dough to pressure.
Brake	A machine to roll pastry or other dough.
Break	That part of the crust formed during oven spring
Bulk Fermentation	Fermentation time between dough kneading and scaling.
Bun	A small yeast fermented or chemically aerated, sweetened cake.
Bun Wash	Eggs brushed on bakery products before baking
Cabinet Pudding	A baked custard containing sponge cake and fruits.
Cake Flour	Fine, white flour made from soft wheat.
Caramelisation	The browning of sugar caused by heat.
Cassata	An Italian-style, usually with three layers of different ice creams, plus a filling of Italian meringue.
Castor Sugar	Sugar that is boiled to hard crack stage and then poured into moulds to harden.
Celsius Scale	The metric system of temperature measurement, with 0 °C set at the freezing point of water and 100 °C set at the boiling point of water.
Chapelure	Crumbs made from dried bread.
Charlotte	(1) A cold dessert made of Bavarian cream or other creams in a special mould usually lined with ladyfingers or other sponge products. (2) A hot dessert made of cooked fruit and baked in a special mould lined with strips of bread.
Cake	A baked mixture of fat, sugar, eggs and flour, with or without milk, baking powder, fruits, etc.

Cake Hoop	A metal ring which supports a cake during baking.
Carbonate of Ammonia	A mixture of ammonium bicarbonate and ammonium carbonate. It completely volatilises, when moistened and heated into ammonia gas, CO_2 and water.
Carbon Dioxide	A heavy colourless gas produced as a result of the fermentation of sugar by yeast. This gas is also evolved from a carbonate or bicarbonate alone or in the presence of an acid, when moistened and heated.
Chaffing	The careful final moulding of buns, scones, etc., to produce a perfectly smooth skin.
Chemical Leavener	A leavener, such as baking soda, baking powder or baking ammonia, which releases gases produced by chemical reactions.
Chiffon Cake	A light cake made by the chiffon method.
Chiffon Method	A cake mixing method involving the folding of egg whites into a batter made of flour, egg yolks and oil.
Chiffon Pie	A pie with a light fluffy filling, containing egg whites and usually gelatine.
Chocolate Liquor	Unsweetened chocolate, consisting of cocoa solids and cocoa butter.
Christmas Pudding	A dark, heavy steamed pudding made of dried and candied fruits, spices, beef suet and crumbs.
Clear Flour	A tan-coloured wheat flour made from the outer portion of the endosperm.
Coagulation	The process by which proteins become firm, usually when heated.
Clarity	A crumb free from cores, seams and streaks.
Clearing	Thorough dispersal of all ingredients during dough making.
Cobbler	A fruit dessert similar to a pie but without a bottom.
Cocoa	The dry powder that remains after cocoa butter is pressed out of the chocolate liquor.
Cocoa Butter	A white or yellowish fat found in natural chocolate.

Compote	Fruit cooked in sugar syrup.
Coat	To cover a cake with icing or cream.
Comb Scraper	A plastic scraper with a serrated edge, which makes a pattern on the surface of the royal icing, chocolate or cream.
Coupe	A dessert consisting of one or two scoops of ice cream or sherbet, placed in a glass and topped with any number of syrups, fruits and garnishes – a sundae.
Couverture	Natural, sweet chocolate containing no added fats other than natural cocoa butter; used for dipping, moulding, coating and similar purposes.
Cones	Coarsely ground rice or maize, used to prevent dough from sticking during manipulation and proving.
Consistency	The "feel" of the dough.
Cores	Hard spots in the crumb structure.
Cream	1. To beat fat and sugar until light and fluffy. 2. To add cream as decoration to a baked cake. 3. Dairycream, buttercream, custardcream, etc.
Creaming	The process of beating fat and sugar to blend them uniformly and to incorporate air.
Cream Pie	An unbaked pie containing a pastry cream-type filling.
Crème Anglaise	A light vanilla flavoured custard sauce made of milk, sugar and egg yolks.
Crème Caramel	A custard baked in a would, lined with caramelized sugar and then demoulded.
Crêpe	A very thin pancake often served rolled around a filling.
Crêpes Suzette	French pancakes served in a sweet sauce, flavoured with oranges.
Croissant	A flaky, buttery, yeast roll-shaped like a crescent and made from a rolled in dough.
Custard	A liquid that is thickened or set by the coagulation of egg protein.

Cream of Tartar	One of the best acidic components of baking powder.
Cream Powders	Various acids to be used in baking powders.
Crumb	All the loaf except the crust.
Crust	That part of the outside of the loaf that is dehydrated and caramelised during baking.
Cup Cakes	Small cakes baked in crimped paper cups or cases.
Curdle	A cake mixture, which has separated and has lost its smooth consistency.
Cutters	Implements, either plain or fluted, used to cut out biscuits and pastries in various shapes and sizes.
Disaccharide	A complex or double sugar such as sucrose.
Diastase	Various enzymes, found in flour and in malt that convert starch into sugars.
Devil's Food Cake	A chocolate cake made with a high percentage of baking soda, which gives the cake a reddish tint.
Dessert Syrup	A flavoured syrup used to flavour and moisten cakes and desserts.
Develop	To thoroughly mix dough, to increase its elasticity by complete hydration and the development of the gluten.
Divider	A machine manual or mechanised, that divides accurately a piece of dough into smaller pieces.
Dough	A yeast-fermented mixture.
Dobos Torte	A Hungarian cake made of seven thin layers filled with chocolate, buttercream and topped with caramelized sugar.
Docking	Piercing or perforating pastry dough before baking, in order to allow steam to escape and to avoid blistering.
Draw	To remove bread or cakes from the oven.
Drained Weight	The weight of solid canned fruit after draining off the juice.
Dredge	To sprinkle thoroughly with sugar or some other dry powder.

Drop Batter	A batter that is too thick to pour but will drop from a spoon in lumps.
Dredger	A small container with a perforated lid used to sprinkle sugar, flour, etc.
Drummed Hoop	A cake hoop across the bottom and side of, which is stretcher a sheet of strong grease, proof paper.
Dust	To sprinkle flour on the tabletop to prevent dough or pastry from sticking.
Dutch Process	Cocoa processed with an alkali to reduce its acidity.
Éclair Paste	A paste or dough made of boiling water or milk, butter, flour and eggs; used to make éclairs, cream puffs and similar products.
Emulsion	A mixture of two or more unmixable substances.
Endosperm	The starchy inner portion of grain kernels.
Egg Wash	To wash dough pastry pieces with beaten egg.
Elasticity	The effect of manipulation on a dough.
Emulsion	An intimate mixture of the fluids that normally would not mix, such as oil and water.
Enrichment	The addition of enriching agents, such as fat, sugar, eggs, etc., to doughs and pastries.
Essences	Aromatic compounds used for flavouring confectionery.
Extensibility	The degree to which dough may be stretched or deformed, without break or rupture.
Extraction	The portion of the grain kernel that is separated into a particular grade of flour.
Face	The side crust of a tin loaf.
Fancies	Small decorated cakes of any kind.
Ferment	A soft sponge used as a preliminary stage for rich fermented doughs.
Fermentation	Fermentation is brought about by the action of yeast on sugars in solution which produces CO_2, alcohol and other by-products.
Final Proof	The fermentation period before baking.
Fingers	Finger-shaped products.

Foaming	The process of whipping air, with or without sugar, to incorporate air.
French Pastry	A variety of small fancy cakes and other pastries, usually in single portion size.
French Style	Ice cream containing egg yolks.
Frozen Mousse	A still frozen dessert containing whipped cream.
Frangipane	A type of almond-flavoured cream.
Fondant	A form of icing made by boiling sugar, water, glucose or a weak acid to 115 °C, then agitating when it is cool until it forms a mass of minute crystals.
Foxy Colour	The red-brown colour of the crust caused by under-fermented dough.
Ganache	A rich cream made of sweet chocolate and heavy cream.
Gâteau	French word for 'cake'.
Gaufre	French word for 'waffle'.
Germ	The plant embryo portion of a grain kernel.
Gelatinisation	The heating of starch in water so that the cells burst. On cooling, a gel is formed.
Genoise	Sheets of good quality plain cake that are cut into small shapes for making genoese, fancies, etc.
Gliadin	A protein in wheat flours that combines with another protein glutenin to form gluten.
Glaze	1. Egg washing before baking. 2. To brush with highly-boiled apricot puree. 3. To wash with sugar solution after baking.
Glucose	Thick viscous, colourless syrup used in boiling sugar to prevent premature graining.
Gram	The basic unit of weight in the metric system; equal to about one-thirtieth of an ounce.
Granité	Coarsed, crystalline frozen dessert made of water, sugar and fruit juice or another flavouring.
Gum Paste	A type of sugar paste or pastillage made with vegetable gum.
Gluten	Insoluble wheat protein after hydration.

Glycerine	A colourless, odourless syrup with a sweet taste.
Grain	The size, shape and arrangement of the cells which make up the crumb surface.
Green Dough	Under-fermented dough.
Handing Up	Shaping into balls of yeasted-dough pieces and scones after weighing, in preparation for final shaping.
Harshness	Dough with tough tenacious gluten.
Hearth Bread	Bread that is baked directly at the bottom of the oven, not in a pan.
High Ratio	1. Term referring to cakes and cake formulas mixed by a special method and containing more sugar than flour. 2. The mixing method used for these cakes. 3. Term referring to certain specially formulated ingredients used in these cakes, such as shortening.
Homogenised Milk	Milk that has been processed, so that the cream does not separate out.
Hydrogenation	A process that converts liquid oils to solid fats (shortenings) by chemically bonding hydrogen to the fat molecules.
Hot Plate	A heated flat, metal plate in which muffins, crumpets and pancakes are baked.
Hygroscopic	The power of attracting moisture.
Hygrometer	An instrument to measure the humidity of the atmosphere.
Ice	A frozen dessert made of water, sugar and fruit juice.
Ice cream	A churn-frozen mixture of milk, cream, sugar, flavourings, and sometimes eggs.
Inversion	A chemical process in which a double sugar splits in two simple sugars.
Invert Sugar	A mixture of two simple sugars, dextrose and levulose, resulting from the breakdown of sucrose.
Italian Meringue	A meringue made by whipping boiling syrup into egg whites.

Icing	The coating and decoration of a cake with royal icing.
Icing Sugar	Finely powdered sugar.
Intermediate Proof	Intermediate proofing is a short rest period between dough dividing and the final moulding.
Japonaise	A baked meringue, flavoured with nuts.
Jelly	A liquid substance thickened by a thickening agent like starch, gelatine, pectin, etc.
Kernel Paste	A nut paste, similar to almond paste, made of apricot kernels and sugar.
Kirsch	A clear alcoholic beverage distilled from cherries.
Knock Back	The operation of degassing fermented dough either by hand or machine.
Lamination	The formation of numerous alternate layers of dough and butter in puff pastry by rolling and folding.
Lean Dough	A dough that is low in fat and sugar.
Lecithin	An emulsifier from egg yolks and soya beans.
Leavening	The production or incorporation of gases in a baked product to increase the volume and to produce shape and texture.
Linzertorte	A tart made of raspberry jam and a short dough, containing nuts and spices.
Liqueurs	Spirits sweetened with sugar and flavoured with essences, fruit juice, distillates or essential oils.
Macaroon	A cookie made of eggs (usually whites) and almond paste or coconut.
Malt Syrup	A type of syrup containing maltose sugar, extracted from sprouted barley.
Marble	To partly mix two colours of cake batter or icing so that the colours are indecorative swirls.
Marron	French word for "chestnut."
Marshmallow	A light confection, icing, or filling made of meringue and gelatine (or other stabilisers).
Marzipan	A paste or confection made of almonds and sugar and often used for decorative work.
Meringue	Thick, white foam made of whipped eggs and sugar.

Meringue Chantilly	Baked meringue filled with whipped cream.
Meringue Glacée	Baked meringue filled with ice cream.
Manipulations	The use of hands or machine in moulding, folding, rolling, shaping and plaiting.
Masking	To cover a cake or such like base with buttercream.
Maw Seed	Seeds to sprinkle on tea breads and rolls.
Mince Meat	A confection for making mince pies and tarts, containing currants, peel, sultanas, raisins, suet, sugar, apples, spices, lemon juice and brandy or rum.
Modeling Chocolate	A thick paste made of chocolate and glucose, which can be moulded by hand into decorative shapes.
Molasses	Heavy brown syrup made from sugarcane.
Monosaccharide	A simple or single sugar, such as glucose and fructose.
Mousse	A soft cream dessert that is made light by the addition of whipped cream, egg whites, or both.
Mould	1. Shaping dough into a hollow form for casting marzipan, biscuit dough, etc. 2. Form to shape chocolate.
Napoleon	A desert made of layers of puff pastry filled with pastry cream.
Net Weight	The weight of total contents of a can or package.
Nougat	A mixture of caramelized sugar and almonds or other nuts used in decorative work and as a confection and flavouring.
No Time Dough	Straight dough with very short bulk fermentation.
Old Dough	A dough that is over-fermented.
One-Stage Method	A cookie-mixing method in which all the ingredients are added to the bowl at once.
Othello	A type of small (single-portion size), spherical sponge cake filled with cream and iced with fondant.

Oven Spring	The increase of volume during the first stage of baking.
Over Developed	Dough, which has fermented too much and has been manipulated excessively.
Overrun	The increase in volume of ice cream or frozen desserts due to the incorporation of air while freezing.
Pain D'epice	A type of gingerbread. French word, meaning spice bread.
Palmier	A small pastry or petit four made of rolled-sugared puff pastry. Cut into slices and baked.
Parfait	1. A type of sundae served in a thin tall glass. 2. A still frozen dessert made of egg yolk, syrup and heavy cream.
Paris-Brest	A dessert consisting of a ring of baked choux paste filled with cream.
Pasteurised	Heat-treated to kill bacteria that might cause disease or spoilage.
Pastillage	A sugar paste used for decorative work, which becomes very hard when dry.
Pastry Cream	A thick custard sauce containing eggs and starch.
Pâte À Choux	Éclair paste.
Pâte Feuilleté	French name for puff pastry.
Peel	A flat wooden shovel, use to place hearth breads in an oven and remove them.
Petit Four	A delicate cake or pastry, small enough to be eaten in one or two bites.
Petit Four Glacé	French name for puff pastry.
Petit Four Sec	An un-iced or unfilled petit, such as a small butter cookie orpalmier (means dry).
Philadelphia Style	Ice cream containing no eggs.
Phyllo	A paper-thin dough or pastry used to make strudels and various Middle Eastern and Greek desserts.
Piping Jelly	A transparent, sweet jelly used for decorating cakes.

Pithiviers	A cake made of puff pastry, filled with almond cream.
Pot De Crème	A rich baked custard.
Pour Batter	A batter that is liquid enough to pour.
Praline	A confection or flavouring made of nuts and caramelized sugar.
Profiterole	A small puff made of éclair paste, often filled with ice cream and served with chocolate sauce.
Paletta Knife	A thin, flat, knife with a rounded end, used for spreading, icing and cake batter.
Pan	Baking tin for bread.
Pectin	A thickening agent found in fruits and vegetables.
Pie	Fruit of meat in dish covered with a pastry lid.
Pinched	The decoration on the edge of short bread.
Pinning	The rolling of dough or pastry into a flat sheet with a rolling pin.
Piping	1. The decoration on a cake. 2. The depositing of batters through a piping bag.
Plaiting	The weaving of one or more ropes of dough into ordered design.
Pound Cakes	All cakes baked in a round hoop or oblong tin.
Press	A scaled piece of dough that is divided into small, equal units in a dough divider.
Profiterole	A small puff made of éclair paste often filled with ice cream and served with chocolate sauce.
Prove	The filling of yeasted-dough with gas.
Proofer	A cupboard with a controlled humidity and temperature for the fermentation of yeasted goods.
Puff Pastry	A very light, flaky pastry made from a laminated structure built-up of alternate layers of dough and butter.
Pulled Sugar	Sugar, that is boiled to the hard-crack stage, allowed to harden slightly,then pulled or stretched until it develops a pearly sheen.

Pullman Loaf	A long, rectangular loaf of bread.
Pumpernickel Flour	Coarse, flaky meal made from whole rye grains.
Punching	A method of expelling gases from fermented dough.
Puree	A food made into a smooth pulp, usually by being ground or forced through a sieve.
Retarding	Refrigerating yeast dough to slow the fermentation.
Recipe	Ingredients and processing method of a certain product.
Recovery Time	The time necessary for dough to lose its toughness manipulation.
Retardation	This is a process of slowing down the final rising in the bread making process, like proofing bread overnight in the refrigerator.
Rice Flour	Finely milled rice used for dusting purposes.
Rice Condé	A thick, moulded-rice pudding, usually topped with fruit.
Rice Imperatrice	A rich rice pudding containing whipped cream, candied fruits, and gelatine.
Rich Dough	Dough high in fat, sugar, and / or eggs.
Rolled-In Dough	Dough in which a fat has been incorporated in many layers by using arolling and folding procedure.
Rounding	A method of moulding a piece of dough into round balls with a smooth surface or skin.
Ripening	The action of fermentation, manipulation, salt water and temperature on gluten, all of which affect its toughness.
Rolls	Small bread shapes used at breakfast, dinner and tea.
Rope	The crumb of the loaf discolours, becomes sticky and emits a bad odour.
Royal Icing	A mixture of icing sugar and egg white, sometimes with the addition of lemon juice.
Rye Blend	A mixture of rye flour and hard wheat flour.

Sabayon	A foamy dessert or sauce made of egg yolks whipped with wine or liqueur.
Sacristain	A small pastry made of a twisted strip of puff pastry, coated with nuts and sugar.
St. Honoré	1. A dessert made of a ring of cream puffs set on a short dough base and filled with a type of pastry cream. 2. The cream used to fill this dessert, made of pastry cream and whipped cream and whipped egg whites.
Savoy Bag	A triangular-shaped bag made of cloth or a plastic material into which a pipe is inserted.
Savoy Pipe	A metal nozzle to be used in a piping bag.
Savarin	A type of yeast bread or cake that is soaked in syrup.
Scaling	Weighing, usually of ingredients, dough or batters.
Scone	A type of biscuit or biscuit-like bread.
Scoop	A big spoon for holding materials like flour, sugar, etc.
Scraper	1. A small oblong piece of plastic, with two round corners, rounded for scraping down mixing bowls. 2. A metal blade in a wooden handle that is used to scrape the surface of a bench, floor or baking trays.
Season	The dulling of the shiny surface of pans and baking tins so that heat will penetrate and not be reflected.
Seasoning	The adding of pepper, salt, spices and herbs to meat and other savoury products.
Sheen	Reflection from the cells in the cut surface of the crumb.
Shell	Or flying top, a loose top crust by too short a final proof.
Sherbet	A frozen dessert made of water, sugar, fruit juice and sometimes milk or cream.
Short	Having a high-fat content, which makes the product very crumbly and tender.

Short Pastry	A friable easily broken pastry made from flour, fat, sugar and egg. For savoury pastry, the sugar is omitted.
Shortening	1. Any fat used in baking to tenderize the product by shortening gluten strands. 2. A white, tasteless, solid fat that has been formulated for baking or deep-frying.
Sour	A dough in which excessive acidity has been allowed to develop.
Soft Wheat	Wheat, low in protein.
Solid Pack	A type of canned fruit or vegetable with no water added.
Soufflé	1. A baked dish containing whipped egg whites, which cause the dish to rise during baking. 2. A still frozen dessert made in a soufflé dish, so that it resembles a baked soufflé.
Sour Dough	1. A yeast type dough made with a sponge or starter that has fermented so long that it has become very sour or acidic. 2. A bread made with such dough.
Shred	Character of the surface of the bread. It may be smooth, ragged or broken.
Sieve	Utensil with a wire or nylon mesh, through which dry materials are passed.
Skinning	The formation of a skin by evaporation of the surface moisture.
Slack Dough	Soft dough.
Slab Cake	Plain or fruitcake baked in rectangular tins or frames.
Snow	Well-beaten egg whites.
Sodium Bicarbonate	The constituent of baking powder that liberates CO_2.
Soft Flour	Flour containing weak gluten.
Spatula	A wooden tool with a flat blade for beating and mixing.
Sponge	A light plain cake produced by whisking eggs and sugar together until stiff and thoroughly aerated, then carefully blending in flour.

Sponge & Dough Method	Dough made with a sponge.
Spun Sugar	Boiled sugar made into long, thin threads by dipping wires into the sugar syrup and waving them, so that the sugar falls off and sets into fine strands.
Stability	The quality of the gluten in dough that enables it to withstand the effects of fermentation and manipulation.
Straight Dough	A method of bread making in which all the ingredients are mixed together at the dough making stage.
Streaks	Continuous patches seen in the crumb structure.
Strong Flour	Flour containing strong, stable gluten.
Straight Flour	Flour made from entire wheat kernel, minus the bran and germ.
Stollen	A type of sweet yeast bread made with fruit.
Streusel	A crumbly topping for baked goods, consisting of fat, sugar and flour rubbed together.
Swiss Roll	A thin sponge cake layer, spread with a filling and rolled up.
Tart	A pastry case baked with a filling.
Tea Breads	Small yeast goods made from enriched dough, shaped in many ways.
Texture	The "feel" of the cut crumb surface.
Turntable	A piece of equipment for icing of the cake which can be rotated at any speed.
Two-Stage Method	A cake mixing method, beginning with the blending of flour, and high-shortening, followed by the addition of liquids. Also called the high-ratio method.
Vacherin	A crisp meringue shell filled with cream, fruits or other items.
Wash	1. To brush with eggs, milk, water, before baking. 2. To brush with a glaze after baking.
Wedding Cakes	A richly fruited cake covered with almond paste, coated and piped with royal icing, usually made in several tiers.

Yield	The calculated units from the total baked weight of a particular formula.
Young Dough	A dough that is under-fermented.
Zabaglione	An Italian dessert or sauce made of whipped yolks and Marsala wine.
Zest	The outer coloured portion of the peel of citrus.

References

1. Bender D.A. "Benders' Dictionary of Nutrition and Food Technology". 8th Edition. Woodhead Publishing. Oxford, 2006.
2. Belitz H.D., Grosch W., Schieberle P. "Food Chemistry". 4th Edition. Springer, 2009.
3. http://www.chinafooding.com
4. List of dairy products, From Wikipedia, the free encyclopedia.
5. Amendola, J., Rees, N. (2003). Understanding Baking: The Art and the Science of Baking. New Jersey. John Wiley & Sons.
6. Banfield, W.T. (1947). Manna: A Comprehensive Treatise on Bread Manufacture. London. Maclaren & Sons.
7. www.google.com
8. David, E. (1979). English Bread and Yeast Cookery. London. Penguin.
9. Baking: The Art and Science First English Edition. by Claus Schunemann (Author) 1.0 out of 5 stars 1 rating. ISBN-13: 978-0969374503.
10. The Professional Pastry Chef: Fundamentals of Baking and Pastry, 4th Edition Bo Friberg ISBN: 978-0-471-35925-8 March 2002, 1040 Pages.
11. Bureau of Indian Standards (1981). Handbook of Food Analysis. Part XI.
12. Dairy Products. Manak Bhawan-9, Bahadur Shah Jafar Marg, New Delhi, India. p. 115.

13. http://oer.nios.ac.in/wiki/index.php/Leavening_Agents
14. https://www.google.com
15. http://www.chemistryindustry.biz/thickeners.html
16. http://www.yourarticlelibrary.com/home-science/bread/10-common-faults-committed-while-making-bread/86685

Index

A
Acesulfame potassium 119
Aerosol cream 21
Albert pudding 283
All-purpose flour 50
Almond cookies 341
Almond oil 73
American frosting 149
Angel food method 159
Apple strudel 305
Apple turnovers 262
Applesauce 114
Apricot kernel oil 71
Apricot puree 116
Armenian cracker bread-
biscocho 244
Arrowroot powder 101
Aspartame 119
Assorted doughnuts 300
Avocado oil 71, 73

B
Baba au Rhum 289
Bachelor buttons 339
Baguettes 240
Baugette bread 328
Baked milk 14
Bakery oven 200
Baking measurements 132
Baking powder 90, 102, 103
  types and uses of 89
  use of filler in 88, 102
Baking soda 89
Baklava 307
Barley flour 49
Barley malt syrup 113
Basic meringues 125
Batch system 7
Baugette bread 328
Bavaroie 288
Beurre Manié 99
Bicarbonate of soda 91
Black forest cake 311
Bleached flour 52
Blended butter 43
Bolillos 242
Breads 199
Bread and butter pudding 282
Bread faults 251
Bread flour 51
Bread improvers 222
Bread making 200
Bread making process 215
Bread recipes 314
Bread rolls 250, 314
Bread sticks 323
Breakfast sugar 110
Brewer's yeast 91
Broiche 249, 321
Brown bread 247, 320
Brown rice syrup 115
Brown rice malt syrup 118
Brown sugar 109, 110

Buck wheat 49
Butter 15, 35
  packing & storage 37
  processing and
    manufacturing 36
  types of 43
  uses of 37
Butter cakes 45
Butter making process 40
Buttercream 126, 147
Buttermilk 4, 13
Butterscotch sponge 161, 269
Byaslag 31

C

Cabinet pudding 286
Cake flour 50
Camembert 32
Candy 194
Caramel and toffee 195
Caramel custard 283
Caramel icing 148
Castor sugar 110
Charlotte royal 298
Cheddar 32
Cheese 15
  classification of 26-27
  storage of 34
  processing of 25
  varieties of 30
Cheese straws 318
Chiffon method 159
Chocolate
  manufacturing and
    processing of 186
  assorted preparation of 197
Chocolate brownie 302
Chocolate buttercream 129
Chocolate buttercream
  frosting 149
Chocolate chip cookie 338
Chocolate cream cheese
  frosting 149
Chocolate cream puff 294
Chocolate fudge 197
Chocolate fudge frosting 150
Chocolate icing 150
Chocolate mocha cream cheese
  icing 151
Chocolate mousse 277
Chocolate parfait 290
Chocolate products 187
Choux paste 264
Choux pastry 138
Christmas pudding 284
Ciabatta bread 333
Cinnamon 114
Cinnamon and raisins rolls 332
Citric acid 91
Clarified butter 43
Clotted cream 19, 20
Clover leaf rolls 316, 326
Cocoa, types of 187
Cocoa powder 104
Coconut biscuits 339
Coconut oil 71
Coconut sugar 115
Coffee buttercream 129
Coffee crème brulee 295
Coffee mousse 278
Compressed yeast 208
Condensed milk 3, 13
Continuous dough method 220
Continuous system 8
Convection ovens 230
Cookies recipes 335
Corn flour 53
Corn meal 53
Corn oil 73
Corn syrup 111, 117

Cornstarch 101
Cranberries 115
Cream
classification of 22
handling 23
processing of 19
storage 23
types of 18, 20
Cream candies 196
Cream cheese icing 126
Cream of tartar (potassium hydrogen tartrate) 91, 104
Cream puffs (Choux a la cream) 265
Cream roll 262
Cream-based desserts 183
Creaming method 157
Crepe Normandy 308
Crepe suette sauce 293
Crepe suzette 292
Crossiants 310

D
Danish blue 32
Danish pastry 136, 263
Date sugar 111
Decorating equipment 145
Decorator's buttercream 126
Diastatic malt 215
Double cream 20
Drawplate ovens 228
Dry yeast 87
Dried milk 13
Dripping 44
Dundee cake 274

E
Eclairs 266
Egg bread and rolls 242
Egg-based desserts 182
Electric oven 226, 229
Emmental 33
Erythritol 114
Evaporated milk 3, 14

F
Fats 65, 211
characteristics of 66
classification 66
composition 67
importance of 70
processing and refining of 76
role of 69
types of 76
Fat-less sponge 162, 271
Ferment and dough process 217
Ferment/sponge and dough method 217
Fillings 147
Flaky pastry 261
Flan pastry 138
Flavour reversion 79
Flour
composition of 47, 201, 203
milling of 47
types of 48
use of 48
Flour batter cakes 158
Foam cakes 158
Foam icings 144
Fondant 124, 144, 196
Food thickeners 94
Fortified skimmed milk 14
French bread 248, 315
French buttercream 128, 144
French ice cream 165
French meringue 254

Fresh-squeezed orange juice 116
Fresh yeast 87
Frozen cream 21
Frozen custard 165
Frozen desserts, types of 164
Frozen juice concentrate 116
Frozen soufflé 165
Frozen yogurt 165
Fruit cake 130, 274
Fruit ice 166
Fruit juice concentrates 118
Fruit tart 130
Fruit-based desserts 183
Fudge-type icings 144

G
Garlic bread 322
Gas ovens 226, 229
Gas-forming bacteria 92
Gateau de Fruit 301
Gelatine-based desserts 181
Gelato / gelati 166
Genoise sponge 159, 266
German buttercream 144
Ghee 16, 44
Ghiradelli chocolate frosting 151
Ginger bread 331
Glazes 144
Gluten-free flours 52
Golden goodies 336
Golden syrup 111
Grain sugar 109
Granita 166
Granité 166
Grapefruit 115
Grapeseed oil 72
Grissini (Italian bread sticks) 244, 325

H
Half cream 21
Hamentashen 130
Hard candy 195
Harlyqueen bread 334
Herbsand potatoes 323
Herve cheese 31
High fat cakes 157
High temperature short time method 8
Holding system 7
Homogenised milk 3, 4, 12
Honey 112
Honey butter frosting 148
Honeycomb mould 276
Hot water pastry 139
Hydrogenation 78

I
Ice cream 164
Ice cream roulade 166
Ice cream-based desserts 184
Icing sugar 110
Icings 142
International bread varieties 238
Italian bread 240, 241
Italian buttercream 143
Italian ice 166
Italian meringue 257

J
Jaggery 111

K
Khara biscuits 340
Khoa 15
Kulcha 319

L
Laminate pastry 132, 134
Lard 44, 79
Lavash 312
Leavening agents
  classification of 84
  types of 100
Leavening, methods of 84
Lemon 114
Lemon soufflé 279
Lemon sponge 270
Limburger cheese 31
Lime 115

M
Madeira cake 275
Malt 212
Malted milk powder 104
Maple syrup 112
Marble chocolate 198
Margarine 44, 45, 79
Marzipan 154
Masala bread 319
Melting moments 336
Meringues 125
Meringue desserts 128
Meringue-type buttercream 127
Milk 3, 212
  clarification of 7
  composition of 16
  freezing of 11
  homogenisation of 9
  kinds of 4
  nutritive value of 15
  pasteurisation of 7-8
  processing of 5, 10
  storage of 11
  uses of 16
Milk bread 324
Milk chocolate frosting 152
Milk powder 5
Milk products 15
Millet flours 53
Mineral bread improvers 223
Molasses 109, 117
Mousse 166
Mousse au chocolate 278
Mozzarella 33
Multigrain cookies 342

N
Nan khatai 335
Natural leaveners 91
Natural sweeteners 118
Non-laminate pastry 132

O
Oat flour 53
Oat meal 53
Oats cookies 341
Oil / diesel ovens 226
Olive oil 72
Organic butter 44
Organic flour 48
Organic improvers 224
Osmophilic bacteria 92
Ovens 224-25

P
Palm oil 74
Palmiers 266
Pasteurisation 7
  role of 9
Pasteurised milk 15
Pastry 130
Pastry creams 123
Pastry flour 51
Pastry recipes 261
Pate des pommes 296
Peanut oil 74
Perfect chocolate frosting 153

Peta bread 244
Pie crust 130
Pigmented bacteria 92
Pineapple soufflé 280
Pistolette rolls 241
Pizza base 329
Plum pudding 285
Pound cakes 45
Powder milk 3
Processed dates 115
Profit rolls 265
Puff pastry 261
Pullman split-top bread 239
Pumpernickel bread and
  rolls 243
Pumpernickle bread 330
Pumpkin seed oil 74
Pure starches 100
Puréed banana 116

Q
Queen of pudding 287

R
Raising agents 83, 99
Raisins 114
Rancidity 79
Raw butter 43
Refined fructose 118
Refined oils 77
Refined sugar 109
Rice 53
Rice desserts 183
Rich-butter cake 162, 273
Rotary ovens 231
Rough puff pastry 136
Round split breads 239
Roux 98
Royal icing 145, 156
Rum 116
Rye flour 52

S
Saccharine 119
Saccharophilic bacteria 92
Sakura cheese 31
Salt 209
Salt delayed bread making
  process 219
Salted butter 43
Savarin des fruit 297
Seed oils 73
Self-rising flour 51
Semolina 49
Sesame oil 75
Short crust pastry 132, 134
Short dough 130
Shortenings 45, 65
  nutritional importance of 70
  plasticity of 70
  role of 68-69
Simple buttercream 126
Single cream 20
Skim milk 3, 4, 12
Skinny doughs 251
Slurry 99
Smoking point 80
Sodium bicarbonate 102
Soft margarine 44
Sorghum 53
Soufflé milanaise 295
Sour cream 19, 20, 21
Sour cream chocolate
  frosting 153
Sourdough breads 220
Specific fats 77
Sponge and dough process 218
Sponge method 158
Steam tube ovens 227
Stevia 118
Stone-ground wheat flour 48
Straight dough method 215
Strong flour 49

Sucanat 116
Sucralose 119
Suet 44
Sugar 107, 210
  importance of 108
  stages of cooking 108
  types of 109
Sugar paste icing 155
Sugar substitutes 112
Sulguni 30
Sunflower oil 75
Sweet and short pastry 140
Sweet paste 261
Swiss buttercream 143
Swiss meringue 257
Swiss roll 271

T

Tapioca granules 102
Tart tartin 291
Thermoduric bacteria 91
Thermophiles 91
Thermophilic bacteria 91
Thickeners 94
Thickening agents 94
  classification of 96
  role of 97
Tiramisu 303
Toppings 146
Travelling ovens 231
Triangular cookies 130
Tricolour biscuits 337
Two-stage mixing method 158

U

UHT cream 21
Ultra-high temperature system 8
Unbleached flour 52
Unsalted butter 43
Unshorten cakes 158
Unsweetened cocoa powder 114

V

Vanilla souffle 281
Vienna bread 242
Vienna ovens 229

W

Walnut oil 75
Wheat
  biological control of insects/ pests in 58
  growing conditions of 58
  structure of 55
  types of 57
Wheat crops 58
Wheat flour 53
  baking process 62
  processing of 59
  protein in 61
Wheat germ 49
Wheat grain, structure of 201
Wheat kernel 54
Wheat plant 53
Whipped cream 20
Whipping cream 20
White bread 246
White chocolate frosting 153
White chocolate ganache 154
White mountain bread 239
White pan bread 238
Whole milk 3, 4, 12
Whole wheat bread 244, 317, 327
Whole-wheat flour 51
Winterisation 78
Wood-fired ovens 226

Y

Yeast 90, 103, 206
Yeast food improvers 224
Yorkchire curd tart 306